Women and Sustainability in Business

Women and Sustainability in Business: A Global Perspective, edited by Kiymet Caliyurt, brings together original research from a dozen countries, concerning the issues and challenges facing women in sustainable business. This is a recurrent topic among researchers, regulators, companies and rating agencies. Governments pay special attention to how women impact the economy when shaping their strategies on economic sustainability. Women's contribution to business is fundamental to creating a sustainable economy, such that businesses try to strengthen 'women's presence' within their organisations, especially on their boards. Today, sustainable companies cannot survive without strategies involving women. Stakeholders, regulators, NGOs and rating agencies track both women-focused strategies and the corporate sustainability reports of companies. Well-designed strategies for women workers help companies to develop their financial and social sustainability initiatives progressively. This book analyses the practice of women in sustainable business, in terms of company performance, social responsibility, board management, entrepreneurship, employment, education, management, social sustainability, environmental politics and technology, from a wide range of diverse, regional perspectives and highlights the differences between the underdeveloped, developing and developed world.

Prof. Dr Kiymet Tunca Caliyurt graduated from the Faculty of Business Administration and Economics at Marmara University, Istanbul, Turkey. Her Masters and PhD degrees are in Accounting and Finance from the Social Graduate School, Marmara University. Her research interests are in accounting, auditing, fraud, social responsibility, corporate governance, finance and business ethics, with a special interest in NGOs and aviation management. She is the founder of the International Group on Governance, Fraud, Ethics and Social Responsibility (IGonGFE&SR) and the president of the National-International-Students' Conference Series on Governance, Fraud, Ethics and Social Responsibility (IConGFE&SR). She also founded the International Women and Business Group, which organizes a global, annual conference. Kiymet has published papers and book chapters both nationally and internationally on fraud, social responsibility, ethics in accounting/finance/aviation disciplines and NGOs.

Women and Sustainable Business

Series Editor: Kiymet Çaliyurt

The series Women and Sustainable Business, edited by Kiymet Caliyurt, researches the issues surrounding women and sustainability in business.

The concept of sustainability hinges on perfecting the balance between society, economy and the environment and this issue is firmly and squarely on the corporate agenda. After many financial crises, corruption scandals, natural disasters and developments in e-trade, companies understand that being sustainable and well governed are more important factors in the competitive market than simply turning a profit and maximizing shareholder value.

Stakeholders, particularly shareholders, have started to review a company's sustainability much more closely, thus, companies know that they have to put this issue high on their list of priorities and become increasingly transparent about their strategies in regard to environmental, gender, social and ethical issues. In order to be funded by these green investors or socially responsible stakeholders, organisations must produce non-financial statements, such as sustainability reports or social responsibility reports, to support their engagement with this agenda.

With books covering topics such as social and environmental sustainability and women's issues, women and entrepreneurship and women and public policy, the series will undoubtedly fill a gap in the existing literature surrounding women in business and appeal to a broad range of readers, including academicians, corporate board members, CSR and sustainability directors, representatives of female NGOs and policy regulators.

Women in Agriculture Worldwide
Key Issues and Practical Approaches
Edited by Amber J. Fletcher and Wendee Kubik

Women and Sustainability in Business
A Global Perspective
Kiymet Çaliyurt

Women and Sustainability in Business

A Global Perspective

Edited by
Kiymet Çaliyurt

Routledge
Taylor & Francis Group

LONDON AND NEW YORK

First published 2017
by Routledge

2 Park Square, Milton Park, Abingdon, Oxfordshire OX14 4RN
52 Vanderbilt Avenue, New York, NY 10017

Routledge is an imprint of the Taylor & Francis Group, an informa business

First issued in paperback 2020

British Library Cataloguing in Publication Data
A catalogue record for this book is available from the British Library

Library of Congress Cataloging-in-Publication Data
Names: Çaliyurt, Kiymet Tunca.
Title: Women and sustainability in business: a global perspective / by Kiymet Çaliyurt.
Description: Burlington : Gower, 2016. | Series: Women and sustainable business | Includes bibliographical references and index.
Identifiers: LCCN 2015025553 | ISBN 9781472448910 (hardback)
Subjects: LCSH: Businesswomen. | Leadership in women. | Sex discrimination in employment—Law and legislation—Europe. | Sustainable development.
Classification: LCC HD6053 .C35 2016 | DDC 338.9/27082—dc23

ISBN: 978-1-4724-4891-0 (hbk)
ISBN: 978-0-367-60600-8 (pbk)

Typeset in NewBaskerville
by Apex CoVantage, LLC

Contents

Figures

Tables

Editor Biography

Professor Kiymet Tunca Çaliyurt graduated from the Faculty of Business Administration and Economics, Marmara University, Istanbul, Turkey. Her Masters and PhD degrees are in Accounting and Finance from the Social Graduate School, Marmara University. Her research interests are in accounting, auditing, fraud, social responsibility, corporate governance, finance, business ethics with special interest in NGOs and aviation management. She is the founder of the International Group on Governance, Fraud, Ethics and Social Responsibility (IGonGFE&SR) and the president of the National-International-Students' Conference Series on Governance, Fraud, Ethics and Social Responsibility (IConGFE&SR). She has published papers and book chapters both nationally and internationally on fraud, social responsibility, ethics in accounting/finance/aviation disciplines and NGOs. She is founder of Edirne City Branch of Turkish Federation of University Women and lecturer for the Master's degree course 'Women and Entrepreneurship'. She has published with the International Women and Business Group since 2009 discussing women and business issues and organizing conferences.

CV details of Professor Kiymet Çaliyurt can be found following website: http://personel-en.trakya.edu.tr/kiymetcaliyurt/#.Um6kVJXTryk/.

Contributors' Biographies

Rute Abreu (Portugal) is an Accounting and Finance Professor in the Business and Economics Scientific and Technical Unit of the Technology and Business Higher School at the Instituto Politécnico da Guarda, Portugal. She received her Master's degree in Industrial Engineering from the Universidade Nova de Lisboa, Portugal (1996), and PhD in Accounting and Finance from the Universidad de Salamanca, Spain (2009). Since 2010, she develops activities with a social responsibility research network, researches and publishes papers in several journals, and participates frequently in conferences and meetings all over the world.

Rahayati Ahmad (Malaysia) holds a Bachelor's and Master's in Accounting from Universiti Teknologi MARA Malaysia. Before she started her career as a lecturer, she worked as a restaurant manager for Pizza Hut for four years. She has been teaching accounting subjects for more than 10 years. She started her career as a lecturer at the Institute Professional Baitulmal (IPB) Cheras, Kuala Lumpur, and is continuing her teaching career at the College University Insaniah (KUIN), Alor Setar, Kedah. She has produced more than five accounting manuals for KUIN undergraduate students and been involved in several Fundamental Research Grants Scheme (FRGS) from the Ministry of Higher Education Malaysia. Ms Rahayati is currently furthering her study with a PhD (Accounting) at Universiti Teknologi MARA Malaysia and her research areas are Corporate Governance, Corporate Social Responsibility and Capital Structure. She has been an Associate Member (AM) of the Malaysia Institute of Accountants (MIA) for more than four years.

Maria Aluchna (Poland) is Associate Professor at the Department of Management Theory, Warsaw School of Economics, Poland. She specializes in corporate governance, strategic management and corporate social responsibility. She teaches 'Corporate governance', 'Transition in Central and Eastern Europe' and 'Strategic management'. She was awarded the Deutscher Akademischer Austauchdienst (DAAD, 2001/2002) scholarship to research at Universität Passau, and a Polish-American Fulbright Commission scholarship to research at Columbia University (2002/2003). Maria Aluchna is a member of the European Corporate Governance Institute (ECGI), European Academy of Management (EURAM), the editorial teams of *Journal of Knowledge, Globalization,* and the *European Journal of Economics and Management* as well as of the Polish journals *Przegląd Organizacji* [*Organization Review*] and *e-Mentor.* She is also the Academic Director of the Community of

European Management Schools (CEMS) programme at the Warsaw School of Economics. She is a team member at the law firm Głuchowski, Siemiątkowski i Zwara.

Syahiza Arsada (Malaysia) is currently a lecturer at the Kulliyyah Muamalat, Insaniah University College and part-time PhD (Accountancy) student at Universiti Teknologi MARA. She obtained her Bachelor of Accountancy (1999–2001) from Universiti Teknologi MARA and MBA (Accountancy) from Universiti Utara Malaysia (2007). She is also a member of the Fundamental Research Grants Scheme (FRGS) and the Exploratory Research Grants Scheme (ERGS). She has presented her research at national and international conferences. Her research interests include corporate social responsibility, corporate governance, human capital and Islamic accounting.

Milen Baltov (Bulgaria) graduated from the University of National and World Economy, Bulgaria, in 2001 and was made Associate Professor in 2009 by the Higher Attestation Commission to the Council of Ministers, Bulgaria. He was appointed Professor in 2014 at the Burgas Free University, Bulgaria, and Vice Rector Research and International Cooperation and Head Business Administration at the Burgas Free University. He is an Evaluator of project applications under the Bulgarian–Swiss Programme for Scientific Exchange, Expert in the Accreditation procedures of Bulgarian universities, Expert in the Working Group designing the Higher Education Strategy of the Republic of Bulgaria, National Contact Point for coordination and implementation of the activities of the thematic priority 'Small and Medium-sized Enterprises' of the EU Framework Programme for Scientific Research and Innovations 'Horizon 2020' (2014–20), International expert in the Accreditation procedure of universities in the Republic of Kazakhstan. He is a Member of the Regional Development Council and the Regional Coordination Committee of the South East Region (R. of Bulgaria). He is author of more than 70 publications, with two monographs, seven books, 10 manuals and teaching tools.

Professor Abdulrazzak Charbaji (Lebanon), a native of Beirut, Lebanon, was the Dean of College of Business Administration in the Hariri Canadian University. He is a member of the Social Responsibility Research Network and the founder and principal of CHARBAJI Consultants (www.charbaji.com). He received a Bachelor's degree in Economics from the Beirut Arab University, a Master of Science degree in Business from University of Northern Colorado and a PhD in Applied Statistics and Research Methods from University of Northern Colorado.

Dr Charbaji has been teaching part- and full-time at AUB, LAU, Notre Dame University, RHU, Kaslik, King Faisal University and the Lebanese University since 1982. His international publications cover corporate governance, leadership, banking, marketing and finance. Professor Abdulrazzak Charbaji has published more than 20 papers in major international refereed journals including *Journal of Applied Economics; Advances in Financial Planning and Forecasting; Advances in Quantitative Analysis of Finance and Accounting; Social Responsibility Journal; Managerial Auditing Journal; Corporate Governance; International Journal of Commerce and Management; Journal of Economic & Administrative Sciences (JEAS); Journal of Managerial Psychology; Journal of Environmental Sciences;* and *International Review of Education.* He is the author of five books: one of them is available at Amazon.com entitled *Applied Econometrics using Eviews, SPSS & Excel with Applications in Arab Countries* (2012).

During his academic years, Professor Charbaji has been working as a consultant and/or as a team leader for different consulting firms in Lebanon and Arab countries since 1980. He has constructed the 'Status of Lebanese Woman Index' for ESCWA and conducted a SWOT analysis for the City Development project on behalf of the Ministry of the Interior and Municipality in Lebanon and the World Bank, and conducted for the Ministry of Economy in Lebanon an investigation for the creation of an enabling environment for the Lebanese small and medium enterprises (SMEs). He worked on establishing a Planning, Monitoring and Evaluation Unit at DGVTE, Ministry of Education.

Biljana Chavkoska (Serbia) PhD holds a doctor of law degree from the state university St Kiril and Metodij in Skopje, Republic of Macedonia. She graduated at the Faculty of Law with special *honor sum laude* and won the Frank Maning prize for the best student of the generation. Biljana Chavkoska is Assistant Professor at FON University. She teaches Labour law, Insurance law and European social law. Since 2011 she has been a head of the Business Law Department at the Faculty of Law. During the past years, she has published important articles in international and national journals and has participated in many scientific conferences. She is a member of the editorial board of the *Journal Jurist*, published by the Law Association of the Republic of Macedonia. In 2013, she was nominated as the National coordinator of the Republic of Macedonia for the action of the COST programme (European cooperation in science and technology) financed by the European Union.

Nesrin Çobanoğlu (Turkey) graduated from Istanbul University, Cerrahpasa School of Medicine. She completed her graduate studies in Public Administration and the History of Medicine, Deontology and Medical Ethics to become an Associate Professor in 2005 and a Professor in 2011. She is the founder of the Department of History of Medicine and Medical Ethics in Baskent University. She is currently working as the Chair of the Department of Medical Ethics and History of Medicine in Gazi University. She is teaching doctoral courses in the Institute of Social Sciences in Ankara University (Faculty of Political Science). Thus, she continues her scientific career in both areas. She has been the president of Women's Studies Centre in Gazi University. She has many national and international publications and books to her name. She worked on the ethics boards of many national and international scientific organizations. She has been invited to the UN, WHO, UNESCO and the EU scientific meetings as the representative of Turkey. She is a member of Health Ministry Scientific Committee.

She has been a member of the administrative board of the Turkish Medical Association and Ankara Medical Association (General Secretary). She is currently a member of the Turkish Medical Association, Biopolitics International Organization (BIOS), BPW (Business and Professional Woman), Sociological Association, AIDS Prevention Society, Hacettepe University AIDS Treatment Centre (HATAM), Public Management Professionals Association, the Philosophical Society of Turkey, Bioethics Association, International Association for Education in Ethics (IAEE), Association of Medical Ethics and Medical Law. She has a son.

Fatima David (Portugal) is an Accounting and Finance Professor in the Business and Economics Scientific and Technical Unit of the Technology and Business Higher School at the Instituto Politécnico da Guarda, Portugal. She received her Master's degree in Management from the Universidade da Beira Interior, Portugal (1996) and PhD in Accounting and Taxation from the Universidad de Salamanca, Spain (2007). Her researches have been published in several journals and she participates in conferences and meetings.

Maja Đokić (Serbia) PhD, graduated from the Faculty of Film and Audio-visual Arts of Catalonia (ESCAC), Barcelona University, Barcelona, Spain. Her Master's degree is in Marketing, about commercial aspects of art products, from the College of Business Economics, Pan European University Apeiron, Banja Luka, Bosnia and Herzegovina. Her PhD, from FIMEK, University Business Academy, Novi Sad, Serbia, is also in the field of Marketing, concerning the marketing of art products on the global market. Her research interests are in marketing, advertising, public relations and art. She is currently a Professor at Pan European University Apeiron, Banja Luka, Bosnia and Herzegovina, and Market Communications College, Belgrade, Serbia. She has published papers, both nationally and internationally, on marketing and advertising. She combines her academic work with jobs in advertising and as a film director.

Amber J. Fletcher (Canada) is a Postdoctoral Research Fellow at the Johnson-Shoyama Graduate School of Public Policy, University of Regina, Canada. She is an interdisciplinary scholar with specialization in political sociology, gender studies, public policy and qualitative methodology. Amber Fletcher's research examines the social and gendered effects of major changes in public policy and climate, with particular focus on women in agriculture. She holds an interdisciplinary PhD from the Johnson-Shoyama Graduate School of Public Policy, a Master of Arts in Women's Studies from York University (Toronto) and a Bachelor of Arts (High Honours) in Women's Studies from the University of Regina. She is a laureate of the Governor General of Canada's Award in Commemoration of the Persons Case for her work on gender equality in Canada.

Henrique Formigoni (Brazil) is an Accounting and Finance Professor at the Center of Applied Social Science of Mackenzie Presbyterian University in São Paulo, Brazil. He received his Master's degree in Accounting from Pontifícia Universidade Católica, Brazil, and his PhD in Accounting from the University of São Paulo, in São Paulo, Brazil, and Postdoctoral Study in Accounting and Finance from the Universidad de Salamanca, Spain. He worked for several companies as an accountant for many years and now he is the Coordinator of the Accounting course and works as a Researcher and Professor in Mackenzie Presbyterian University.

Professor Zorka Grandov (Bosnia and Herzegovina) graduated from the Faculty of Economics, Belgrade University, Belgrade, Serbia. Her Master's degree is in Monetary Economics from Belgrade University, and her PhD is in Economic Policy and Development from Novi Sad University, Serbia. Her research interests are in international economics, international commerce and management. She was a professor at the Faculty of Economics, Pristina, and Faculty of Commerce and Banking, BK University, Belgrade. She is currently a Professor at FIMEK, University Business

Academy, Novi Sad, Serbia, the College of Business Economics, Pan European University Apeiron, Banja Luka, Bosnia and Herzegovina, and Faculty of Commerce and Banking, Alfa University, Belgrade, Serbia. She is the Chief Editor of the scientific journal *Economy and Market Communication Review*, published by Pan European University Apeiron, Banja Luka, BiH. Also, she is the president of 'EDASOL: Economic Development and Standard of Living' series of international conferences. She has published books and papers, both nationally and internationally, on international economics, international commerce and management.

Nevena Jovanović (Serbia) was born in 1985 in Kragujevac. After finishing grammar school – language department, she graduated from Belgrade University – Faculty of Philosophy with a Master's degree in Psychology in 2010. Currently she is pursuing her second Master's degree in Human Resources Management at the Faculty of Management in Belgrade. During her studies she has engaged in various activities such as human resources, marketing, education and research. Her research area is human resources and social and organization psychology. She is currently employed at Dunav Insurance Company, Belgrade, as a psychologist in the Human Resources department, where she is engaged in various strategies and procedures regarding human resources.

Radica Jovanović (Serbia) gained her first work experience and expertise in business and trade after graduation from the High School of Economics. Dr Jovanović has worked in the trade company Mercator and Emona-Agropromet where she was in charge of planning and analysis. In order to further her education, Radica enrolled and graduated from the Faculty of Trade and Banking, Department of Trades, at the University Braca Karić. She also took a Master's degree in the Department of Trade Management in the same faculty. Radica earned the degree of Doctor of Economic Sciences from the University Business Academy in Novi Sad in the Faculty of Economics and Engineering Management. At the University Union-Nikola Tesla where she has worked, she was elected Assistant Professor in Economics and Management. Currently she is working at Belgrade Business School as a Professor of the subjects in the field of commerce (Foreign Trade Management, Foreign Exchange Management, Sales Management). She has participated in several international conferences and seminars at home as well as abroad. Radica is author of several articles published in national magazines and a co-author of the textbook *Foreign Trade*. She also was a mentor of undergraduate and graduate students. The area of her academic interest is international trading.

Verica Jovanović (Serbia), PhD, graduated from the Faculty of Economics and industrial management in Novi Sad, Serbia. She received a Master's degree in economics and a PhD in Business Planning, both from Pan European University Apeiron, Banja Luka, Bosnia and Herzegovina. Her research interests are focused on Education, Business planning, Development and Entrepreneurship. She was a professor in R&B College and Elite College in Belgrade. In 2007 she became Vice Principal of the School of Economics and Management, Pancevo, Serbia. She is also a board member of Pancevo Municipality Development Public Agency.

Milena Krumova (Bulgaria) works as Assistant Professor, PhD, at the Technical University, Sofia, Faculty of Management, Department of Economy, Industrial Engineering and Management. She teaches economics, business economics, cost management and business administration projects. Since 2005, when she started work at the TU-Sofia, she has been supervisor of more than 50 Bachelor and Master degree students. For the last three school years she has studied in the College for Fashion and Design (Sofia), and worked part-time at Telebid Ltd. as Cloud Computing Business Analyst.

In 2011, she gained a PhD in Economics at the Chemical, Technology and Metallurgy University, Sofia, and in October 2014 she defended her PhD thesis in Engineering ('Automation of non-material areas'), at the TU-Sofia, Faculty of Electronic Engineering and Technologies. She has participated in many international scientific initiatives – conferences, workshops and summer schools in Austria – Krems (2007), Poland – Warsaw (2007), Spain – Gijon (2008), Lithuania – Vilnius (2008), England – London (2009), Netherlands – Delft (2010), Ohrid – Macedonia (2011), Tübingen – Germany (2011), Thessaloniki – Greece (2010, 2011), Oslo – Norway (2012) and Albany – New York, USA (2012; 2013). She has more than 50 published papers, some of them presented at international conferences. She has taken part in more than 10 research projects. Her interests for future research are in the field of open data.

Olivera Karić Nedeljković (Serbia) started to gain her rich work experience in 1979, the year when she founded the company Kosovouniverzum in Pec, where she worked until 1987. After that she created two companies, also in Pec: Metalac in 1988 and Inox in 1989. She also founded the company Karić Turist in Belgrade in 1989, where she worked as a director. Olivera gained her work experience and expertise working in the company Saint Nikola Putnik in Belgrade and at the Institute Braca Karić as Social Advisor from 1991 to 1993. Oivera was the vice president of the Fund Braca Karić from 1993 to 1995. From 1995 to 1997 she worked in the Europa International Company and in the Cita-Tel company as a consultant. From 1999 until 2002 she worked as executive director at Astra Tourist in Astra Simit Group. In 2002 she founded the Family Tourist company, where she works as the President. In the field of education, Olivera Nedeljković earned a Bachelor's degree in Economics from the Faculty of Commerce and Banking Janicije and Danica Karić in Belgrade in 2002. In 2008 she earned a Master's degree in Management from the same faculty in Belgrade.

Meltem Onay (Turkey) PhD, graduated from the Faculty of Business and Economics in Adnan Menderes University, Aydın (Turkey). She earned a Master's degree in Business and Management, and a PhD in Management and Organization in Adnan University. Her research interests are focused on Women Entrepreneurship, Organization Culture, Organization Image, Women leaders. She was a Professor in Celal Bayar University in Turkey. Since 2000, she has worked in the School of Applied Science in Manisa. She gives lessons in entrepreneurship and management in her university.

Arzu İrge Özyol (Turkey) from 1983 to 2002 worked in the Construction Company as an Environmental Engineer after she had graduated from Middle East Technical University. She received an MBA degree from İstanbul Bilgi University in 2002 and established the International Project and Consulting Company. She has prepared and managed almost 50 EU-funded projects since 2003. In 2006 she accepted the request of BPW International to establish first BPW-Club in Ankara. She was a member of the executive board of the BPWI Environmental Standing Committee between 2006 and 2011, and a member of the European Coordination Committee of BPW between 2007 and 2009, furthering the efforts that she has made for the expansion of BPW in Turkey. In 2012, BPW gained Federation status in Turkey. Arzu Özyol is the UN Representative of BPWI; member of the board of the UNESCO Center for Women and Peace in Balkan Countries; and coordinator of the South Eastern Europe Leadership Centre for Women in Business, which was established through the cooperation of BPWI and the UNESCO Center in 2011. She is a member of the African Business Council in the TR Foreign Economic Relations Committee and advisor to the Global Platform of International Trade Centre for action on sourcing from women vendors. Since 2009, she has advocated Women Empowerment Principles, the common initiative of UN Women and the UN Global Compact, at international, regional and national levels. She translated the official booklet of UNWEPs. She is working to provide equal opportunities for women and men throughout the world as a member of the advisory board of the B-MENA Initiative (Broader Initiative for Civil Society in North Africa and Middle East) that was started by the ex-Minister of the US Department of State, Hillary Clinton, and as a member of the work group that was established by the TR Ministry of Family and Social Policies and co-organized by World Economic Forum. Arzu Özyol has completed her PhD study on Bioethics and Environmental Politics.

Vesna Pavlićević (Serbia) was born in 1974 in Belgrade. After finishing grammar school – natural sciences department – she was already determined to pursue science, choosing research studies as her favourite field of work. She gained a Master's degree in psychology at the state University of Belgrade Faculty of philosophy in 2001. Further education was directed by professional opportunities, so she took a two-year course of system family therapy of alcoholism and upgraded her skills in some specific psychological instruments. She participated as co-author in several scientific publications, mostly contributing with statistical analysis and data interpretation within theory. Her research areas are methodology, psychometrics and statistical analysis and their use in scientific research regarding social and medical areas. Vesna Pavlićević has more than decade of experience in psychology and human resources in several companies, including in the most stressful and demanding professions, such as the police and rescue services. She currently employed at Dunav Insurance Company, Belgrade.

Diana Sabotinova (Bulgaria) is Assistant Professor in Bourgas Free University. Her PhD degree is from Department of Macroeconomics, Institute of Economics, Bulgarian Academy of Science, Sofia, Bulgaria. Her thesis title is 'Macroeconomic Consequences of Population Ageing' and her Master's degree is in Economics from the University of National and World Economy, Sofia, Bulgaria. She has been on the academic staff in Burgas Free University, Burgas, Bulgaria, since 2000. She teaches in Macroeconomics, Microeconomics, International Economics and Economic Theories.

Roshima Said (Malaysia) PhD is an Associate Professor of Universiti Teknologi MARA, Malaysia. She acts as an Accounting Research Institute (ARI) Associates Fellow of Universiti Teknologi MARA, Malaysia. Her research interest is in the area of Corporate Governance, Corporate Social Responsibility, Corporate Reporting, Ethics and Financial Criminology. She has conducted research that has been presented at international and local seminars, conferences and colloquia and published in proceedings and journals. She also has published papers, books and book chapters both nationally and internationally. She also acts on the editorial advisory board for *Social Responsibility Journal*, published by Emerald Group Publishing Limited. She also acts as Member of Board in *Issues in Social and Environmental Accounting (Issues in SEA)*.

Liliane Segura (Brazil) is an Accounting and Finance Professor at the Center of Applied Social Science of Mackenzie Presbyterian University in São Paulo, Brazil. She received her Master's degree in Business Strategy from the University of São Paulo, Brazil (2003), her PhD in Accounting and Finance from Mackenzie Presbyterian University in São Paulo, Brazil, and Postdoctoral Study in Accounting and Finance from the Universidad de Salamanca, Spain. She worked as a director and manager in several Brazilian companies for 15 years and now works as a Researcher and Professor in Mackenzie Presbyterian University.

Duygu Türker (Turkey) is an Assistant Professor in the Department of Business Administration in Yasar University. She has a BA in Business Administration from Dokuz Eylül University, an MSc in Environmental Sciences from Ankara University, an MBA from Dokuz Eylül University, and a PhD in Public Administration from Dokuz Eylül University. She has been involved in various projects as researcher or administrator. Her research interest includes CSR, business ethics, interorganizational relations and entrepreneurship.

Snežana Videnović (Serbia) was born in 1966 in Belgrade. After graduating from the Faculty of Law at Belgrade University, she completed a Master's degree in Strategic Management at the Faculty of Strategic Management at BK University. In 2013 she defended her doctoral thesis entitled 'Possibility of Applying the Concept of Coaching in Serbia' at the Belgrade Banking Academy at University Union. She has participated as a speaker at numerous conferences in the country and abroad. She is the author of numerous articles published in national and international journals and publications. Her research areas are strategic management and human resources. Snežana Videnović has 20 years of experience in human resources in various positions, and is currently employed at Dunav Insurance Company, Belgrade. She is Assistant Professor at the Faculty of Bijeljina in Bijeljina.

Senem Yılmaz (Turkey) is a Research Assistant in the Department of Business Administration and the Head of Career Centre in Yasar University. She has a BA in Economics from Dokuz Eylül University and an MBA from Ege University. Currently she is a PhD candidate at the department of Business Administration in Ege University. Her research interests include CSR, leadership and management, interorganizational relations and organizational aesthetics.

Mine Yılmazer (Turkey) PhD, graduated from the Faculty of Economics and Administrative Science in Hacettepe University in Ankara, Turkey. She received a Master's degree and PhD in Economics. Her research interests are focused on human development, economic growth and sustainable development and international trade. She is working in the School of Applied Science as an Associate Professor in Celal Bayar University in Manisa, Turkey. In 2014 she became Head of the Department of International Trade at this university.

Why Women Are Important for a Sustainable World

Kiymet Tunca Çaliyurt

'Women in business' is an emerging issue among the business world, academicians, NGOs, governments and other parties. Each party takes the issue from a different perspective. However, everyone agrees that women in business have many, many problems. These problems become bigger and bigger every day because of war, economic crises, globalization and bankruptcies. Everyone also agrees that we all have to solve these problems for a better world. Many national and international regulations are being promulgated and solutions are being served every day. For example, according to a draft paper prepared for United Nations Research Institute for Social Development titled 'Beyond the Business Case: A Community Economies Approach to Gender, Development and Social Economy':[1]

> if economy is divorced from capitalism, if development governance is divorced from neoliberalism, and if care and cooperation are divorced from their gender essentialist dimensions, we can begin to imagine a process of development that is directed to the totality of interdependant relationship – in households, firms, communities, commons, in and non-market exchange that allows us a chance of a future worth living in.
>
> (12)

However, women in the world cannot survive against problems by 'if'. Women need radical decisions, strict applications and cooperation in the world. In the first book of this series, group members of International Women and Business have decided to discuss 'women and sustainability' for many reasons:

- An increasing number of studies indicate that gender inequalities are extracting high economic costs and leading to social inequalities and environmental degradation around the world (Stevens, 2010).
- Sustainability is an issue that women workers are an important part of.
- Most of the innovative companies started to send surveys to women customers to ask about their opinion on the company's sustainability, so women customers have more importance than before.
- Publishing sustainability reporting has a positive effect on customers if it includes issues on women workers.
- Many countries support companies' women-oriented social programmes.
- Customers like to shop and invest in women-friendly companies.

In Chapter 1, Diana Sabotinova discusses the invisible work of women in the economy. She complains that the current development model is focused on profit rather than on people. She notes that economic indicators like GDP do not reflect the contribution of women through unpaid work.

In Chapter 2, Zorka Grandov, Radica Jovanović and Olivera Karić Nedeljković discuss that although the equality of women and men in the labour market is regulated by law, more indicators show that Serbia is among the countries with high levels of gender inequality in the labour market when the data are compared with the situation in neighbouring countries, especially the countries of the European Union.

In Chapter 3, Mine Yılmazer and Meltem Onay discuss women's social and employment status in Germany and Turkey. The purpose of their study is to uncover the activities that are carried out to increase women's employment in the spirit of social municipality in Germany and Turkey. In the study, first the importance of the matter and the content of the studies conducted on this subject are emphasized. Then, indicators of gender inequality in Turkey and Germany are compared. Methods, models and hypotheses are discussed after presenting research findings. Finally, after the social benefit-cost analysis is performed, each country's SWOT analysis is made to identify situations, strengths and weakness that will shape their future policies.

In Chapter 4, Zorka Grandov, Verica Jovanović and Maja Đokić state that in university education in the past four decades the number of women has increased 200% more than the number of men. Accordingly, it is logical to expect that since the educational competence is increased, the number of women in high management positions will also increase. However, numerous clues gained by analysing different statistical data and relevant international research undoubtedly indicate that this did not happen, so women must overcome many other barriers in order to increase their participation at high management functions.

In Chapter 5, Abdulrazzak Charbaji has researched Lebanese women's senior professional positions in Lebanon. The aim of his chapter is to make a survey of a large sample of graduate working women undertaken using a questionnaire specifically developed for this study. The study finds that 'empowerment', 'job satisfaction', 'financial barriers' and 'number of children' are the most important discriminating variables. Finally, the study identifies two issues that need to be addressed if change in the status of Lebanese women is to occur: (1) ensuring that women have equal access to training and empowerment opportunities; and (2) removing the cultural stereotype barriers that block the advancement of women.

In Chapter 6, Snežana Videnović, Vesna Pavlićević and Nevena Jovanović consider that since the beginning of the twenty-first century men and women, willingly or not, have become accustomed to the fact that employers' expectations are unambiguous – each one of us has to contribute to business goals and has to do their job successfully. On the other hand, traditional understanding of division of labour by gender, based on both biological differences and cultural studies, prejudice and stereotypes has been deeply rooted. The subject matter of their chapter is the analysis of respondents' attitude towards the status of employed women in Serbia. Their chapter aims to depict the profile of a successful woman in Serbia based on the analysis of research results, and determine the current level of prejudice against women in our society.

In Chapter 7, Rute Abreu and Fatima David examine how, the world over, the economic success of banks is based on men and women working together. Their research investigates women's labour in general, and in the bank sector in particular, and how historical data is improving public awareness and the tendency toward gender equality in the present. These data allow critical examination of several issues affecting women's labour in the Portuguese banking system and show, that despite the progress overall, there are difficulties in obtaining true equality, and this affects professional achievement. The empirical analysis provides important insights into bank disclosure information and stakeholders' perception of the benefits of legal and ethical responsibilities about working women that go beyond maximizing economic gains and, then, banks truly balance their interests.

In Chapter 8, Maria Aluchna discusses women's positions on boards and the situation in Poland. The financial crisis and the economic slowdown which started with the credit crunch on American subprime mortgages led to the sovereign debt crisis and the severe uncertainty on stock markets in the majority of developed economies. Growing economic challenges triggered the formulation and adoption of many codes of best practice and a set of recommendations that are intended to improve the performance of companies and countries. The adoption of more restricted regulations, the discipline of national budgets, and greater supervision of public debt policies and the stock market belong to the most debated recommendations. Maria Aluchna reviews recommendations to increase female participation in business and on corporate boards. Corporate boards are essential bodies for governance and management and their efficiency determines the company performance.

In Chapter 9, Liliane Segura, Henrique Formigoni, Fatima David and Rute Abreu discuss how earnings management brings the problem of smoothing profit and manipulating earnings of the company.

In Chapter 10, Zorka Grandov, Verica Jovanović and Maja Đokić try to find out why there are not many women in high positions in companies.

In Chapter 11, Biljana Chavkoska considers Gender Equality Law in the EU context based on primary and secondary law and the case law of the European Court of Justice. Major improvement was made with the Treaty of Amsterdam by including Article 13, which impairs discrimination with new legal bases apart from gender. Harassment and sexual harassment within the meaning of this directive shall be deemed to be discrimination on the grounds of sex and therefore prohibited. Defining harassment and sexual harassment was necessary because of the increased number of victims of sexual harassment in the workplace in member states. Her chapter analyses the scope of the concepts, the importance of including the definitions of harassment and sexual harassment in the national law of the member states and the best practices.

In Chapter 12, Duygu Türker and Senem Yılmaz mention that women in most developing countries have struggled with numerous problems including poverty, unemployment, crime, illiteracy or various forms of discrimination. Today, most business organizations recognize the existence of women stakeholders and initiate CSR projects towards them. However, the literature provides almost nothing on the nature, structure or, more importantly, effectiveness of such projects. The purpose of their study is to address this issue by analysing how CSR towards women stakeholders are practiced in a developing country, Turkey.

In Chapter 13, Amber Fletcher states that since the late 1800s, family farms have populated the vast agricultural region of the Canadian prairies. Since these early days, farm women have played a crucial but often invisible role in sustaining family farms through economic and environmental challenges. She discusses how a new productivist paradigm has affected rural societies and farming practices, and she suggests the importance of preserving historical forms of social capital to ensure environmentally sustainable farming into the future.

In Chapter 14, Arzu İrge Özyol and Nesrin Çobanoğlu consider that 70 per cent of 1.3 billion people in developing countries living on less than a dollar a day are women, and therefore that it follows that energy poverty is a problem that has a disproportionate effect on women because women are responsible for supplying their families with food, fuel and water, often without the benefit of basic modern infrastructure. They are exposed to harmful levels of gases, particles and dangerous compounds. Indoor air pollution is responsible for more than 1.6 million deaths per year due to pneumonia, asthma, bronchitis, tuberculosis, lung cancer and heart disease. In 2013, research indicates that women continue not to be accounted for in any planned environmental policy actions including legislation and programmes and, moreover, environmental politics haven't been prepared by using gender lenses. However, it is impossible to provide sustainable development if the role of women in environmental decision-making is not taken into consideration.

In Chapter 15, Roshima Said, Syahiza Arsada and Rahayati Ahmad investigate the relationship between boards of directors, ownership structure and women on boards on the extent of CSR reporting in Malaysian public listed companies. This study has demonstrated that, in order to mitigate agency problems between firms and shareholders, society and stakeholders, and particularly environmental impact, the inclusion of corporate governance characteristics may help to decrease the expected costs and the negative impact on firm value, and also show society and stakeholders that individual firms are doing their part to help solve social and environmental problems through additional disclosures.

In Chapter 16, Milena Krumova shows that the Internet has fundamentally changed the practical and economic realities of distributing knowledge. Web 2.0 led to the development and evolution of Web-based communities that allow people to connect, create, collaborate and share knowledge more rapidly, effectively and efficiently through networking. Web 2.0 has the potential to deliver rich interactions among users, enable collaborative value creation across business partners and create new services, business models and vast opportunities for women entrepreneurship. Her chapter discusses the potential of open resources within Web which can be utilized by women when starting up businesses.

In Chapter 17, Milen Baltov examines how company growth is a function of organizational inputs, and gender differences are attributable to individual abilities and decisions. Nevertheless, social feminism asserts the existence of gendered access to resources and differences in values between men and women. Thus, feminist theories stress that women face financial and social barriers when they run a company. Previous research has consequently pointed to underperformance on the part of companies headed by women when compared with companies headed by men. His study pursues three main goals. First, the impact of start-up capital and external financing on growth in companies run by men or by women is studied. Second, the existence of or otherwise the gender impact on these variables is analysed in relation to a selected industry. Third, the performance in terms of growth of companies run by women is explored in an attempt to identify the existence or otherwise of underperformance over a given period.

As the International Women and Business Group, we hope that this book will help to solve problems for women in business life and help readers to have a 'women-oriented' point of view. We hope to meet with you at future conferences and through books published by the International Women and Business Group.

Note

1 Draft Report Beyond the Business Case: A Community Economies Approach to Gender, Development and Social Economy UNRISD Conference, Potential and Limits of Social and Solidarity Economy, 6–8 May 2013, Geneva, Switzerland.

References

Stevens, Candice. (2010), *Are Women the Key to Sustainable Development?* The Frederick S. Pardee Center for the Study of the Longer-Range Future, Boston University. Available at: http://www.bu.edu/pardee/files/2010/04/UNsdkp003fsingle.pdf (Retrieved 22 April 2014).

UNRISD. (2013), Beyond the Business Case: A Community Economies Approach to Gender, Development and Social Economy. *UNRISD Conference, Potential and Limits of Social and Solidarity Economy*, Draft Report, 6–8 May 2013, Geneva, Switzerland.

Part I

Women and Economic Sustainability

Chapter 1

Making Visible the Invisible

Women's Unpaid Labour

Diana Sabotinova

Introduction: Visibility and the Measurement in the National Accounts

There have been attempts from the United Nations and from academic and feminist circles for care and domestic activities in the home to be classified as value-generating work, and as an immeasurable component of wealth. Few efforts have been made in this direction both because of technical and methodological difficulties and of what the statistical measurement of unpaid social reproduction work would require – a conceptualization of the economic system that allows the scale and quality of this work to be properly recorded.

The system of national accounts (adopted by the United Nations Statistical Commission in 1993) recommends that the concept of 'production' should include not just goods and services produced for the market, but also goods produced in the home for family consumption. These are left out of classification, and activities associated with the production of personal and domestic services by household members for their own consumption are consequently treated as 'non-economic'.

One consequence of this is that these activities are not included in conventional censuses and surveys. In 1995 the United Nations Development Programme (UNDP) *Gender and Human Development Report* revealed that women were responsible for over half of the total time spent on working in the world and that they carried out more work in total (in terms of physical units of time) than men. The report also highlighted the fact that three-quarters of men's working time was spent on paid activities, while only a third of women's working time was paid. In other words, women do more work than men, but the current economic and political system does not record, measure, value or reward it. Studies dealing with household income, and particularly those concerned with poverty, explicitly consider the contribution of family members to income but continue to ignore the contribution made by social reproduction work.[1]

The inclusion of unpaid work (household, caregiving or subsistence activities) in the systems of national accounts would have major consequences, given the importance of these instruments for policy-making and economic decision-making, at both the national and international levels. National accounts quantify all the areas deemed to be part of the national economy, and resources are allocated on the basis of the information they provide. This means that any economic activities not included in this system, or in the satellite accounts, are not only invisible but will not receive the vital resources they need to improve their performance, while the policies and programmes that target them will not reflect their real needs or their contribution to national development.

There is little experience of national accounts systems that shows the non-monetary contribution of social reproduction work done by women and some men, in the way that Canada's Total Work Accounts System (TWAS) does. This system was created against a background of heated political debate about budgetary constraints on social security and social policies, and was based on three observations:

1   wealth-creating work is not confined to the activities measured by conventional labour-market surveys;
2   the strong links between paid and unpaid work make it difficult to isolate their behaviour when only the economically 'active' population is considered;
3   paid work is a subset of 'work of economic value'.

The TWAS was based on the 1998 General Social Survey on Time Use, which collected time use data. One of its greatest contributions was to assign the estimated output of each activity classified as unpaid work to a specific beneficiary or group, while also allowing domestic responsibilities and the needs of family members to be taken into account in any studies dealing with labour issues.

Some progress has been made since the decision by the Directing Council of the Pan American Health Organization (PAHO) to encourage governments to include as appropriate in the National Health Accounts indicators for the unremunerated time devoted by men and women to health care in the home, as a function of the total expenditure of the health care system.

There are different views on the necessity of including unpaid household work in satellite accounts, which would alter the traditional composition of the national accounts. Another ongoing debate concerns possible methodologies for valuing domestic and care work. One of the most controversial aspects is the use of market prices to set a monetary value on unpaid work.

The invisibility of women's unpaid work is only a part of the problem. The extent and economic value of such work are not easy to calculate because the very fact that it is unpaid means there are no obvious monetary measures, it is generally undervalued in the market, and there are no obvious measures of output, as it is often intangible. This being the case, the most commonly used method has been to employ time use surveys to measure the number of people carrying out such work and the time they spend on it.

Time Use Surveys and Their Potential Policy-making Input

Analysing labour market data in isolation from those relating to domestic work has prevented observation of the strong interrelationships between the two and has helped to perpetuate the erroneous and widespread belief that male and female workers participate in the labour market on similar economic terms, while family constraints and the gender division of labour are related to the 'non-economic' realm. The evidence shows that no category could be less appropriate than 'inactivity' when applied to 'housewives'.

Time use surveys are a useful instrument for analysing work in the light of the links between the public and private spheres, and for studying the 'social contract' governing day-to-day relations between men and women within the home and in society.

Care Needs and Shared Responsibilities: Can Policies Reconcile Work and Family Life?

Even as governments from all over the world were proclaiming their desire to reconcile work and family life at the Fourth World Conference on Women in 1995 – Action for Equality, Development and Peace (UN, 1995), the policies actually being implemented ran counter to the concept of protection and the rights-based approach characterizing the agenda of the United Nations. The prevailing tendency was to shrink the state, deregulate markets and increase employment flexibility. The measures adopted in most countries redefined the relationship between these three elements and, although at the social level the stage was set for the creation of governmental mechanisms for the advancement of women, these were not given a central place on public agendas but developed mainly thanks to pressure from women's movements and the contributions of multilateral and bilateral cooperation agencies.

The lack of debate during the 1990s on the issues identified in Beijing may have been attributable to the difficulty of finding common ground between dialogues based on apparently irreconcilable paradigms. It was not only the difficulties inherent in the interdisciplinary approach that complicated the analysis of the linkages between the social and political realms; another contributory factor was the abandonment of the rights-based approach in the face of the urgent need to meet macroeconomic targets.

A genuine policy of reconciling work and family responsibilities must be aimed at men as much as at women and must firmly promote the active involvement of men in domestic and caregiving work, thereby contributing to a redistribution among household members of the time spent on such tasks and helping to banish stereotyped roles associated with the traditional sexual division of labour. Arrangements of this type enable more women to enter the labour market on better terms. In many countries, however, such policies target only women, and this can undermine their rights as workers and reinforce the cultural pattern that assigns social reproduction tasks to them.

Reconciliation of Family and Work Responsibilities in the Beijing Platform for Action

Strategic objective F.6 of the Beijing Platform for Action deals with the need to harmonize the working and family responsibilities of women and men. Among the measures to be taken by governments are the following:

a   Adopt policies to ensure the appropriate protection of labour laws and social security benefits for part-time, temporary, seasonal and home-based workers; promote career development based on work conditions that harmonize work and family responsibilities.
b   Develop policies, inter alia, in education to change attitudes that reinforce the division of labour based on gender in order to promote the concept of shared family responsibility for work in the home, particularly in relation to children and elder care.

c   Improve the development of, and access to, technologies that facilitate occupational as well as domestic work, encourage self-support, generate income, transform gender-prescribed roles within the productive process and enable women to move out of low-paying jobs.
d   Examine a range of policies and programmes, including social security legislation and taxation systems, in accordance with national priorities and policies, to determine how to promote gender equality and flexibility in the way people divide their time between and derive benefits from education and training, paid employment, family responsibilities, volunteer activity and other socially useful forms of work, rest and leisure.

According to national mechanisms for the advancement of women, it is recognized that there is a need to harmonize family and work through legislation and through public policies and programmes, and there is a concern about the proper functioning of institutions and instruments that support such harmonization, including childcare services and leave from work for breastfeeding mothers. However, this concern is not necessarily reflected in an adequate supply of services, programmes and funding. Furthermore, the concept of reconciliation policies is still a subject for debate and analysis, complicated by diverse policies designed to facilitate women's access to the labour market and those that actually promote the sharing of responsibilities between women and men. There is also a divide between countries that see this as primarily a matter for private negotiation among family members and countries that lean towards giving the state a regulatory role reflected in employment legislation and even in the laws governing the operation of businesses.

A challenge to higher female employment is unpaid work: see Figure 1.1.

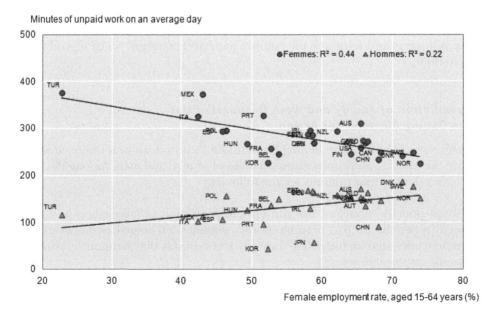

Figure 1.1 Minutes of unpaid work on an average day

Source: OECD (2011). *Doing Better for Families.*

The very different situations existing with respect to the care of young children, along with the relatively low proportion of women working in occupations covered by employment legislation, have created childcare difficulties for families at a time when the state has withdrawn from several areas of social provision. The ideal model of social policies inspired by the welfare state was underpinned by the assumption that families contained a 'male breadwinner' and a 'housewife', with childcare needs being covered by the woman's domestic work. This system, where the 'wage earner' was assumed to be the man, was promoted by income transfers in the form of family allowances or social insurance; in addition, it was the male worker's formal employment that gave the rest of his family access to health and social security systems. All this was supplemented by universal health and education policies in many countries. Although this context was changed substantially by the sector reforms of the 1990s, laws and contracts persist in conferring on women both labour rights that are shared with men and other 'gender-related rights' that entail a greater workload. The right to work is merged with the obligation of care.

The three key components for analysing caregiving capacity are 'time to care, money to care and caregiving services'. Although the public policy implications of these components go beyond employment legislation and they concern more the early months of the life cycle, they are indicative of the links between maternity and paternity leave, childbirth and adoption benefits and the regulation of day-care centres and crèches attached to parents' workplaces. The way these three components are structured will generate alternatives that in some way or other help to consolidate different models of care in the dynamic of gender relations within families. The role of the state is far from neutral, whether in formulating childcare policies or in regulating employment relations between the market and male and female family members.

In employment legislation, the first key element (time to provide care) ties in with the second, namely the availability of financial resources to allow adults to devote their time to caring for a newborn child. Most parental leave (meaning periods of time for which workers may be absent from their employment, while retaining the right to resume it, because of the birth, adoption or guardianship of a child or the need to care for a child, so that the availability of time and money is guaranteed) is granted to working women for periods that vary considerably in the different countries (but are generally no less than 12 weeks). The situation for men is strikingly different. They are allowed only two or three days off after the day of the birth and do not have the option of taking more time off to look after the newborn child. Numerous initiatives have been put forward in recent years (and many of them have now been passed into law) to extend paternity leave to between 10 and 20 days.

The existence of day-care centres or crèches is related to the third key component: childcare services for the children of working people. The regulations on childcare facilities attached to the workplace vary enormously from one country to another, but the great majority oblige employers to provide such facilities based on the number of female workers they employ. The law therefore not only assumes that it will be the working mother who brings her child to work, but also allows them to restrict the number of women they employ to avoid the extra burden of providing a new childcare facility.

The European Union has devised a basic set of nine indicators, some quantitative and others qualitative, to follow up the Beijing *Platform for Action* agreements on harmonization of family and working life. As a report produced for the European

Parliament points out, the most interesting feature is that time use is the basic unit in six of the nine indicators, while others refer to aspects of care for children and dependent adults and one deals generally with integrated policies, especially those concerning employment.

In the private sphere, there has been an upsurge in recent years of what is known as corporate social responsibility, by which is meant an active, voluntary contribution by companies to social, economic and environmental development with a view to improving their competitiveness in the market and hence their value. Corporate social responsibility means more than obeying laws and regulations – indeed, strict compliance with these is taken for granted. It encompasses a whole set of practices, strategies and business management systems intended to strike a new balance between the economic, social and environmental aspects of corporate activities.

Characteristics of corporate social responsibility include an interest in the sustainability of corporate governance practices, a spirit of cooperation with customers, suppliers, competitors and governments, transparency commitments made to society and followed up by accountability measures, usually in the form of annual reports that can be audited by outside agencies and, lastly, corporate citizenship, meaning the rights and obligations that belong to the firm within the community it is part of. Good practices designed to harmonize family and working life for male and female employees are conspicuous by their absence, however.

The EU: Reconciling Family and Working Life, Qualitative And Quantitative Indicators

The qualitative and quantitative indicators proposed by the European Union to measure the degree of reconciliation between family and working life include the following:

1   Employed men and women on parental leave (paid and unpaid) as a proportion of all employed parents.
2   Allocation of parental leave between employed men and women as a proportion of all parental leave.
3   Children cared for (other than by the family) as a proportion of all children of the same age group:

  • before entry into the non-compulsory preschool system (during the day);
  • in the non-compulsory or equivalent preschool system (outside preschool hours);
  • in compulsory primary education (outside school hours).

4   Comprehensive and integrated policies, particularly employment policies, aimed at promoting a balance between working and family life.
5   Dependent elderly men and women (unable to look after themselves on a daily basis) over 75:

  • living in specialized institutions;
  • who have help (other than the family) at home;
  • looked after by the family.

6   Opening hours of public services during the week and at weekends.
7   Opening hours of shops during the week and at weekends.
8   Total 'tied' time per day for each employed parent living with a partner, having one or more children under the age of 12 years or a dependent:

- paid working time;
- travelling time;
- basic time spent on domestic work;
- other time devoted to the family (upbringing and care of children and care of dependent adults).

9   Total 'tied' time per day for each employed parent living alone, having one or more children under the age of 12 years or a dependant:

- paid working time;
- travelling time;
- basic time spent on domestic work;
- other time devoted to the family (upbringing and care of children and care of dependent adults).

The increase in the older adult population and the gradual rise in life expectancy have aroused interest in the functioning of care systems and the role of women in providing unpaid care services, but there is not yet full public backing for social services to support the social reproduction of the older adult population, which means that the family and, to a lesser extent, the market act as the main absorption mechanism for risks associated with old age.

Generally speaking, care is associated only with children and other types of care are therefore overlooked. In addition, it is generally thought that the burden of care falls mainly on the young, since it is young women who have to care for children. The evidence shows, however, that women can also be caregivers at other stages of life and that they provide care more than once in their life cycle, starting with their children, continuing with their parents and ending with their sick spouse. These three stages of care generally correspond to three different stages in a woman's life: youth, adulthood and maturity. The fact is that tradition, socialization and financial relationships combine to give women the central role in caring for older people (and indeed for other social groups), and this tends to hold true whether the woman is in paid employment or carries out domestic work only.

Approaching gender equality from the perspective of unpaid care work allows the world of work to be analysed from a standpoint that is usually ignored in economic and social analyses. This analytical perspective transcends the dichotomy between the public and private spheres, which leads to a focus on unpaid activities and assigns caregiving a subsidiary, complementary and natural role based on the prevailing gender order. But we must consider all the dimensions that affect gender equality, such as employment, unpaid work, social security and, most importantly, the essential and unrecorded contribution of work in the private sphere, which is a vital pillar of development. Although the dichotomy between the public sphere and the private one (the non-business family realm) has a very long history, it is only in the last few decades that the situation has begun to become critical because women have been entering the labour market in large numbers, have little choice but to remain there, and wish to develop their autonomy on the basis of financial independence, something that has also been driven by demographic changes, particularly their control over their fertility and reproductive life, their educational attainments and the growing demand for participation in democratic life.

This change in analytical perspective makes it possible to focus on women's contributions rather than on what is lacking to them, and reveals the non-monetary subsidy they provide over time in the form of unpaid care for children, the sick, the elderly and other family members. Not only that, but the excessive burden of work to which most women are subject yields earnings from employment that are essential for overcoming poverty and achieving well-being, but that result in situations which are extremely distressing for poor women who have to relinquish the care of their own loved ones to work in other households or leave their own countries. This represents a sort of informal social insurance that makes up for the lack of universal, solidarity-based public policies.

The Role of Unpaid Work in the Economy and in Economics

Unpaid work done by men and women throughout the world on average encompasses at least as much of their time as does paid work. A very substantial share of human needs is satisfied by the fruits of unpaid labour. This simple fact could be taken to imply that the economic significance of unpaid work must be gigantic. Economists, however, have had great difficulties in integrating unpaid work in their intellectual endeavours.

In Marxist economics, unpaid work, especially women's housework, is labelled 'reproduction'. The concept of reproduction in Marxist economics refers to the reproduction of the labour force, both on a daily basis and between generations. Reproduction is to be distinguished from production that is characterized by the phenomenon of surplus value. Both spheres, however, are interdependent, as the organization of production presupposes and reinforces a certain way of organizing domestic work. Depending on the changing interest of capital and the state, parts of the reproductive functions of the family sometimes are taken over by public facilities and at other times transferred back to the family. Marxist philosophy also gives reproduction an immaterial meaning: women's caring role in the family reinforces the existing social relations.

Neoclassical economics looks at unpaid work essentially as a form of consumption – a logical consequence of the emphasis put on market phenomena. Unpaid work, especially of married women, is taken into account in the study of (female) labour supply, but it is still treated as a form of leisure (the so-called labour-leisure analysis). John Kenneth Galbraith (1974), however, called the post-war American housewife a 'crypto-servant' for her critical role in the expansion and administration of private consumption. Ivan Illich (1981) became famous for his rather critical analysis of women's 'shadow work' that became a necessary complement to wage labour in modern industrialized economies. Gary Becker's famous article 'A theory of the allocation of time' (1965) marked the beginning of a new school of thought: the New Home Economics. Becker considered the family as 'a small factory' where households divide their time between paid employment, unpaid household production and leisure.

The school of New Home Economics explicitly or implicitly rejected the dichotomy between production and consumption. They envisaged a production function of the household that reflects the production of commodities by combining market goods and time. Becker and his followers have been criticized by feminist economists for taking the household as a unit of analysis, and in that way obscuring conflicts of interest and conflicts over power inside the household.

Economists interested in unpaid work have mostly concentrated on micro-analysis of household work. Far less is known of the macroeconomic significance of unpaid work. At the macro-level, 'an iceberg view of the economy' prevails: what is visible is actually only a very small part of what goes on in the economy. Feminist economists, however, are very rapidly making up for this omission by highlighting the overall economic importance of non-market work, such as subsistence production and caring activity. Fewer economic data and analyses are available on various forms of voluntary community work; voluntary work – translated in the catch-all term 'civil society' – is more the domain of political philosophy.

Unpaid Work and Policy-making

Unpaid work has been given increased attention since the 1960s and '70s, when it (partially and hesitantly) reached the research agendas of mainstream economics and sociology. For a long time economists had equated work with paid employment, while sociologists specializing in labour questions had left the issue for their (often less prestigious) colleagues occupied with the sociology of the family. Years later, the issue of unpaid work was heatedly discussed at two United Nations World Conferences, the Social Summit (Copenhagen, March 1995) and the Fourth World Conference on Women (Beijing, September 1995). Government diplomats and non-governmental organization (NGO) lobbyists not only negotiated language on measuring and valuing unpaid work, but also agreed (all be it implicitly) on a new way of looking at the world's work, i.e. comprising both paid and unpaid work. The controversy concerning the incorporation of unpaid work in national accounts and other statistics, however, has obscured the fact that recognizing unpaid work as work is a revolution in itself. The consequences of this new vision have hardly been explored in the follow-up processes emanating from the two world conferences. Although it seems hardly possible to speak of unpaid work without discussing its counterpart, paid work, the relationship between both is not much studied. The role unpaid work could or should play in socio-economic policy-making has not yet been adequately discussed.

Unpaid work does not simply consist of one specific type of activity, for instance housework, but encompasses a variety of activities. Critical for the definition of the concept of unpaid work is the so-called 'third person criterion'. This criterion implies a production boundary containing non-market activities that in principle could be replaced by market goods and services. United Nations studies and other research have estimated how much unpaid work is done and by whom. On average, unpaid working time amounts to hours a week which are comparable to hours worked in paid employment. The burden of unpaid work and paid work respectively are distributed unequally between men and women.

It is not some inherent trait which causes some activities to be paid or unpaid. The same activity may be paid or unpaid, depending on the social context. Economists have highlighted technological innovation, changes in productivity and relative prices. Women's studies have concentrated on the gender division of labour. The unequal distribution of unpaid work between women and men is substantially linked to the gender-segregated labour market and the prevailing gender discrimination and domination of men's values in society at large. The paid and the unpaid sectors of the economy are interconnected and interrelated, and changes in one part cannot be brought about without changes in the other.

A very substantial share of human needs is satisfied by the fruits of unpaid labour. The economic significance of unpaid work must be gigantic. Economists, however, have had great difficulties in integrating unpaid work in their scientific research. Unpaid work should not be confused with the concept of the informal sector. Most work in the informal sector generates income, however small and unrecorded that may be. The informal sector can be seen as an intermediate zone between unpaid work and regularly paid employment. A portion of the citizens counted as doing unpaid work are in fact 'discouraged workers' and should be counted as 'hidden unemployed'. Because they do not receive a social security benefit or welfare, their unemployment seems to cost nothing.

It is often said that the issue of unpaid work is very different for industrialized and developing countries. This is true as far as the sort of activities performed as unpaid work differs very much in societies of different stages of development. A common denominator, however, seems to be the infinite elasticity of unpaid work: apparently it can be stretched or contracted, if need be. The costs of shifts between these two sectors of the economy are largely invisible.

Unpaid Work as a Gender Issue

Unpaid work as a women's or gender issue has a long UN history. Originally it was perceived as 'women's double burden', but after the First Women's Conference (Mexico City, 1975) another paradigm prevailed. Since then, the question of unpaid work has been seen as an issue of unjust distribution and/or inefficient allocation between the sexes. This should be brought back into balance by (a) promoting equal sharing of family responsibilities between women and men, and (b) providing a better infrastructure of public or social services. Gender equality at the workplace and the sharing of domestic and parental responsibilities are interrelated. Therefore only combined strategies – aiming at both the sphere of unpaid work and the world of formal gainful employment – might be successful in changing the uneven distribution of unpaid work.

Unpaid Work as a Social Issue

Unpaid work as a social issue has a much shorter history in the UN; it really dates back to the preparatory process of the Social Summit itself. The boundaries of paid and unpaid work are influenced by market forces determining the range of the private service sector and by political and budgetary factors determining the range of the public service sector. The choice between paid and unpaid work and profitability/political feasibility of social servicing are two sides of the same coin. The way public policies affect this choice is an important issue.

In order to create more conceptual clarity and to illustrate what we know and what still has to be more deeply researched, the policies related to unpaid work are divided into two groups: specific or direct policies and indirect or 'mainstreamed' policies.

Direct or Specific Policies Related to Unpaid Work

Specific policies are those explicitly aimed at unpaid work. Such an aim might be recognizing or making it more visible, influencing the quantity of unpaid work in society or changing the distribution of unpaid work among different groups.

Various instruments can contribute to *better recognizing unpaid work*: quantitative and qualitative data collection, presentation and analysis; imputation of the value in monetary terms and giving allowances for unpaid work, or actually paying for it.

Four elements of *modern gender equality policy* have been discussed: (1) promoting a more equal sharing of unpaid work between women and men; (2) recognizing of all sorts of 'useful activities' as work or employment in a broader sense;[2] (3) providing of public services, such as childcare; (4) commercializing of domestic labour.

Measures which governments can take to stimulate citizens to participate in *voluntary community work* include a very radical alternative option: compulsory social service. There is practically no literature on voluntary work written from a policy perspective. Compared to the abundance of work on the unpaid housework and caring tasks of women and related issues, this may be called a striking gap.

Indirect or 'Mainstreamed' Policies Relating to Unpaid Work

Affecting unpaid work is not the primary objective of these policies, but they do have (implicit) effects on unpaid work. Sometimes influencing unpaid work is built-in as an explicit secondary objective of a policy design. Mostly, however, mainstream socio-economic policies will have implicit effects on unpaid work. The ways in which wage and income policies, employment and labour market policies, taxation, social security and welfare affect unpaid work in one form or the other are discussed. The implicit influence of mainstream socio-economic policies on unpaid work is an unexplored area. References in the scientific literature are scarce, fragmentary and difficult to track down and coherent research and analysis in this field has hardly started. Analysis from a gender perspective has evidently made most progress, but that is not proportionately reflected in mainstream literature. The assumed dependency of women on the male breadwinner – implicit in social security and taxation systems – is a case in point.

Partly conflicting policy considerations play a role here. On the one hand policymakers have sometimes tried to do justice to existing patterns of allocation of paid and unpaid work and to protect the weaker party. On the other hand, in doing so they have (intentionally or unintentionally) built up barriers to change. This paradox – well known to experts in the field of gender equality policy – lacks the interest of the leading actors in these fields.

Another theme is the recognition of unpaid work as 'socially useful activities' in social benefit regulations and activating labour market policies. Policy questions in this field involve difficult choices between respecting private preferences and demanding a quid pro quo. Policy programmes such as 'workfare' could easily pass the point where the citizen's right to choose employment freely would be at stake. This exercise in exploring the implicit effects of socio-economic policies on unpaid work does not allow a firm conclusion. Effects are diversified, depending not only on the policies concerned but also on the type of unpaid work that one has in mind.

Not only is such an acceptance among policy-makers far away, we also have only a very primitive insight into the interplay of non-market production and market production and how that is affected by government policies. Different groups of activists and academics use the concept of unpaid work for their own purposes. While they speak of 'unpaid work' as such, they are in fact focusing on specific unpaid activities by specific parts of the population and putting their favourite policy issues up front. The UN has offered a forum for all these different groups and tendencies to spread their views. Lacking an integrating theory and a shared body of knowledge, the result is vague and fragmentary.

The unpaid work issue should not be left to the 'women's sections' of national governments, NGOs, international organizations and the academic community. Although the importance of the issue from a gender perspective obviously stands out, it wouldn't be sensible to leave it in this way. Even in a hypothetical world of perfect gender balance unpaid work has to be taken into account as a necessary element of private freedom and as a pillar of civil society and political democracy. In addition, even in a world of full employment, a certain part of human needs would still be met by non-market activities. So, unpaid work should be recognized, valued and factored in as a regular element in policy-making. Social policy that leaves the unpaid work issue out as if it were 'something else' is beside the mark.

Conclusion

All work can be done both as wage (or self-employed) labour and as unpaid activity: it is the specific historical and local context that makes some work paid and other types of work unpaid. Given the variety of activities that makes up the rather amorphous concept of unpaid work, it is important to specify what forms of unpaid work seem relevant in specific policy discussions. In fact, this is not always done. Different groups of activists and academics use the concept for their own purposes; while they speak of 'unpaid work' as such, they are in fact focusing on specific unpaid activities by specific parts of the population and advocating their favourite policy issues.

Women-in-development and some other development experts concentrate on the role of women's subsistence labour and domestic production as an indispensable factor of economic growth and human development. Women's empowerment and reform of macroeconomic adjustment strategies are their prime goals. Gender equality experts, especially those from industrialized countries, focus on women's economic independence and advocate equal sharing of paid employment and unpaid caring work between women and men. They lobby for policy reforms that would support such change and help eliminate hidden gender bias in existing regulations. A segment of the women's movement – those who don't believe in reallocation of work – still wants women's housework to be 'recognized', if not financially then statistically. They collide with statisticians and economists fighting each other on an arena of their own. Some welfare experts and advocates for the unemployed – those who don't believe in full employment – are concerned about a legitimate place for volunteer or alternative work and argue for 'socially useful activities' to be recognized under a broader concept of work.

Last but not least, some policy-makers jump on that bandwagon, pleading for 'work-fare' to solve their problems in financing the burden of social benefits and reducing unemployment. This rough sketch pictures different actors, all claiming the unpaid work issue from their particular perspective and for their particular political goal. Looked at in this way, what happened and is still happening becomes more under-standable. Questions about the different aspects of the issue and using an integrated approach in dealing with it arise.

The importance of the issue of unpaid work from a gender perspective obviously stands out, but it wouldn't be sensible to leave it in this way. The first argument is that a gender perspective must be mainstreamed in all policy areas, including social policy. Second, it is important to realize that the issue of unpaid work would not 'disappear' if the gender aspect could be reconsidered. Even then a certain part of human needs would still have to be met by non-market activities. Even in a hypotheti-cal world of perfect gender balance, unpaid work will have to be taken into account as a necessary element of private freedom and as a pillar of civil society and political democracy. Social policy that leaves the unpaid work issue out as if it were 'something else' misses the point.

In addition, even in a world of full employment, people would continue to engage in work outside the labour market. It is neither feasible nor desirable that all work should be done for the market. Therefore, unpaid work should further be studied in all its different forms and should be recognized, valued and factored in as a regular element in socio-economic policy-making. Further studies on this issue should have two thrusts.

First, the concept of unpaid labour and its place in the economy at large deserves more in-depth research and analysis. What does that broader picture of the economy look like, and will it be possible to develop some paradigm of unpaid work that tran-scends the diversity of all the different unpaid activities and the various perspectives of their advocates in theory and practice? And what would that mean for mainstream economic theory and modelling?

Second, the concept of unpaid work should be elaborated on and attention focused on the different sorts of unpaid work. If the three broad components – subsistence production, domestic work and voluntary activities – are compared, the last of the categories is the most underexposed. Much high-flown philosophy on 'civil society' has not yet yielded concrete insights into questions such as why people work 'for nothing' and how their willingness to do so fluctuates with, for instance, economic circumstances and government intervention.

Further unravelling the economics of unpaid labour could essentially contribute to a broader recognition and understanding of work and employment issues.

Notes

1 Social reproduction is a concept originally proposed by Karl Marx in *Capital*, and is a devel-opment of his broader idea of reproduction. According to sociologist Christopher B. Doob, it 'refers to the emphasis on the structures and activities that transmit social inequality from one generation to the next'. According to Bourdieu there are four types of capital

that contribute to social reproduction in society. They are financial capital, cultural capital, human capital, and social capital.

2 The consequences of this broadening of the concept of work have not been examined, however. All energy went into the controversy of the valuation of unpaid work and its incorporation in national accounts. The outcomes of both conferences implied that unpaid work and its relation with paid work had to be taken into account in the formulation of socio-economic policies, but neither of the conferences spelled out how that goal had to be accomplished.

References

Becker, G.S. (1965), A Theory of Allocation of Time. *The Economic Journal* 75(299): 493–517.

Galbraith, J.K. (1974), 'Consumption and the concept of the household', in *Economics and the Public Purpose*. Harmondsworth: Penguin Books.

Illich, I. (1981), *Shadow Work*. London: Marion Boyars Publishers.

OECD. (2011), *Doing Better for Families*. Available at: http://www.leavenetwork.org/fileadmin/Leavenetwork/Links_publications/OECD_DoingBetterForFamilies_2011.pdf/ (Retrieved 31 May 2013).

UN. (1995), Platform for Action. Action for Equality, Development and Peace. *Fourth World Conference on Women*, Beijing. Available at: http://www.un.org/womenwatch/daw/beijing/platform/ (Retrieved 28 August 2013).

Chapter 2

Employing Women in the Western Balkans

Zorka Grandov, Radica Jovanović
and Olivera Karić Nedeljković

Introduction

Throughout history men and women have contributed to the reproduction of the social world, but the nature of this partnership has changed over time. Paid work has long been associated with men, but the steady disintegration of the traditional family model in which only men perform work outside of the home has been accompanied by a greater income equality for women, both at home and in the professional sphere.

This increase in female employment has been observed in structural social development throughout the twentieth century. A greater number of women now form part of the labour force. Between 35 and 60 per cent of women aged 15 and over in most European countries now work for wages (Gides, 2005: 393). Despite the adoption of progressive legislation which has improved the social status of women in many countries, many traditional forms and norms of behaviour still remain:

> [The] gap is especially apparent when it comes to the economic status of women. In addition to this, the influence of tradition, occasional tendencies of women to 'return home to their families', demands to abandon job positions for the sake of men, the disregard of double work burden of women (at work and at home), informal occupational segregation (a greater proportion of women in lower-paid occupations, and a smaller proportion of women owners and female entrepreneurs) are all equally topical issues asking for the economic emancipation of women in the nineteenth and twentieth century.
>
> (Sekulic, 2007: 144)

In the Western Balkans, women face many problems and are in a difficult situation with regard to the labour market. The major changes that have taken place here – the construction of democratic political institutions, the move towards a market system of free competition and dealing with the consequences of these changes – have created consequences that manifest themselves in the increase of unemployment, poverty and job insecurity. The experience of many countries shows that in dealing with the negative consequences of the processes of structural adjustment and operation of the market women are far more affected than men, and that risks and opportunities are unevenly distributed.

The Serbian labour market is characterized by a declining rate of female activity and high unemployment, the most important factor in an unequal position. Female unemployment in Serbia is similar to that of other countries in the Western Balkans and is far higher than female unemployment in the European Union (EU).

Immediately after attaining EU membership, Bulgaria and Romania increased their employment rates for women to 57.6 per cent in Bulgaria and 52.8 per cent in Romania. Clearly the employment incentives within the EU are reflected in the increased participation of women in the labour market. In these countries, it has also increased the participation of women in management positions.

Involvement of Women in Paid Work

The material, social and psychological dependency of women on their husbands is significantly reduced by the mass employment of women. In practical terms this has made them independent of men and the revenues they raise. Mass employment of women, as well as the separation of a wife's work in the home from outside it, has happened because of modern industry. The need to employ a woman has two sources: on the one hand, the need of capital for cheap labour, dramatically demonstrated during the Industrial Revolution, and on the other hand, the need for additional pay in order to secure decent financial conditions for the family.

Since the 1950s, developed countries have been open to new jobs that require those skills and traits that women express a greater suitability for, such as empathy, teamwork, tolerance, creating the opportunity to increase women's employment, and bringing transformations in many sectors of the economy, particularly the service sector.

Women are increasingly employed for the fulfilment of personal needs, but also to provide funds for the family's survival, particularly where women are the sole provider (single-parent families, couples without children, singles, etc.) (Garhammer, 1997).

Women, in addition to the young and uneducated, are in the worst position in the formal labour market, and therefore mostly employed in the informal sector. In societies undergoing a period of transition, those most at risk of poverty are mothers with children, women over 40 years of age who lose their jobs, rural women, single mothers, the unemployed, the sick, housewives and the uneducated.

Although women in the Western Balkans are facing many problems due to social and individual transitions such as divorce and single parenthood, men and women are forced to do more types of work, and this is reflected in the organization of family life and relationships between family members.

Although there is an evident increase in women's employment and their *formal* legal equality with men in all spheres, women still experience segregation in employment. 'Women are no longer employed in the public sector, clerical work, in educational, health care institutions' (Puljiz et al., 2005: 326). Despite the principle of equality with men, women often face the 'invisible' barriers that impede their progress in occupying key positions in public life.

However, equality has been achieved in the labour market; women with the same level of education and doing the same job have the same salary as men. Those business sectors that stereotype so-called women's work clearly show the difficult progression of women to better-paying jobs (Gabrić Molnar, 2002: 179).

It might be expected that women in the workplace would be treated as equal with men. However, companies exclude women from the ruling relations of production and legitimate government structures and organizations. They are usually trapped in sectors with no prospect of improvement, a practice which justifies their lower salaries and supports the view that their salaries are simply extra household income.

The problems of women are reflected in the low availability of management jobs and the best-paid jobs, the traditional division whereby 'male' work is better paid and more prestigious, and 'female' work less well-paid and less prestigious, with many women working in the 'grey' economy, and a high concentration of female labour in lower-paid jobs (Official Gazette of the Republic of Serbia, 2008: 65).

Economic equality between women and men is required to achieve a balance in the relationship between them. If you do not have equal conditions and opportunities for economic independence, all other measures to promote gender equality are less likely to succeed. Under-used female labour is one of the obstacles to faster economic growth, and there is room for women to become an important resource for developments which contribute to the overall betterment of society.

Statistical data and reports on unemployment show that it affects women more than men. Female unemployment in the total labour force is 1.5 times higher than unemployment of men in the same period.

The position of unemployed women was determined by a weak outlook for permanent employment, low and irregular payment of compensation for those out of work, little chance for professional retraining, and the increased likelihood that they will engage in unpaid work in the home — or resume doing business in the 'underground economy' (e.g. babysitting and caring for older people, housekeeping in other houses, selling goods in public or flea markets, etc.), which is still a significant source of income for unemployed women.

Female unemployment in the Western Balkans is far higher than in the rest of the EU. Female unemployment in the EU increased from 7.4 per cent in 2008 to 8.0 per cent in 2009, suggesting that the female unemployment rate is slightly higher than the male (Eurostat, 2009). In accordance with the proactive intervention espoused by the EU document (diverse documents, rulebooks, regulations, decrees, legislations talking about gender equality and woman employment), it should also provide for the Western Balkan countries' coordinated efforts to suppress all forms of discrimination, as social rights would not be a barrier to its inclusion in employment.

Hiring and the Female Labour Market in the Western Balkans

Economic security and the rights of women is a top priority of the United Nations Agency for Gender Equality and the Empowerment of Women – UN Women, both globally and in the countries of the Western Balkans.

The importance of the economic empowerment of women and the benefits that flow from it are undisputed, from the perspective of women's rights and from the standpoint of economic growth and productivity. However, when it comes to formal employment and enjoying the fruits of their labour, equality between women and men has yet to be achieved.

Although the working population is reduced and unemployment rate increased because of wars, NATO bombing, the disintegration of Yugoslavia and the privatisation of public companies, women in the Western Balkans are still one-third less likely than men to be employed: about half of the female population is economically inactive.

In addition, there are significant differences in the level and type of economic engagement of women, depending on age, level of education and where they live.

Better employment opportunities, especially for women, are still the biggest long-term challenge for the Western Balkans. Western Balkan countries enjoyed rapid growth until 2008, and this was followed by a decline in the unemployment rate, but countries in the region have developed in different directions. Recent data on women's employment in the Western Balkans shows that the labour market is characterized by a low activity rate.

Since the 2008 economic crisis, unemployment in Serbia has increased from 14.4 per cent to 20 per cent in 2010 – the highest level since 1997 (*The Labour Force Survey*, 2010). Bosnia and Herzegovina experienced the same trend – in 2010 unemployment grew to 27.2 per cent. Unemployment in Albania increased as a result of the crisis, but fell to 12.5 per cent in 2010. Despite the decline in production in 2009 and the slow recovery in the meantime, the unemployment rate in the former Yugoslav Republic (FYR) of Macedonia has remained constant at 32 per cent in 2009 and 2010. Kosovo has not carried out a survey of the labour force since 2009, when unemployment stood at 45 per cent, but it is expected that conditions in the labour market will lead to moderate growth and increased public infrastructure investments. Data from the *Labour Force Survey* for 2011 show that unemployment continued to rise in Bosnia and Herzegovina (27.6 per cent), Montenegro (20.1 per cent) and Serbia (where it hit a record 22.8 per cent). In FYR Macedonia, the unemployment rate fell to 31.3 per cent (World Bank, 2011).

The Western Balkans are characterized by the scant involvement of women, who in several countries in the region are largely excluded from the labour market. Activity rates and, consequently, the employment of women is noticeably low in Kosovo and Bosnia. Kosovo and Bosnia are the regions in the Western Balkans which are culturally most specific – women are mostly treated in traditional ways – not allowed to be educated or to work for a salary. The main role for a woman is taking care of a family, giving birth and raising children. Families usually have more than seven children.

Labour market indicators in the countries of the Western Balkans are much lower than the EU average, while the employment rate of women is far below the Lisbon target. Table 2.1 provides a comparative overview of labour market indicators in the countries of the Western Balkans.

Recent data on the employment of women in the Western Balkans confirm that the labour market is characterized by a low activity rate for women. According to the same data source, female employment increases with the level of education, so that the lowest employment rate is for women with the lowest education level (this is significantly lower than for men of the same educational level), and the highest employment rate is for women with higher or university education – even higher than that for men (see Table 2.2).

In the Western Balkans, women's employment activities differ significantly across the region. Women's employment by occupation in Macedonia in 2011 shows most similarity with the structure of employment in the Republic of Serbia in the agricultural sector. In Montenegro, a high proportion of women are employed in the service sector and in trade. Like Montenegro, Croatia has the most female employees in the service sector. Generally, it can be said that in the Western Balkan countries most women are employed in the service sector. Women are most widely represented in health and social welfare, education, catering and trade (see Table 2.3).

Table 2.1 Key labour market indicators: WB (2009–2011) (per cent)

	Activity rate		Employment rate			Unemployment rate			
	2009	2010	2011*	2009	2010	2011*	2009	2010	2011*
Albania	61.9	62.2	–	53.4	53.4	–	13.8	14.2	–
Women	**51.8**	**52.8**	**–**	**43.6**	**44.4**	**–**	**15.9**	**15.9**	**–**
Bosnia and Herzegovina	43.6	44.6	44.0	33.1	32.5	31.9	24.1	27.2	27.6
Women	**31.9**	**33.2**	**32.8**	**23.7**	**23.3**	**23.0**	**25.0**	**29.9**	**29.9**
Macedonia	56.7	56.9	56.8	38.4	38.7	38.9	32.2	32.0	31.4
Women	**43.7**	**44.0**	**44.7**	**29.4**	**29.4**	**30.9**	**32.8**	**32.8**	**30.8**
Montenegro	51.1	50.1	48.7	41.3	40.3	39.1	19.1	19.7	19.7
Women	**43.3**	**42.6**	**42.1**	**34.5**	**33.8**	**33.6**	**20.5**	**20.7**	**20.0**
Croatia	47.3	46.6	45.7	43.2	41.1	39.5	8.7	11.8	13.5
Women	**41.6**	**40.6**	**39.1**	**37.8**	**35.6**	**34.0**	**9.2**	**12.2**	**13.2**
Serbia	49.1	46.9	46.4	41.2	37.9	35.8	16.1	19.2	23.0
Women	**41.4**	**39.0**	**38.0**	**34.0**	**31.1**	**29.0**	**17.8**	**20.2**	**23.7**

Source: National Institutes of Statistics Labour Force Survey, 2009, 2010, 2011.

Note: *data for Albania are from administrative sources and for 2011 are not available.

Table 2.2 Employment by education level of women in the Western Balkan countries 2010–2011 (%)

	Primary school and lower	Primary school and lower	Secondary school	Secondary school	College, university	College, university
	2010	2011	2010	2011	2010	2011
Albania*	–	–	–	–	–	–
Bosnia and Herzegovina	23.6	23.0	56.5	55.3	19.9	21.7
Macedonia	23.2	23.3	50.9	50.1	25.9	26.8
Montenegro	7.9	5.9	64.8	64.5	27.3	29.5
Croatia	19.7	19.2	55.2	54.8	25.1	26.0
Serbia	19.7	17.2	52.6	46.2	27.8	36.7

Source: National Statistical Offices, ARS, 2010, 2011.

Note: *data are not available for Albania.

Table 2.3 Employment of women by sectors in the Western Balkan countries 2010–2011

	Agriculture (%)	Agriculture (%)	Industry (%)	Industry (%)	Services (%)	Services (%)
	2010	2011*	2010	2011*	2010	2011*
Albania	52.6	–	10.8	–	36.6	–
Bosnia and Herzegovina	22.8	26.0	16.4	16.0	60.8	58.0
Macedonia	19.7	18.8	25.1	25.5	55.1	55.9
Montenegro	5.0	4.2	9.8	9.4	85.2	86.4
Croatia	16.3	16.2	13.3	15.3	68.6	67.3
Serbia	16.9	19.4	17.0	16.4	66.0	64.2

Source: National Statistical Offices, ARS, 2010, 2011.

Note: *data for Albania are from administrative sources and for 2011 are not available.

Status of Women in the Labour Market in Serbia

Although the equality of women and men in the labour market is regulated by law, indicators show that Serbia is among those countries with a high level of gender inequality in the labour market when data are compared with the situation in neighbouring countries, especially those of the EU.

The level of education for women and men is the same in Serbia, which is expected to contribute to gender-equal opportunities in employment, given that education is defined as both the most important factor of vertical mobility and a powerful instrument for the prevention of social exclusion. However, the data show that women do not succeed to the same extent as men in finding quality employment and a successful working career. Typically women are losing the race in the competition, in which there are still gender-specific jobs, which leads to new tensions due to the vulnerability of women at work and at home.

The Serbian labour market is characterized by a declining rate of female activity and an unemployment rate which is one of the highest in Europe for both men and women, an important factor in an unequal position.

The activity of women in the labour market compared to the overall female population is very low, and their economic activity is significantly lower than that of men. Accumulated problems of women from the past are being transmitted and reinforced during the transitions in society, and economic insecurity, fear of job losses and declining living standards are becoming a reality for most families.

Statistical data and reports on unemployment show that it affects women more than men. Unemployment rates in Serbia range from 21 to 30 per cent, depending on the method of calculation, and unemployment is a major problem. Existing economic activity and the slow rate of growth of gross domestic product in the republic are failing to provide increased employment. From 2008 to 2011, coinciding with the global economic crisis, the total number of unemployed has increased.

According to the data from the National Employment Service of the Republic of Serbia (NES) 2011, of the total registered unemployed at end of 2010, 52.69 per cent are women, and most of these women are aged 25 to 29 years (14.5 per cent).

In the current economic conditions, Serbia cannot expect better results in terms of the self-employment of women. Although female entrepreneurship is widely promoted by public and private organizations, according to government data Serbian women own or have a stake in the ownership of 25 per cent of all businesses, while 17 per cent of companies in Serbia are both owned by women and perform managerial functions.

Women in Serbia are inhibited by various barriers, as suggested by the data on educational and career choices, the absence of women in leadership roles and other prestigious jobs that bring higher wages, as well as data on the willingness of women to start their own businesses and become entrepreneurs.

Data from the *Labour Force Survey* for the three-year period 2008 to 2010 point to shifts in the educational structure of employed, unemployed and inactive persons aged over 15 years (RSO, 2008, 2009, 2010). Among employees there is an increasing trend in the proportion of individuals with higher education, stagnation of the share of people with secondary vocational and general education, as well as a trend of declining participation of persons with primary education and no education.

Although the legal framework is largely in line with the legislation of the EU, so that it is possible to evaluate trends in the improvement of the legal status of women, reform of the legal sector has not been completed in all areas; the legal position of women in Serbia is still contradictory and inconsistent. In line with the European perspective and Strategy for the Advancement of Women and Gender Equality, adopted in early 2009 (Official Gazette of the Republic of Serbia, 2008) as well as a number of international declarations and other strategic documents signed by Serbia, all planned activities of state institutions and civil society in this area will need to be aligned with the EU.

Serbia, as a member of the United Nations, the Council of Europe and other international organizations, and also party to a number of international instruments relating to women's rights and gender equality, needs a commitment to constantly work on the equality and rights of women and men, to enable equal opportunities in all walks of life.

National Employment Serbia (Official Gazette of the Republic of Serbia, 2008) provided the expected rates of employment (and unemployment) by 2020. The rate is 61.4 per cent (10.8 per cent) of the working age population of 15–64 years, a slower pace than the employment rate of 70 per cent provided for in the strategy 'Europe 2020' for the 27 countries of the EU, which gives a figure of 64.6 per cent in 2010. Special attention will be required to improve the labour market in certain categories, such as the young, old and women.

Conclusion

Economic and social changes bring new job opportunities for women and provision of well-paid jobs, while changes in the labour market lead to increased unemployment and economic uncertainty that affects women more than men. Various barriers hinder women in employment, and this is apparent in data on the economic activities of women, their educational and career choices, and information on the high level of unemployment. Economic equality between women and men is required to achieve a balance in the relationship between the sexes. Brain waste of the female labour force is one obstacle to faster economic growth.

Better employment opportunities, especially for women, are still the biggest long-term challenge for the Western Balkans. Labour market indicators in the countries of the Western Balkans are much lower than the EU average that the employment rate of Lisbon Strategy 2020 targets 70 per cent.

In the current economic conditions the unemployed can expect better results in terms of employment of women in the Western Balkans. Women's employment policies and activities of the institutions of the labour market must fully comply with the EU acquis. Employment incentives in the EU are reflected in the increased participation of women in the labour market.

References

Eurostat. (2009), *Eurostat*. Available at: http://ec.europa.eu/eurostat/statistics-explained/index.php/Unemployment_and_beyond (Retrieved 14 June 2014).

Gabrić Molnar, I. (2002), 'Presence of the patriarchal pattern in the market economy and business sphere', in M. Dokmanovic (ed.), *Transition, Privatisation and Women*. Subotica, Serbia: Women's Centre for Democracy and Human Rights, p. 179.

Garhammer, M. (1997), Familiale und Gesellschaftliche Arbeitsteilung – ein europäischer Vergleich. *Zeitschrift für Familienforschung* 9: 28–70.

Gides, E. (2005), *Sociology*. Belgrade: University of Belgrade.

Puljiz, V., Bezovan, G., Sucur, Z. and Zrinscak, S. (2005), *Social Policy: History, Systems, Glossary*. Zagreb: Faculty of Law.

Republic Office for Statistics of Serbia. (2008, 2009, 2010).

Sekulic, N. (2007), *Sociological Dictionary*. Belgrade: Institute of Textbooks.

World Bank. (2011), *Southeast Europe: Regular Economic Report*. Available at: www.worldbank.org (Retrieved 15 February 2013).

Websites

www.dzs.hr
http://www.instat.gov.al
https://ask.rks-gov.net
www.stat.gov.mk
www.fzs.ba
www.monstat.org

Chapter 3

A Different View of Women's Employment

The Case of Turkey and Germany

Mine Yılmazer and Meltem Onay

Introduction

The main objective of women's empowerment is to increase health, education and employment. It will not only improve their own opportunities, but also provide benefits for a new generation that will be healthy and educated. Women who participate in vocational training and employment and receive a regular income contribute to the country's development. In developed countries gender discrimination is less and women's socio-economic power is greater. As women's level of education increases the age of marriage is later; fertility and child death rates decrease; healthier, well-fed and educated children increase; and participation in the labour force and the portion of women's national income increases.

The first condition of troubleshooting women's problems is to acknowledge the problem's existence. It is necessary to be aware of the social gender concept and to examine the result of gender prejudice. Women's rights are a human entitlement. Within the context of fundamental rights and freedoms, women need to demand their implementation, but embodiment of the demands of women depends upon their gaining competence and strength.

Only after women have the strength to give direction to their lives will their input in the mechanisms of economic and political decision-making increase. However, this implementation relies on other aspects of society's support. With the support of all individuals and institutions women will be able to begin to act to address their problems. In terms of awareness, benefiting from vocational and technical education and inclusion in employment, public institutions support women to have vocational and technical education and be employed.

In each community, boys and girls or men and women have different roles. With regard to gender discrimination, historical and cultural features, religious structures, health, social security and education priorities, there is a time and space difference depending on access to resources. In countries, measures to be taken by local institutions should show some differences in accordance with the intensity of gender discrimination (Lahn, Hayen and Unterberg, 2008: 13). The boundaries of gender discrimination must first be determined, then training and job-finding activities should be planned and implemented.

Women's social and employment status is much higher in Germany in comparison to Turkey. However, because of external migration in some regions of Germany and internal migration in Turkey, it is observed that the problem of women's employment is increasing in cities. The purpose of this study is to uncover the activities that are carried out to increase women's employment in the spirit of social municipality in Germany and Turkey. Thus the difference in women's living standards between Germany, a country with a developed welfare system, and Turkey will be discussed. We will first examine the key issues of importance and the content of the studies conducted on this subject.

Fundamental Economic Data and Gender Inequality in Turkey and Germany

Once the indicators of human development and women are considered, serious differences between Germany and Turkey are apparent. For example, according to the Human Development Index, which ranks countries with regard to their education, health and income levels as determined by the United Nations Development Programme (UNDP), Germany is at number 5, Turkey at 90 and Niger is the last on the list at 186. The UNDP has a similar determination on issues affecting women. According to the Gender Inequality Index Germany ranks 6, Turkey 68 and Yemen is last at 148 (UNDP, 2013: 152–9).

Table 3.1 illustrates the fundamental indicators for women in both countries for 2012.

The gender gap index which is represented in Table 3.1 examines the gap between men and women in four categories: economic participation and opportunity, educational attainment, health and survival and political empowerment (World Economic Forum, 2013: 4). According to the index ranking, Turkey is listed at 120 and Germany at 14 amongst 136 countries.

Turkey's population growth rate (1.21 per cent) and fertility rate (2.06) is significantly higher than Germany's (0.03 per cent and 1.41). In parallel, while the age of marriage for women is 32 in Germany, it is 23 in Turkey and, while the birth rate is 7 per 1,000 girls aged 15–19 in Germany, it is 32 in Turkey (Table 3.1). In Turkey, women marry and have children at an early age, which has an adverse effect on their professional and training success and development.

Table 3.1 Women indicators in Germany and Turkey, 2012

Indicator (2012)	Germany		Turkey	
Gender Inequality Index rank	6		68	
Gender Gap Index rank	14		120	
Population growth (%)	0.03		1.21	
Fertility rate	1.41		2.06	
Age at first marriage, female	31.7		23	
Adolescent fertility rate (births per 1,000 girls aged 15–19)	7		32	
Literacy rate	99 (W)	99 (M)	90 (W)	98 (M)
Estimated earned income	30,378 (W)	40,000 (M)	8,053 (W)	27,597 (M)
Women in parliament	33 (W)	67 (M)	14 (W)	86 (M)

Sources: World Economic Forum (2013); UNDP (2013).

In Turkey, the ratio of literate adult women that live in rural areas is low (90 per cent) but for men it is at the level of developed countries (98 per cent). In Turkey compulsory education was up to year 7 in the 1990s and was increased to year 12 in the 2000s: accordingly, literacy issues were resolved to a great extent in the younger generation. Income inequality between men and women is a problem throughout the country. In 2012, women's income level was 24 per cent less in Germany and 70 per cent less in Turkey in comparison to men (Table 3.1). The figures show that women's access to resources in Turkey is very low compared to Germany. In Turkey the women's labour force participation rate is very low, and in general women work in informal sectors or take part in unpaid work at home. According to the women's labour force participation rate, Turkey is last amongst the Organization for Economic Cooperation Development (OECD) countries and in twentieth position amongst the worst countries, while in Germany, women's labour force participation rate was 72 per cent in 2012; this ratio was 30 per cent in Turkey (World Bank, 2013).

In Germany in 2012, 46 of every 100 people who are employed were women. Because 51 per cent of the total population is female, women in Germany think that they are not represented in economic life (Federal Statistical Office of Germany, 2012a: 10). In Turkey 30 out of every 100 workers are female (World Bank, 2013). When you consider that women represent 51 per cent of the population, it is clear that women's representative rights are lower in Germany. In both countries, women are at the forefront of domestic responsibilities. The most important difference between Germany and Turkey is that in Turkey, due to a traditional perspective, women prefer to work in their houses rather than to have a paid working life, whereas in Germany women's participation in the workforce changes according to their plan to have children and the number of children they have. In Germany, 91 per cent of fathers aged 20–49 and 57 per cent of mothers are employed. On the other hand, 78 per cent of mothers with preschool children and 88 per cent of fathers work full-time. Childbirth is one of the major causes for women to leave their jobs in Germany; 61 per cent of women with one child, 46 per cent of women with two children and 24.5 per cent of women with three or more children participate in employment. In Germany, 54 per cent of women and 10 per cent men work part-time in order to look after their children and other family members and to take care of the household duties (Federal Statistical Office of Germany, 2012a: 33). Although women have children they work part-time and maintain their connection to working life. In Turkey, the family responsibilities of women lead women to leave work or work informally at home, while in Germany women work part-time to continue to have social security.

One of the most important factors for women's participation in working life is the average length of working hours. Weekly working hours in Germany (35.5 hours) are lower than the European average (37.4 hours). Working hours in Turkey are 48.9 which is well above the European average (Federal Statistical Office Germany, 2012a: 25). As the age of the workers increases, the working hours also increase.

In Germany unemployment insurance is administered in an efficient manner. Despite this, in recent years there has been an increase in the inequality of unemployment insurance payments. While the proportion of those who benefit from unemployment insurance payments was 87 per cent both for German and foreign workers in 2001, it was 85 per cent for Germans and 80 per cent for foreign workers in 2011 (Federal Statistical Office of Germany, 2012a: 48).

In this study, two regions that have a similar structure in Turkey and Germany have been chosen and the effectiveness of activities for women employed at municipalities which are local institutes has been assessed. In this context, the activities of Konak Municipality in Izmir, Turkey, and the Bremen Municipality in Germany, which are 'sister cities' and both have 'women-friendly' features, are examined.

With a population of 4 million, according to its economic size and human development, Izmir is the third-largest city in Turkey. Izmir's 'sister city' Bremen's population is only 547,340. Both cities from past to present are harbours and trading cities. In Bremen in 2010 12.5 per cent of the population was under 15 years of age, 66 per cent of the population was aged 15–65 and the population over the age of 65 was 21 per cent. In Izmir, these ratios are 19.5 per cent, 71.5 per cent and 9 per cent respectively (Federal Statistical Office of Germany, 2012b: 11; TUİK, 2012).

The fact that Izmir's young and active population is greater than Bremen's suggests an emphasis on employment in Izmir. Immigrants come from 27 European Union countries, making up 4.5 per cent of the population in Bremen.

Five per cent of the population in Bremen is Turkish and represents the highest percentage of immigrants; the rest of the population are immigrants from Poland, Serbia, Russia, Portugal, Bulgaria and Italy. Izmir is also a city of immigration from countries such as Ukraine, Belarus, Korea, Iran, Syria and many others.

Determinants of Women's Employment

In developing countries there are three factors that adversely affect women's participation in the labour market: economic, social and demographic. Economic factors are low rates of wages, social insecurity, high working hours, lack of childcare and elderly care services. Social factors are outlined as gender discrimination against women, women's low level of education and the quality of vocational education, women's role in the household and negative attitudes towards working women. Some of the demographic factors are early marriage, giving birth to children at an early age, and rural–urban migration.

Women's labour force participation rate depends on the decisions that are taken in the household and the environment's perspective towards women (Gornick and Hegewisch, 2010). Decision-makers need to apply policies that will eliminate gender inequality for women and enable them to benefit from work and social security rights while also establishing a balance between in-house responsibilities and work life (Budig, Misra and Boeckmann, 2012; Katz, 2008; Sundstrom, 2002). To resolve the differences between men and women, a wide range of vocational and technical training opportunities should be provided, social security measures should be expanded, the challenges that women face in the labour market should be reduced and these activities should apply in all countries. In developed countries, women's issues are relatively less and social services are more common, making implementation for eliminating gender disparity even more important for developing countries.

It is emphasized in many studies in the literature that if women receive assistance in childcare and family responsibilities their participation level in the labour force can be increased (Alonso-Almeida, 2014; del Boca, 2002; Haan and Wrohlich, 2011; Kreyenfeld and Hank, 2000; Lee and Lee, 2014). In particular, in developed countries child benefit and social services are quite advanced. For example, Schober and

Schmitt (2013) came to the conclusion that childcare services have an overall positive impact on family life, health, income level and parent satisfaction. However, in the wake of the 2008 global financial crisis, Germany, Great Britain, Ireland and many other European countries sought to reduce childcare and other social services. On the other hand, in the same period in developing countries such as Chile, South Africa, Egypt and Turkey, women's employment was subsidized, quotas were applied and financing and training was provided: Turkey created 65,000 jobs for women in the year 2009–10 (ILO, 2012: 31–4). However, it is not so easy to provide a solution to the female employment problem in Turkey. Women's labour force participation in Turkey increases during periods of economic crisis, but is reduced again when the crisis is over (Ozdemir and Dundar, 2012: 3).

In Turkey women are generally poor and work in informal jobs, mostly in the agricultural sector. This situation suggests that institutions provide inadequate policies to address gender inequality and protection (Karadeniz, 2011: 83; Ozdemir, Yalman and Bayrakdar, 2012: 116). Institutions allocate greater resources for employment activities to be carried out, but the projects do not provide the desired results. In Turkey, the effectiveness of the institutions that provide employment to disadvantaged groups is measured only by the number of participants and not the outcome (Gursel and Uysal-Kolasin, 2010: 3).

However, in recent years the rapid growth in ongoing immigration from rural areas to cities has caused uneducated women to stay away from work: either that or it leads to them working informally. Women in urban areas do not work in part because of immigration, but also because priority is given to child and family care (Dayioglu and Kirdar, 2010: 13). In this context Germany is in a similar situation. The difference for women in Germany is that in addition to meeting their family responsibilities they also engage in part-time jobs, and thus they do not fall out of the labour force. According to Simonson, Gordova and Titova (2011), in West Germany women prefer to work part-time while they still largely work full-time in East Germany. The income gap between the two regions is seen as the most important cause of this condition.

Ultimately, economic and cultural characteristics of the countries shape the perspectives of institutions and individuals and bring women's employment and gender inequality with them. The biggest difference between Germany and Turkey is that while in Turkey women's labour force participation rate is low and informal employment is high, in Germany women prioritize children and family responsibilities but still work part-time and remain part of work life and social security.

Method and Scope of the Research

The purpose of this study is to compare the work completed on women's employment at the Konak Municipality (population of 405,580) in Izmir, Turkey, with Bremen, which has a busy harbour and a population of 547,340. Because Bremen and İzmir are 'sister cities', this research will also deliver significant results in the development of bilateral relations.

Different resources from both cities were used to carry out this research. We decided to contact the Bremen Municipality: it operates in conjunction with the Goethe Institute which works actively in Izmir. A survey prepared by us was sent to the Department Responsible for Women's Issues and Employment of Bremen Municipality. However, rather than completing the survey, five reports and website links that indicate the status of the country and the city in general were sent to us, and the Konak Municipality submitted documents and reports from its Social Services Unit. The scope of the survey was intended to address 18 questions.

In our study, the factors thought to affect women's employment were examined in three groups. As shown in Figure 3.1, three basic hypotheses are based on the model of study:

- **Hypothesis 1:** When municipalities and institutions that cooperate with them offer vocational training programmes, women's employment opportunities increase.
- **Hypothesis 2:** When municipalities find solutions to women's family issues (childcare, fertility, disability, poverty), women's employment increases.
- **Hypothesis 3:** When municipalities address the requirements of women's social activities (awareness, human rights, psychological counselling), women's employment increases.

Hypothesis 1: When municipalities and institutions that cooperate with them offer vocational training programmes, women's employment opportunities increase.

Konak's Affairs Directorate of Social Assistance department is working in order to meet the economic and social needs of society, but especially women and children

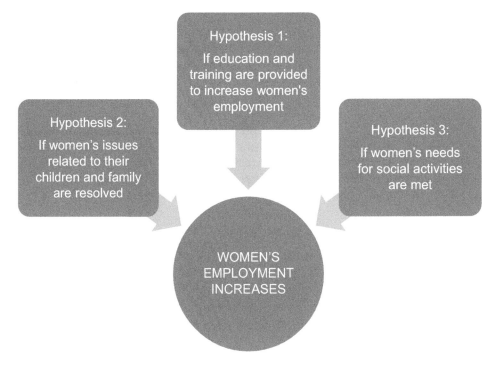

Figure 3.1 The research model and the relationship between the established hypotheses research findings

that are vulnerable groups. Its municipal social services aims at increasing employment by working in collaboration with ISKUR (the Business Association of Turkey), KOSGEB (for the Development and Support Administration of Small and Medium-sized Enterprises) and civil society organizations. These services are based on the aim of ensuring that women benefit from technical and vocational training, child development and education assistance, adaptation to culture and art, and integration into social life.

The Bremen 'job centre' organizes basic assistance for job seekers, and these needs are met by the City of Bremen and the Employment Agency, working jointly. The Employment Agency's role is to provide vocational counselling and work placement, and the City of Bremen provides shelter, heating and education, all of which are significant aspects of attending work. The main purpose of these institutions is to eliminate gender disadvantage; therefore, the aim is to maintain a balance between women's family life and work life.

Konak Municipality has opened courses in patient care, confectionery, tourism, sign language, executive assistance, styling, aesthetics, clothes sewing, being an admissions secretary and cookery courses for female employment. The municipality usually holds these courses with ISKUR. ISKUR helps trainees to find employment after training. KADER (Association for Support of Women Candidates) provides life-coaching and personal development for women, and KOSGEB gives vocational training and provides employment opportunities.

There has been intense participation in these courses, and in recent years an increase in the demand has become self-evident. The training offered is in line with the expectations of the society, but the courses do not help women participate in working life actively because working life requires different qualifications and skills.

The municipality has a 'home pool' and if there is a need for guidance to other institutions, women will be referred to them. In 2013, 50 of the 60 people who attended the Patient Care course were placed in jobs (in private nursing homes, hospitals and dealing with patients in their own homes).

The Bremen Municipality usually supports women who are economically dependent and uneducated; they refer women to the employment agency and to vocational courses to find jobs according to their skills. They provide consulting services to the unemployed and to those who want to improve their careers. In this context, together with Work Agencies, activities such as employment according to their qualifications, support to those who left their jobs, professional and vocational training are carried out. Gender equality is also emphasized. Thus, the disadvantages of women in labour market are tried to be eliminated.

Women who are connected to the social and health services by the City of Bremen are generally divided into three groups:

1   those undergoing financial hardship;
2   single mothers who brought up their children without a spouse; and
3   women over the age of 65.

In Bremen Municipality, the Equal Opportunities Commission actively directs their focus towards women. Their objectives are: providing vocational training for women; giving them a career path and helping them to rise in their career path; training women how to reduce their domestic responsibilities; advising on returning to work after a break; and advocating flexible working hours to increase women's employment. Female university graduates in Bremen have usually been trained in the fields of medicine and dentistry, as health personnel assistants, and in law, teaching and logistics. However, it has been observed that women who want to have careers based on their vocational training choose hairdressing, office administration and sales work.

Both municipalities organize activities to increase employment and apply positive discrimination for women.

Our hypothesis that when municipalities and cooperating institutions offer vocational training programmes, women's employment opportunities increase, can be accepted as a valid.

Hypothesis 2: When municipalities find solutions to women's family issues (childcare, fertility, disability, poverty) women's employment increases.

Information and counselling services are provided by Konak Municipality in regard to the development and education of children aged 1–6. Each month seminars are held by the child development staff in the neighbourhoods on different topics to address various issues. Due to the schools' requests, within the budget of Konak Municipality stationery and clothing assistance are provided to those students who are identified as in need.

In primary schools, trips are organized in order to contribute to the development of cultural and artistic awareness in the students. Similarly, trips are organized to develop women's consciousness of city life and culture, which also helps with their participation in social life.

In Bremen in 2010, 47,049 (of the total population of 94,243 women) were women that were in need of social services; 72 per cent of these needed assistance although they are able to work (Statistisches Landesamt Bremen, 2012).

In addition to counselling for women, the City of Bremen also has counselling centres for children, youth and families. When families are in need of financial assistance, municipalities can provide child support to families. A family will receive €70 a year to purchase school supplies, and €10 and school transport fee towards the children's involvement in sports, culture and entertainment.

In addition, parental leave and financial support for children with disabilities are provided. The City of Bremen also provides counselling services and mediates for children who have dropped out of school. In 2010, figures show that the number of children in childcare was 17,531; 3,205 of these were aged 0–3 years, and 14,326 aged 3–6 (Statistisches Landesamt Bremen, 2012).

It is clear that both countries municipalities have taken measures to facilitate improvement in women's, children's, and young people's lives. However, these benefits are directed to overcoming the financial difficulties of poor families and are not sufficient to increase women's employment. In this instance there was no evidence to substantiate the hypothesis.

In both countries, women consider 'family responsibilities' before employment. However, women in Turkey, due to their lack of education, inability to find work or because of family pressure, prefer home-based or unregistered work. As a result, they try to generate revenue by both being involved with their families and working parallel to their household. While the portion of working women with no children is high in Germany, as the number of children increases, women choose part-time work and remain connected to work life and social security, rather than being separated from them because of family responsibilities.

Hypothesis 3: When municipalities address the requirements of women's social activities (awareness, human rights, psychological counselling), women's employment increases.

Konak Municipality does not have a specific budget for women, but there is an allocation of funds to provide support to women's social welfare and activities. In the City of Konak, under the title 'Leaders of Women's Education' in the district centres, 10 women are chosen to 'identify the needs of their neighbourhood', such as the required parks, lighting, health centres and installation of surveillance. Konak's project KADER has identified young women aged 20–30, victims of abuse that have vocational training and live in disadvantaged areas, and have offered these young women a chance to be employed by the municipality.

Enquiry subjects at the Family Counselling Unit of Konak Municipality usually concern communication problems in marriage, violence and anger management issues.

Although other municipalities in the province of Izmir have shelters, there is no women's shelter in Konak. In 2013 one male asylum-centre building was added to these temporary shelters. In Izmir women who arrive from overseas (Ukraine, Belarus, Korea, Iran, Syria, Greece, Libya and Kazakhstan) are given Turkish language education. Foreign women have not requested support with regard to employment and adaptation to the society.

The Municipality has established a commission of equality for men and women. Prevention of obesity, cleanliness of the street toilets, building guesthouses for children, vocational training and retirement neighbourhood homes are amongst the decisions that have been taken. Annually 600 people apply to seek support from the municipalities' consulting services. Generally, they apply for support in psychological counselling, adolescent issues and family communication issues. District centres also offer women's human rights education at regular intervals.

Turkey's first female museum was created by Konak Municipality. This museum presents female pioneers in their respective careers and is both informative and encouraging. The Municipality has a women's soccer team and this team is sixteenth in the European league.

There are 123 women's shelters in Bremen. Emergency calls and counselling services are provided to women and children. The fee for staying one night at this accommodation is €11.64 and, depending on the applicants' unemployment security status, this fee is either paid by the government or the woman. Women are reluctant to stay at these houses due to the financial burden. The budget that has been allocated by the government for shelters has increased from €150,000 to €168,000 in 2012/2013 because it was felt that they needed more staff and services available. In Bremen it is thought that the proportion of the immigrant population in general, and women in particular who have suffered violence, is high. In contrast, it is thought that the services offered to abuse victims are not sufficient in financial terms and are not offered by specialists in the field.

Municipalities always provide help to children and immigrants. In some cases, municipalities are forced to close or reduce social facilities that help the poor or reduce the budget spent on public services, a situation which can cause adverse reactions by local citizens.

As a result, in either country when measures for social activities are taken, it raises awareness among women and it also raises awareness in regard to their rights. Although there isn't sufficient data to show that social activities increase women's employment, this kind of work is expected to provide opportunities for women's employment indirectly.

Conclusion

The purpose of development is to provide a human-oriented progress which emphasizes individual rights and freedoms. Within this context every individual in society should have access to an egalitarian development. This will mostly involve children, adolescents, the elderly, the disabled, women, the unemployed, the poor and immigrants. In other words, what needs to be addressed is the vulnerable portion of society and their access to resources, their participation level in employment and the freedom of choice to manage their lives.

In this study, the effectiveness of the measures to increase woman's employment in Turkey and Germany has been carried out by comparing these two micro-level municipalities. In general, based on micro and macro data, a significant difference in human values between Turkey and Germany is observed in relation to the woman-oriented data.

The above information is summarized in accordance with the information received from the two country's municipalities. A lack of information on how much the municipal projects and activities that are carried out affect women's employment has made it difficult to test the validity of these hypotheses. Therefore, in the light of the findings, both municipalities' social benefits and the costs that affect female employment are shown in Tables 3.2 and 3.3.

Based on the information obtained in Table 3.2, the municipal social benefits of activities to increase women's employment were revealed.

Although the activities and services for women by the municipalities comprise costs, they are very important in terms of social welfare benefits. As shown in Tables 3.2 and 3.3, directly or indirectly, the social benefits of women's activities are much higher than the costs. Women who lack rights and freedoms will obtain a share of income by gaining vocational skills and employment. According to the survey, the results are poor in comparison to the provided services (employment and social security). In contrast, direct or indirect non-financially social benefits arise, and it is clear that these benefits might not contribute to women's empowerment in the short term but will in the long term.

Despite Turkey's socio-economic structure towards women, which is threatening and demonstrates weaknesses, social contributions will continue (Table 3.4). However, it is still difficult to change and eliminate negative views with regard to women socio-culturally.

The activities that are carried out by the Konak municipality have an impact on employment; mostly the change is in women's self-confidence and world vision. It is

Table 3.2 Social benefits of activities carried out to increase women's employment in the Bremen and Konak municipalities

Social benefits

Direct benefits	Indirect benefits
Financial • Opportunities for skills, occasional and professional training • To be employed and to have a social security • Assistance for the prevention of low income • Flexible working conditions • First providing job opportunities to international or domestic immigrants	Financial • Increase in Gross Domestic Product (GDP) • Employment opportunities provided to trainers and consultants • Financial assistance for children and youth • Support for disabled children's families • Increase in district services to support women (parking, lighting, health centres)
Non-financial • Social communication skills • Awareness of individual rights • Skills to give direction to their own life and career planning • Positive discrimination of women in public policy implementation • 'Women-friendly' activities conducted in district centres • Increase in financial opportunities and activating women's counselling centres	Non-financial • Obtaining a social status • Productivity in the family • Increase in children's literacy and technical training • Decrease of fertility rate • Reduction in teenage marriages • The creation of role models in the society • The creation of urban culture and urban consciousness • The prevention of violence and awareness practices in the family • Encouraging women to find their places in society

Table 3.3 Social costs of activities carried out to increase women's employment in the Bremen and Konak municipalities

Social costs

Direct costs	Indirect costs
Financial • Spending on education and other social services • After the spending, not being able to obtain the expected result • Inability to provide women employment	Financial • Increase in unemployment • Restrictions on other social services
Non-financial • Inability of women's empowerment • Discouragement of women if unsuccessful in receiving results from these services	Non-financial • Municipalities do not follow the results of their activities • Data deficiencies

thought that this will also have a positive impact on future generations and that the social benefits are always higher than the social costs.

In the activities of the Bremen Municipality the strengths and opportunities are greater than the weaknesses and threats. While the high level of immigration in Germany and the insufficiency of social services are the greatest weaknesses (despite the level of sophistication of services) women's social status is still better than in any other country (Table 3.5). Germany is relatively in a better position than Turkey.

Table 3.4 SWOT analysis of the activities performed by Konak Municipality

Strengths
- The existence of women who want to benefit from the social support mechanism
- The financial resources and technical support that the municipality has
- Municipalities in cooperation with organizations that provide direct employment
- The support of civil society organizations and some public institutions

Weaknesses
- To provide sufficient employment from vocational and technical training activities
- To prefer to stay at home although sufficient income of women (some women prefer to stay at home when their income is enough)
- The low level of employment and the high rate of unemployment in the country
- Rapid urbanization and inadequate infrastructure
- High income inequality between working women and men
- The high number of working hours

Opportunities
- Positive discrimination for women within the social municipality concept
- To become a women-friendly city
- Improvement of women's empowerment and social status
- The changes in a positive direction in the point of view of society towards women
- The option of benefiting from domestic and foreign funds
- Priority to support immigrants

Threats
- Being a developing country and having low incomes
- Negative points of view about working women in the society
- Family and environmental pressure
- Family violence
- The large number of children and early marriage
- Lack of courage and self-confidence of women
- Lack of access to opportunities of social security
- Lack of morale for women who cannot find a job

Table 3.5 SWOT analysis of the activities performed by Bremen Municipality

Strengths
- Being a developed country and having high incomes
- Positive attitude towards women in the community and in work life
- To cooperate with institutions that provide employment opportunities for women
- Having unemployment insurance and an improved social security system
- To give priority to gender equality
- Working hours that are lower than the European average
- Having financial resources and technical support by municipality
- The large number of people that received vocational training

Weaknesses
- To reduce the budget as a result of increase in financial costs due to domestic and international immigration
- Insufficient funds in the women's budget
- The lack of staff and services in social services
- The shortage of funding allocated to shelters

Opportunities
- Positive discrimination for women
- To be a women-friendly city
- Late marriage and decrease in the birth rate
- Low income inequality between women and men
- Women have a relatively high share of employment
- Part-time work opportunities being higher
- Opportunities to benefit from domestic and foreign funding
- Priority to support the immigrants

Threats
- The negative attitude of the German community towards granting social assistance immigrants
- The negative effect on other social services due to use of resources in such areas
- Family violence being high
- Women prefer to stay at home after they have a child in comparison to work life

In Germany women's participation in education and work life, social security and flexible work conditions are greater than in Turkey; in addition Germany has more ability to provide consultants for people facing financial difficulties than Turkey. In Germany two issues are discussed frequently: the fact that gender equality is not at the desired level and the inadequate representation of women in employment.

Turkey is amongst the countries experiencing serious problems in relation to gender inequality and women's empowerment issues. In Turkey there is a large young population and a lack of equal opportunities in access to resources, family pressure, a low labour participation and injustice in income distribution. Turkey has serious problems, and to overcome these problems more effective women's employment policies are needed.

In conclusion, if women, who are the most vulnerable portion of the society in regards to reaching individual rights and freedom, become stronger, their ability to participate in employment will increase accordingly. In addition the fertility rate and infant deaths will decrease and finally the healthier, well-nourished and educated child population will increase. In summary, women who are courageous, contentious and productive will achieve the freedom of choice to direct their lives and as a result this will have an impact on society's development.

References

Alonso-Almeida, M. (2014), Women (and Mothers) in the Workforce: Worldwide Factors. *Women's Studies International Forum*. Available at: http://www.sciencedirect.com/science/article/pii/S027753951400020X (Retrieved 12 June 2014).

Budig, M., Misra, J. and Boeckmann, U. (2012), The Motherhood Penalty in Cross-national Perspective: The Importance of Work–Family Policies and Cultural Attitudes. *Social Politics* 19(2): 163–93.

Dayioglu, M. and Kirdar, M.G. (2010), Turkiye'de Kadinlarin Işgucune Katiliminda Belirleyici Etkenler ve Egilimler. *Refah ve Sosyal Politika Calisma Raporu*. T.C. Devlet Planlama Teskilatı ve Dunya Bankası (Report by Turkish Government and World Bank).

del Boca, D. (2002), The Effect of Child Care and Part Time Opportunities on Participation and Fertility Decisions in Italy. *Journal of Population Economics* 15: 549–73.

Federal Statistical Office of Germany. (2012a), *Quality of Employment 2012*, Wiesbaden. Available at: https://www.destatis.de/EN/Publications/Specialized/LabourMarket/QualityEmployment0010016129004.pdf?__blob=publicationFile (Retrieved 10 May 2014).

———. (2012b), *Statistical Yearbook, 2012*, Wiesbaden. Available at: https://www.destatis.de/EN/Publications/Specialized/Population/StatYearbook_Chapter2_5011001129004.pdf?__blob=publicationFile (Retrieved 15 May 2014).

Gornick, J.C. and Hegewisch, A. (2010), *The Impact of 'Family-Friendly Policies' on Women's Employment Outcomes and on the Costs and Benefits of Doing Business. A Commissioned Report for the World Bank*. Washington, DC: World Bank.

Gursel, S. and Uysal-Kolasin, G. (2010), İstihdamda Dezavantajlı Grupların Isgucune Katılımını Artırma. Bahcesehir Üniversitesi. *Ekonomik ve Toplumsal Arastırmalar Merkezi*, Istanbul, Turkey.

Haan, P. and Wrohlich, K. (2011), Can Child Care Policy Encourage Employment and Fertility? Evidence from a Structural Model. *Labour Economics* 18: 498–512.

ILO (International Labour Organization). (2012), *Global Employment Trends for Women*. Geneva, Switzerland: International Labour Organization.

Karadeniz, O. (2011), Turkiye' de Atipik Calısan Kadınlar ve Yaygın Sosyal Guvencesizlik. *Çalışma ve Toplum Dergisi* 2: 83–127.

Katz, E. (2008), *Programs Promoting Young Women's Employment: What Works? The Adolescent Girls Initiative: An Alliance for Economic Empowerment*. Available at: http://siteresources.worldbank. org/INTGENDER/Resources/GenderYouthEmploymentKatz.pdf (Retrieved 15 June 2014).

Kreyenfeld, M. and Hank, K. (2000), Does the Availability of Child Care Influence the Employment of Mothers? Findings from Western Germany. *Population Research and Policy Review* 19(4): 317–37.

Lahn, S., Hayen, D. and Unterberg, M. (2008), *Fostering Gender Equality: Meeting the Entrepreneurship and Microfinance Challenge. National Report Germany*. Available at: http://www. microfinancegateway.org/sites/default/files/mfg-en-paper-fostering-gender-equality-meeting-the-entrepreneurship-and-microfinance-challenge-dec-2007.pdf (Retrieved 9 September 2014).

Lee, G.H.Y. and Lee, S.P. (2014), Childcare Availability, Fertility and Female Labor Force Participation in Japan. *Journal of the Japanese and International Economies* 32(June 2014): 71–85.

Ozdemir, D. and Dundar, H.C. (2012), Turkiye' nin Kriz Sonrası Eve Donen Kadınlari. *Turkiye Ekonomi Politikalari Arastirma Vakfı-TEPAV Degerlendirme Notu* N201240.

Ozdemir, Z., Yalman, I.N. and Bayrakdar, S. (2012), Kadin Istihdami ve Ekonomik Kalkinma: Geçiş Ekonomileri Ornegi. *International Conference on Eurasion Economies*, 2010–2015 Eurasian Economists Association, pp. 115–122. Available at: http://avekon.org/papers/476.pdf (Retrieved 15 June 2014).

Schober, P.S. and Schmitt, C. (2013), Day-care Expansion and Parental Subjective Well-being: Evidence from Germany. *SOEP – The German Socio-Economic Panel Study at DIW Berlin*. Available at: http://www.diw.de/documents/publikationen/73/diw_01.c.431283.de/diw_sp0602. pdf (Retrieved 20 May 2014).

Simonson, J., Gordova, L.R. and Titova, N. (2011), Changing Employment Patterns of Women in Germany: How do Baby Boomers Differ from Older Cohorts? A Comparison Using Sequence Analysis. *Advances in Life Course Research* 16: 65–82.

Statistisches Landesamt Bremen. (2012), *Frauen im Land Bremen*. Available at: http://www. statistik.bremen.de (Retrieved 14 March 2014).

Sundstrom, E. (2002), National Policies, Local Policies and Women's Right to Work. *UMEA Studies in Sociology* 118. Available at: http://www.diva-portal.org/smash/get/diva2:142635/ FULLTEXT01.pdf (Retrieved 15 March 2014).

TUİK-Türkiye Istatistik Kurumu. (2012), *İzmir İli Göstergeleri*. Ankara: Türkiye Istatistik Kurumu.

UNDP (United Nations Development Programme). (2013), *Human Development Report 2013*. Available at: http://hdr.undp.org/sites/default/files/reports/14/hdr2013_en_complete. pdf (Retrieved 15 March 2015).

World Bank. (2013), *World Development Indicators*. Available at: http://data.worldbank.org/ indicators (Retrieved 15 March 2014).

World Economic Forum. (2013), *The Gender Gap Index 2013*. Available at: http://www3. weforum.org/docs/WEF_GenderGap_Report_2013.pdf (Retrieved 15 March 2014).

Chapter 4

A Comparative Analysis of Women's Education and their Representation in Higher Management

Zorka Grandov, Verica Jovanović and Maja Đokić

Introduction

Dynamic changes begun by the process of globalization and continued under the influence of the world economic crisis affect economic, social and political world-views. The uncertainty caused by these changes has led to women taking an active part in global social processes, according to their biological need for self-preservation.

Unlike the male population which is stunned by present economic crisis, they have a more active attitude as far as the new problems are concerned (http://phys.org/news/2012–10-crisis-men-women-precarious-leadership.html and Rink et. al., 2013). Their enthusiasm, determination and open mind toward innovations on one hand, and rationality, devotion and responsibility on the other, mean women are capable of being leaders in a crisis. Accordingly their status and social role are strengthened, so that the majority of workers in education and healthcare are women who are steadily taking over those positions usually occupied by men.

The greatest advances in the equality of women are being made in education. Taking into account the number of students enrolled in college as well as the number of graduates, women make up the majority, which in some countries is more than 60 per cent (United Nations, 2012). Research conducted recently has established that companies with a majority of women in leading positions had better economic results (Governancemetrics International, 2010), which suggests it would be logical for more women to work in those positions.

Analysis conducted in this chapter shows that there were more women working in education and healthcare in 2012. It also demonstrates that their influence is growing in economics and politics, where there are more women in middle management and leading the boards of public companies (Grant Thornton, 2013). However, there are fewer women in the highest leading positions, and this is out of balance with their education. It means that their knowledge is not fully used, and that they are working in positions where they do not have opportunity to show their full capabilities. The first woman in the history of the American car industry, Mary Barra, chief executive officer and chairman of the General Motors Company who was also the leader of General Motors at the end of 2013, may be a positive sign that things can be changed in this field.

Methodology

The main subject of this chapter is the comparison of the education level of women in the world and their presence in both the senior and leading positions of executive and high management. We have used a method of context analysis, i.e. analysing the data as far as the educational status of women in the field of higher education is concerned as the independent variable and their presence in leading positions as the dependent variable. According to the data gained by statistical analysis, the disparity of the observed variable is obvious. In addition to the global analysis in this chapter, comparative analysis of the educational level of women and their position in leading positions is also used, in certain regions, groups of countries and certain countries, and is the influential factor for the analysis in this chapter. To see this result more clearly there are both data on the number of women in middle management and on their presence in higher and senior management.

Results are given in the form of charts and graphics. Conclusions about this work are made using an inductive method as well as analysis and synthesis methods.

Education and the Position of Women

It is often said that in the world of education a silent revolution started in the 1970s, and this is supported by the numbers of enrolled pupils at all educational levels. In 1970 in world educational systems there were only 647 million students while in 2009 their number was 1.397 billion (World Atlas of Gender Equality in Education, 2012). Unexpectedly, the number of women doubled in comparison with men. This means that women seized the opportunity to create a better, more humane, healthier and more economically competitive society. Supported by international organizations such as UNESCO, they have bravely approached whole fields of society, but the greatest progress has been made in education. In more than two-thirds of the world, there is now no gap between women and men in education, or it is minimal. The main reason women have made the greatest progress in this field is more opportunity to make independent decisions, i.e. if and where should they study.

All over the world from 1970 to 2009, it is important to analyse the number of enrolled students at tertiary level, which in observed decades has increased in all more than 500 per cent (United Nations, 2012). Statistics show that in this level of education women have made the greatest progress, and throughout the world there are more enrolled and graduated women in this kind of education. From 1970 to 2009, the number of men who participated in the tertiary sector increased from 11 to 26 per cent, i.e. by 230 per cent, while the number of women increased more than 300 per cent (from 8 to 28 per cent). In practical terms this means that there are 2 per cent more women in higher education. According to data from UNESCO, women are the majority among the students in 93 countries, men in 43, and in 10 countries there is an equal number of students of both genders. Activities should facilitate an increase in the educational level of both genders so that in the future there will be no gap between them that might endanger either sex (Calvo, 2014).

However, although women are dominant in the field of higher education, the educational structure in this field differs in different regions. Traditionally, positive attitudes towards women in this field are found in North America and Western Europe, as well as the former communist countries of Central and East Europe. The most dynamic increase in numbers of women participating in higher education is in Latin America and the Caribbean, where there are more women than men enrolled. Unfavourable conditions are still to be found in the region of sub-Saharan Africa, where the rate of participating women is steadily growing, but is not as great as that for men. The situation is slightly better for women in East Asia and the Pacific, where women and men are equal as far as educational levels are concerned (UNESCO Institute for Statistics, 2010).

Research conducted by the UN makes a connection between the economic state of the country and the gender structure of enrolled students, according to which it can be concluded that there are more women than men students in highly developed countries and countries that are in a state of intense development. The greatest disproportion as far as student gender is concerned in higher education is in Iceland where the ratio is almost 1.5:1 for women. In tertiary studies in the US there are 30 per cent more women and in Russia 26 per cent more. Similar ratios are to be found in Argentina, Brazil and Venezuela. In China, the country which has the most intense economic growth in the world, there are more women students. According to China's twenty-first century *Business Herald*, the number of women graduates has grown from 43.8 per cent in 2004 to 49.6 per cent in 2012. On Master's programmes, even in 2010, there were 50 per cent women, and in doctoral studies 35.4 per cent. In some countries there are more men than women in higher education, and the most unfavourable situation for women is in Ethiopia, Eritrea and Guinea, where the ratio of enrolled women in higher education is less than one-third.

There is a hypothesis that the level of economic development of the country is the key factor for the number of women students in higher education, but this is not entirely true. This is because in some countries with a high level of social gross production there are more men than women, although the enrolment rates are almost equal. This primarily applies to the extremely rich Arabic countries such as Qatar and Kuwait, who, as far as GDP is concerned, are at the top of the world's list, but Qatar is in 53rd place as far as educational equality is concerned, and Kuwait 57th (World Economic Forum, 2013). Japan and Brazil have a gender gap in education between male and female, together with a distinctive difference in the unequal number of male and female workers. There are major differences as far as the number of students enrolled in tertiary education is concerned, where the trend is that the number of women students is highest at the undergraduate and Master's level, but lowest in doctoral studies. The only exception is Latin America and the Caribbean, where there are more women even in these programmes.

The basic conclusion from the given data is that women, thanks to their education, became a precious human resource and with their knowledge and abilities can contribute significantly to the social and economic development of a world economy in crisis.

The Presence of Women in Top Management

As already stated, the number of women who graduate from universities is almost in every part of the world greater than the number of men. Thanks to their better education they may be able to find so-called higher jobs in medicine, law, education and architecture (Blackburn, Racko and Jarman, 2009), and in these fields women are in the majority.

For example, in the US in 2012, there were 85% women in health professions, 79% in education, 77% in psychology (Institute of Education Science, 2013). In 2010 in

Greece there were 57% women in architecture, in Croatia 56%, Bulgaria and Slovenia 50% (survey conducted by the Architects' Council of Europe 2010). There are even more women who are the founders and co-founders of their own business. Women are also becoming economically more powerful and so appear on the lists of the richest and the most powerful people in the world. A plethora of research conducted in previous years shows that companies with women as their leaders are more powerful in the market and that their share price increases faster than the share price of companies without women as their leaders. For example, in the most pronounced period of the still-active economic crisis, the share price of big companies with a market price higher than US$10 billion with women on their boards increased by 26 per cent while others could not maintain their value at the same level as before the crisis.

In addition, research conducted by the European Commission showed that 90 per cent of Europeans think that women who are equal with men as far as their professional and educational competences are concerned can be equally successful in the leading positions in big companies (European Commission, 2012). It is justified to expect, according to these facts, that women will conquer the highest leading positions. However, the opposite situation also exists. Although women have better education and work in highly professional places, lowering the gap that exists in senior management positions is a very slow process. The most important business decisions are made by men, while the potential of highly competent women remains unused.

The educational position of women described in the previous chapter shows that there is a significant superiority of women in tertiary education, while for women in positions of leadership the situation is entirely different. Data for this chapter show that the greatest progress for women is made in conquering senior management positions: in some countries more than 50 per cent of senior positions. China has made the greatest progress in comparison to the previous year, increasing the number of women in senior management from 25 to 51 per cent, making it the leading country in this area (Grant Thornton, 2013). In second position is Poland with 48 per cent, followed by several countries of the former Soviet Union, as well as the Philippines, Thailand and Vietnam. In the group of countries that have 30 per cent and more of women in senior management positions are Botswana, Russia, Germany, Taiwan, Turkey, Hong Kong and Greece.

The Pacific is the region with the most female senior managers (in all 29 per cent). Women are slightly below the average in Latin America (23 per cent), while in North America the figure is 21 per cent. Countries with the least number of women senior managers are Japan (7 per cent), the UAE (9 per cent), the Netherlands (11 per cent) and Switzerland (14 per cent). There are more women senior managers in healthcare where they occupy 45 per cent of principal positions, and in education and social services (44 per cent). Then there is the field of hospitality (41 per cent), cleantech (33 per cent) and financial services (29 per cent). It is interesting to note that during 2013 women made the greatest progress in comparison to 2012 in the field of finance, where their number increased from 13 to 31 per cent in principal positions. In addition, great progress is being made in the field of human resources, where the number of women increased by 9 per cent from 21 to 30 per cent.

Although these figures appear to be optimistic and indicate the possibility that the number of women in these positions is growing, there is also the fact that the number of women in middle management has varied recently. In 2004 19 per cent of women held these positions, in 2007 and 2009 there were 24 per cent as today, but in 2011 the number fell to 20 per cent and rose slightly in 2012 to 21 per cent. These turbulences are greatest in highly developed countries in which women have greater possibilities as far as their employment is concerned and can make their own decisions not to fight for a job. For example, in Japan 72 per cent of women stop working when they give birth to their first child and usually never return to the working world (Fujimura-Fanselow, 2011). In many countries, especially in the US and the UK, there are programmes for selecting women who are talented managers. Through innovative competitions, women are put into special competitive conditions of work, which demand devotion and overtime, where women role-play being managers: making decisions, navigating the environment, for example. They are supposed to give their best and strive to be nominated as the real leader. It is considered that women who accept these conditions of competition and prove themselves suitable for senior positions will also have the necessary predisposition to be a successful manager at even higher levels (Barsh and Yee, 2011).

It is estimated that today the participation of women in high-level leadership positions is lower than their participation in senior management positions. Data about the number of women in high-level leadership positions indicate that as far as the executive (higher) management level is concerned there are between 14 and 16 per cent of women. Many people think that this relatively low level is because of a widely applied quota system, i.e. the legitimate obligation for companies to employ a certain percentage of women on their corporate boards. For example, France set the highest scale for the participation of women in steering committees of companies and its goal for the period starting from 2011 is that in the first three years female participation will be 20 per cent, and in the following six years could rise to 40 per cent. In year 2012, the percentage of women board members in committees increased by almost 4 per cent, from 12.7 to 16.6 per cent, and there is hope that the goal will be completely fulfilled.

Opinions differ as to whether or not quotas are desirable. According to data in European Commission research published in the edition of *Women in Senior Management*, 9 out of 10 examinees had a positive attitude to the quota system.

The introduction of quotas is often justified because when a person is to be chosen for a leading position and there are two candidates with similar qualifications and abilities, a special commission, which consists mainly of men, usually chooses a male candidate (Adams, Gray and Nowland, 2011). On the other hand, it is obvious that the reaction of the market to the fact that there are more women in the positions of managers is positive, which is proved through the better financial results of companies with women leaders. Although it is said that the quota is useful and that the participation of women in steering committees of companies lowers business risks, there are also differences of opinion as to whether to use quotas in big industrial companies (Gladman and Lamb, 2012). According to data gained by GMI Ratings' 2012 Women on Boards Survey, the percentage of those who use quotas for market-oriented companies is 55 per cent. Negative attitudes are not confined to men, however. The majority of women think that they should deserve their positions and that the quota system only distracts them in their goal because others may think that they are in a certain position only because of legal obligations and not because of their professionalism. However, it is difficult for women to find a way to overcome the

Table 4.1 Percentage and average number of women directors and women executive officers by North American Industry Classification System (NAICS) industry

NAICS industry	Number of board seats	Women directors (%)	Number of executive officer positions	Women executive officers (%)	Number of companies	Average number of women directors	Average number of total directors	Average number of women executives	Average number of total executive officers
Accommodation and food services	127	14.2	118	14.4	12	1.5	10.6	1.4	9.8
Admin and support, waste management, and remediation services	81	21.0	67	13.4	8	2.1	10.1	1.1	8.4
Agriculture, forestry, fishing, and hunting	58	15.5	63	14.4	5	1.8	11.6	1.8	12.6
Arts, entertainment, and recreation	10	0.0	16	6.3	1	0.0	10.0	1.0	16.0
Construction	62	8.1	46	4.3	6	0.8	10.3	0.3	7.7
Finance and insurance	909	17.9	866	17.6	75	2.2	12.3	2.0	11.5
Health care and social assistance	97	12.4	89	14.6	10	1.2	9.7	1.3	8.9
Information	369	16.3	270	14.1	33	1.8	11.2	1.2	8.2
Management of companies and enterprises	51	9.8	29	6.9	5	1.0	10.2	0.4	5.8
Manufacturing—durable goods	985	15.6	948	11.2	92	1.7	10.7	1.2	10.3
Manufacturing—non-durable goods	898	20.3	830	15.2	79	2.3	11.4	1.6	10.5
Mining, quarrying, and oil and gas extraction	167	13.2	160	16.9	16	1.4	10.4	1.7	10.0
Professional, scientific, and technical services	108	18.5	97	15.5	10	2.0	10.8	1.5	9.7
Real estate and rental and leasing	53	17.0	51	9.8	5	1.8	10.6	1.0	10.2
Retail trade	572	18.2	515	18.6	56	1.9	10.2	1.7	9.2
Transportation and warehousing	256	15.2	194	13.9	23	1.7	11.1	1.2	8.4
Utilities	345	17.7	237	12.7	28	2.2	12.3	1.1	8.5
Wholesale trade	298	14.1	227	12.3	29	1.4	10.3	1.0	7.8
Total	**5.446**	**16.9**	**4.823**	**14.6**	**493**	**1.9**	**11.1**	**1.4**	**9.8**

Source: 2013 Catalyst Census: Fortune 500 Women Board Directors.

numerous obstacles they face in this area and to prove that they are capable of making decisions and leading large companies as men do.

There is statistical data on the number of women in the highest positions in the biggest companies. According to data gained by Catalyst Fortune only 20 out of 500 of the most powerful companies have women as their leaders: only 4 per cent. These companies have slightly more women in their steering committees, about 16.9 per cent, while the percentage of women working as executive managers is 14.6. This means that in all the percentage of women in leading positions in the largest world companies is about 9.8 per cent (see Table 4.1).

The main results gained by the data analysis in this chapter are:

- The number of women with higher education is more than 50 per cent of the whole population.
- Participation of women in senior management is 24 per cent.
- Participation of women in executive management is 14.6 per cent.
- Percentage of women in senior management of larger companies is 4 per cent.
- The disproportion between the educational level of women and their participation on management positions is greater than 300 per cent.

Conclusion

The analysis carried out in this chapter shows that women have gained an advantage in comparison with men as far as higher education is concerned. In opposition to this, when we compare the educational level in the tertiary sector with their participation in the leading positions in companies, the results are disproportionate. The smallest gap between female and male managers is in middle management where women occupy a quarter of the leading positions. However, their participation in higher levels of management, in leading positions in big companies, is very low. This is the most difficult obstacle to overcome: to attain the highest positions in big companies, 95 per cent of which are filled by men. This inequality is present all over the world, but it has been established that world regions with the most highly educated women have the fewest women in leading positions compared to regions or countries which have a lower percentage of educated women.

In consequence there is huge potential in highly educated, professional and talented women that is still unused or is used irrationally by employing highly educated women in less demanding positions. It is obvious that their leading position does not depend on their level of education, so it is necessary to conduct additional research to find the real reasons that prevent women from overcoming this problem.

References

Adams, R, S. Gray, and J. Nowland. 2011. *Does Gender Matter in the Boardroom? Evidence from the Market Reaction to Mandatory New Director Announcements*. Retrieved from http://ssrn.com/abstract=1953152.

Aud, S., Wilkinson-Flicker, S., Kristapovich, P., Rathbun, A., Wang, X., and Zhang, J. (2013). The Condition of Education 2013 (NCES 2013-037). U.S. Department of Education, National Center for Education Statistics. Washington, DC. Retrieved June 2013 from http://nces.ed.gov/pubsearch.

Barsh, Joanna, and Lareina Yee, 2011. "Unlocking the Full Potential of Women in the US Economy." McKinsey & Company. Retrieved fromhttp://www.mckinsey.com/client_service/organization/latest_thinking/unlocking_the_full_potential.

Blackburn, R. M. Racko, G. and Jarman, J. (2009) 'Gender Inequality at Work' *Cambridge Studies in Social Research 11*, Cambridge: Social Science Research Group.

Calvo, Jahir. (2012), Women's Access to Higher Education. *Global University Network for Innovation.* United Nations Scientific, Educational and Cultural Organization (UNESCO). Available at: http://www.guninetwork.org/resources/he-articles/women2019s-access-to-higher-education, and in http://herstoria.com/?p=535 (Retrieved 2 January 2014).

European Commission. (2012), *Women in Decision-Making Positions.* Special Eurobarometer Survey 376. Available at: http://ec.europa.eu/public_opinion/archives/ebs/ebs_376_en.pdf (Retrieved 20 December 2013).

Fujimura-Fanselow, K. (ed) (2011) *Transforming Japan: How Feminism and Diversity are Making a Difference.* New York, NY: The Feminist Press.

Gladman, K. & Lamb, M. 2013. Director Tenure and Gender Diversity in the United States: A Scenario Analysis. New York: GMI Ratings.

Governancemetrics International. (2012), Women on Boards: A Statistical Rewire by Country, Sector and Super Sector, New York: GMIRatings.

Grandov, Z., Jovanović, V. and Djokić, M. *Women in Top Management.* (2012), Third International Women and Business Conference, Organised by Pan-European University Apeiron, Oct 10, 2012, Banja Luka.

Grant Thornton. (2013). *Women in Senior Management: Setting the Stage for Growth. International Business Report.* Chicago: Grant Thornton International Ltd http://www.grantthornton.ie/db/Attachments/IBR2013_WiB_report_final.pdf(Retrieved January 22, 2014).

Institute of Education Science.

Kelley, Donna J., Brush, Candida G., Greene, Patricia G. and Litovsky, Yana. (2012), Global Entrepreneurship Research Association, *Global Entrepreneurship Monitor, 2012. Women's Report,* Babson College, Wellesley, Massachusetts College.

Rink, Floor, Ryan, Michelle K. and Stoker, Janka I. (2013), Social Resources at a Time of Crisis: How Gender Stereotypes Inform Gendered Leader Evaluations, *European Journal of Social Psychology,* 43(5), 381–92.

UNESCO Institute for Statistics. (2012), *World Atlas of Gender Equality in Education.* Montreal, Quebec, Canada.

UNESCO Institute for Statistics. (2010), *Global Education Digest.* Montreal, Quebec, Canada.

World Economic Forum. (2013), *The Global Gender Gap Report 2013.* Geneva: World Economic Forum.

Part II

Women and Management

Perception of Lebanese Working Women Regarding the Barriers Preventing Their Attainment of Senior Professional Positions

Abdulrazzak Charbaji

Introduction

In many countries, women have been successful in securing senior positions in such fields as physiology, biology and social sciences (Wadhwa, 2006). Moreover, many women have become successful entrepreneurs, and the number of female business owners is rapidly increasing (Woldie and Adersua, 2004). Indeed, according to the United Nations Economic Commission for Europe (UNECE), 70 per cent of self-employed women in Western Europe operate businesses that employ five or more people (UNECE, 2004).

However, despite the increasing prominence of women in a variety of fields in many countries, the same picture does not hold true in countries where women face legal and socio-cultural barriers to success – such as in many developing countries, in Eastern Europe or in Arab countries. For example, Adriana and Manolescu (2006: 76) noted that: 'So far, Women are not well represented in all the sectors of the Romanian economy and they are less likely than men to work in the private sector and their own businesses'.

The situation in Arab countries is also difficult for women. McElwee and Al-Riyami (2003) have noted that employers in many Arab countries give priority to men in terms of employment and promotion, even if women have the same qualifications, and Al-Madhi and Barrientos (2003) have reported that several Arab countries maintain discriminatory policies with respect to employment, education and training, and workplace regulations. Al-Mandhry (2000) noted that the low percentage of women participating in the labour force is mainly attributable to a lack of work opportunities, rather than lack of interest. Family law norms in Arab countries often limit the freedom of movement of women, and Arab women have to be accompanied by their husbands or male relatives if they wish to participate in meetings. If they wish to launch their own businesses, Arab women find that their access to credit is very limited.

However, the obstacles encountered by potential female entrepreneurs in Arab countries are usually socio-cultural, rather than legal. The law in many Arab countries ostensibly prohibits gender discrimination and various articles of employment codes in Arab countries explicitly state that the norms of training apply equally to men and women. However, practice is often not consistent with theory, and the reality is often quite different from the legal fiction. Nevertheless, Arab societies and governments are not homogeneous, and any discussion of the role of women in Arab countries must take account of this complexity. Arab women living in Lebanon or in Tunisia have a different political, social and economic status from that of their counterparts in the Gulf region or in Africa. As Barron (2007) observed: 'In Jordan, Syria, Egypt and most other Arab countries, a man who murders his female relative to defend family "honor" receives a reduced penalty – or may not be sent to prison at all'.

In Lebanon, women share similar problems to those of women living in advanced societies in being less likely than men to become employers or be self-employed workers. As Al-Lamky (2007: 49) observed with respect to the situation of women in Oman: 'If professionally inclined, their participation is expected to be in the areas of education, health (mainly nurses) and other support or clerical jobs; leadership positions are typically reserved for men'.

Similarly, Jamali, Sidani and Safieddine (2005: 585) reported that: 'Although women in Lebanon are increasingly recognized as full-fledged partners in the family economy, decision-making positions in Lebanon continue to be monopolized by men'.

The presence of a role model or mentor can influence women in their decisions and choices (Brynin and Schupp, 2000). In this respect, the commitment of the American University of Beirut to the education of Lebanese girls dates back 90 years. Today, there are more Lebanese girls than boys undertaking postgraduate studies. However, although self-employment requires no prior experience or qualifications, Lebanese women face obstacles in starting their own businesses because they lack relevant entrepreneurial and managerial skills. If a Lebanese woman seeks self-employment, she has difficulty finding answers to such questions as: How do I begin? How long will it take? How much will it cost?

Although the position of Lebanese woman has been fundamentally changed by globalization, and although their presence at work and university is rapidly becoming more prominent, the question that remains unanswered is why policy-making and politics remain a 'man's domain' in Lebanon.

The purpose of the present study is to understand the obstacles that prevent women in Lebanon from assuming positions of leadership. More specifically, the objective of the study is to investigate whether working women in Lebanon perceive themselves as lacking skills (and therefore unprepared to stand for policy-making positions) or whether they perceive that gender stereotypes and societal expectations to conform are the main factors that prevent them from reaching positions of power.

Background to the Study

The Lebanese civil war and the conflict between supporters of the governing coalition and the Hezbollah-led opposition have ended. There is an expectation that the Lebanese government will offer jobs to ex-militiamen to discourage them from forming street gangs and continuing the violence. However, economic factors – such as the depreciation of the US dollar against the euro, the escalating price of real estate and the high rate of unemployment in Lebanon – are pushing young educated Lebanese men to seek work in other countries. As Williams (2007) reported:

> In an April [2007] survey of 1,600 Lebanese – half who want to emigrate and half who have [emigrated] – 31 per cent blamed their exit on political instability, 24 per cent cited politics, and 18 per cent said a need to secure their future. Just over 73 per cent didn't plan to return permanently.

It is apparent that many young men are leaving Lebanon, many of them permanently. The question that therefore arises is whether this will provide opportunities for women to alter the balance of political and social power between men and women. It is thus imperative to ascertain whether socio-cultural stereotypes or a lack of real skills is the main factor that hinders Lebanese women from achieving senior policy-making positions in Lebanese society.

Literature Review

Based on a review of the literature on the subject of women and leadership, Rhode (2003) has stated that there have been two main research streams in this area. The first is concerned with differences in opportunities and the existence of so-called 'glass ceilings' that exclude women from leadership positions. The second involves the study of gender differences in the exercise of leadership – such as different styles, effectiveness and priorities between men and women. Rhode (2003) concluded that too little work has been done on the relationship between gender and situational forces, such as race.

Historically, the primary job of Arab women has been to raise children, and their participation in leadership positions has been limited. However, the picture has changed in more recent times. As the United Nations Development Programme for Arab States has reported (UNDP, 2005: 1):

> By early 2006, women held 25.5 per cent of the seats in Iraq's parliament, while in Tunisia's last elections in 2004 women claimed 23 per cent of the seats. In Morocco, the percentage of women in parliament jumped from 1 per cent in 1995 to 11 per cent in 2003; in the same eight-year period in Jordan it went from 2.5 per cent to 5.5 per cent.

Nevertheless, the situation is not as good in Lebanon. As Russeau (2008) has observed: 'In a country where over half of the population are women, Lebanon lacks political representation even more than some of its other Arab neighbours'.

Moreover, socio-cultural factors continue to inhibit the promotion of Lebanese women. As Varia (2008) has noted:

> Lebanese women are caught in an unenviable position. While their participation in the workforce has increased, gender stereotyping and discrimination mean that they have retained the primary burden of household work.

Methodology

Questionnaire

Following a review of literature and discussions with university colleagues who specialized in management studies, the present author developed a pilot questionnaire on the barriers facing Lebanese working women. The pilot instrument used a Likert-style five-point scale and asked female participants to respond to 27 items by circling the one number that most closely matched their level of agreement or disagreement with a particular statement. The scale ranged from one through five and was presented as follows:

1 = Strongly Disagree; 2 = Disagree; 3 = Neither; 4 = Agree; 5 = Strongly Agree

This was distributed on a trial basis, however, because the pilot questionnaire was found to be lengthy, wordy and inappropriately scaled, a revised final questionnaire was developed to correct these problems. Thirteen items (almost half of the items in the instrument) were omitted and 520 of the final compact version were completed and collected in person.

Working Lebanese women were asked to respond to 14 items. The responses to these items were factor analysed and Factor Scores were used as new variables in simple discriminant analysis.

The dichotomous dependent variable in the study was the respondents' perceptions of the barriers that block the advancement of women. A large sample of graduate working women were asked to choose one of two reasons: (i) stereotypes and societal expectations of the role of women; or (ii) lack of skills and knowledge among women to advance in power positions.

Sample

Female employees working for a variety of Lebanese organizations in both the public sector and the private sector constituted the population for this study. A large non-probability sample was selected from this population. Kerlinger states that 'the smaller the sample the larger the error, and the larger the sample the smaller the error' (Kerlinger, 1973: 27). Inevitable to any study are its limitations, as goes for this study. To start with the basics of this study, the concept of 'glass ceilings' is a new phenomenon in Lebanon and selecting a relevant population from which to draw information is difficult if not impossible using this type information. To increase the likelihood of respondents being aware of issues relating to the obstacles that prevent women in Lebanon from assuming positions of leadership, the survey population comprised female graduate students at different universities in Lebanon, who work for different public and private firms and from whom 520 valid questionnaires were collected. Data collection was carried out over a five-month period during 2008, with the help of different graduate research assistants. Working female graduate students were asked to respond to a self-administered questionnaire on various issues related to obstacles encountered by potential female entrepreneurs in Lebanon. This voluntary aspect has some disadvantages and may lead to a biased response rate as only educated females who are aware of obstacles that face working women in Lebanon did subsequently fill it in. However, this is not a problem since not all women in Lebanon understand the concept of obstacles that prevent women in Lebanon from assuming positions of leadership. Factor analysis was based on 438 valid responses. Discriminant analysis was based on 401 valid responses (due to some missing values on demographic variables).

More than one-third of the female graduate respondents (39.2 per cent) were partially involved in voluntary social work. Approximately a quarter (25.1 per cent) did not use the Internet. Less than one-third of the respondents (27.2 per cent) were single.

Conclusion

Factor Analysis and Construct Validation

Factor analysis was carried out as a data-reduction technique. Two statistical tests were conducted to determine the suitability of factor analysis as shown in Table 5.1. First, the Kaisers-Meyer-Olkin (KMO) measure of sampling adequacy score was 0.637, which was well above the recommended level of 0.5. Secondly, Bartlett's test of sphericity was significant (chi square = 2376.06, $p < 0.01$), which indicated that there were adequate correlations among the items to allow factor analysis.

Principal axis factoring was used as an extraction method and oblique rotation was used as a rotation method. Tables 5.2 and 5.3 show that five factors were extracted. The five-factor solution accounted for 72.792 per cent of the total variance. The five factors were easy to label (see Table 5.3). The first factor (which was labelled 'women

Table 5.1 Factor analysis

KMO and Bartlett's Test		
Kaiser-Meyer-Olkin Measure of Sampling Adequacy.		.637
Bartlett's Test of Sphericity	Approx. Chi-Square	2376.060
	df	91
	Sig.	.000

Table 5.2 Total variance explained

Component	Initial Eigenvalues			Extraction Sums of Squared Loadings			Rotation Sums of Squared Loadings[a]
	Total	% of Variance	Cumulative %	Total	% of Variance	Cumulative %	Total
1	2.824	20.171	20.171	2.824	20.171	20.171	2.494
2	2.578	18.417	38.588	2.578	18.417	38.588	2.468
3	1.971	14.076	52.664	1.971	14.076	52.664	1.828
4	1.497	10.694	63.358	1.497	10.694	63.358	1.915
5	1.321	9.434	72.792	1.321	9.434	72.792	1.911
6	.913	6.521	79.313				
7	.596	4.256	83.568				
8	.586	4.189	87.757				
9	.402	2.869	90.626				
10	.369	2.638	93.264				
11	.289	2.063	95.327				
12	.229	1.635	96.962				
13	.220	1.574	98.536				
14	.205	1.464	100.000				

Extraction Method: Principal Component Analysis.

[a] When components are correlated, sums of squared loadings cannot be added to obtain a total variance.

Table 5.3 Structure matrix

	Component				
	1	*2*	*3*	*4*	*5*
My work requires that I work hard	**.816**	.028	−.056	.136	−.168
Self-employment requires skills in finance and marketing	**.796**	.040	.003	.169	−.145
Self-employed woman has control at work of her working hours	**.693**	.092	−.216	.193	−.024
I can balance work and family responsibility	**.559**	.054	.245	−.114	−.210
Women are good at communicating and building relations at work	**.551**	−.094	.397	−.239	−.249
Polygamy in Lebanon is now unthinkable	−.077	**−.912**	.032	.056	.085
Young girls are persuaded into early marriage	.054	**.893**	.099	−.090	−.040
A man can murder his female relative to "defend" family honour	.036	**.878**	.068	−.131	−.053
Girls in our society lack confidence to start-up their own business	−.015	.037	**.872**	−.175	.108
Girls should be forced to marry their assailants to "protect" the family's reputation	.009	−.068	**−.845**	.073	−.186
I would be very happy to spend the rest of my life in my business	.088	−.061	−.097	**.929**	−.085
I feel as if my business problems are my own	.171	−.153	−.130	**.900**	−.106
It is legal for a bank not to give loan to a woman without a man co-sign	.170	.099	−.139	.101	**−.919**
Women lack the necessary start-up finance	−.147	−.039	.157	−.109	**.913**

Extraction Method: Principal Component Analysis.

Rotation Method: Oblimin with Kaiser Normalization.

empowerment') accounted for 20.17 per cent of total variance and was defined by five items. The second factor (labelled 'social barriers') accounted for 18.42 per cent of total variance and was defined by three items with factor loadings greater than 0.70. The third factor (labelled 'lack of confidence') accounted for 14.08 per cent of total variance and was defined by two items with factor loadings greater than 0.70. The fourth factor (labelled 'job satisfaction') accounted for 10.694 per cent of total variance and was defined by two items with factor loadings greater than 0.70. The fifth factor (labelled 'financial barriers') accounted for 9.43 per cent of total variance and was defined by two items with factor loadings greater than 0.70.

Discriminant Analysis

Discriminant analysis was used to distinguish between the two segments of the dependent variable: (i) stereotype; and (ii) lack of skills.

Table 5.4 indicates that by squaring the canonical correlation of 0.733, we see that the function accounts for 53.7 per cent of the variance in the dependent variable. Table 5.5 point towards its significant (chi-square = 300.973; p = 0.0000; Wilks'

Table 5.4 Summary of canonical discriminant functions

Eigenvalues[a]

% of Variance	Cumulative %
100.0	100.0

[a] First 1 canonical discriminant functions were used in the analysis.

Table 5.5 Wilks's lambda

Wilks' Lambda

Test of Function(s)	Wilks' lambda	Chi-square	df	Sig.
1	.462	300.973	8	.000

Table 5.6 Classification results[a]

		Factors preventing working women from reaching top positions	Predicted Group Membership	
			Stereotype	Lack of Skills
Original	Count	Stereotype	180	27
		Lack of Skills	24	165
	%	Stereotype	87.0	13.0
		Lack of Skills	12.7	87.3

[a] 87.1% of original grouped cases correctly classified.

Table 5.7 Standardized canonical discriminant function coefficients

	Function
	1
Marital Status	.050
Children	.215
Do you use Internet Internet	.155
REGR factor score 1 for analysis 1	.969
REGR factor score 2 for analysis 1	−.050
REGR factor score 3 for analysis 1	.000
REGR factor score 4 for analysis 1	.596
REGR factor score 5 for analysis 1	.166

lambda = 0.462) and discriminates well between the two groups (hit rate = 87.1 per cent) as shown in Table 5.6. The standardized discriminant function coefficients and pooled within-groups correlations are given in Table 5.7 and Table 5.8. The test of equivalence for the group covariance matrices using Box's M test in Table 5.9 shows

Table 5.8 Structure matrix

	Function
	I
REGR factor score 1 for analysis 1	.775
REGR factor score 4 for analysis 1	.347
Children	.263
Marital Status	−.063
REGR factor score 5 for analysis 1	−.042
Do you use Internet Internet	−.031
REGR factor score 3 for analysis 1	−.012
REGR factor score 2 for analysis 1	.001

Pooled within-groups correlations between discriminating variables and standardized canonical discriminant functions.

Variables ordered by absolute size of correlation within function.

Table 5.9 Test results

Test Results		
Box's M		158.764
F	Approx.	4.316
	df1	36
	df2	513551.967
	Sig.	.000

Tests null hypothesis of equal population covariance matrices.

that covariance matrices are different from each other (Box's M =158.76, p = 0.00). Using Factor Scores as discriminating variables in addition to demographic characteristics showed that 'Women Empowerment', ' Job Satisfaction', ' Financial Barriers' and number of children are the most important variables in discriminating between the two segments of the dependent variable: (1) stereotypes and the roles our society expect women to conform to and; (2) women lack of skill to advance in power positions.

The other variables (such as 'social barriers' and 'lack of confidence') were not significant.

Conclusions and Recommendations

The findings of this study have shown that 'social barriers' and 'lack of confidence' were not significant variables in determining whether women perceived 'stereotype' or 'lack of skills' as the factor hindering Lebanese women from advancing in power positions. These findings are consistent with Lebanon being different from other Arab countries and reflects the fact that Lebanese people are facing different challenges. For example, CBC News (2007) reported on Lebanon in the following terms: 'From its independence to the start of the civil war in 1975, Lebanon was the wealthiest country in the region and was held up as an example of co-operation between different cultures and religions. Beirut was sometimes called the "Paris of the Middle East"'.

It is apparent that a lack of empowerment and training is hindering the progress of women in Lebanon. The future focus in Lebanon should be on 'empowerment of women', 'job satisfaction' and 'financial barriers'. The findings of this study reveal that a majority of women who are low on the 'job satisfaction' scale perceive that a lack of skills is a barrier to their attainment of senior positions. The study has also found that a majority of women who are high on the 'financial barriers' scale perceive that a lack of skills is a barrier to their attainment of senior positions. It can be concluded that, although Lebanese women have improved their status with respect to participation in education and work, they have still not acquired leadership positions in their own right because they lack the requisite skills to do so.

It is apparent that two issues need to be addressed if change in the status of women is to occur in Lebanon. The first is to ensure that women have equal access to training and empowerment opportunities. The second is to empower women and remove the financial barriers that are impeding the advancement of women to senior positions. Further research is required to establish what leadership means to different women in different situations and how to reach top positions.

References

Adriana, P. and Manolescu, I. (2006), Gender Discrimination in Romania. *Journal of Organizational Change Management* 19(6): 766–71.

Al-Lamky, A. (2007), Feminizing Leadership in Arab Societies: The Perspectives of Omani Female Leaders. *Women in Management Review* 22(1): 49–67.

Al-Madhi, S. and Barrientos, A. (2003), Saudisation and Employment in Saudi Arabia. *Career Development International* 8(2): 70–7.

Al-Mandhry, Z. (2000), Development of Women in the Sultanate of Oman. *Al-Markazi*, Central Bank of Oman, Muscat 25(5): 20.

Barron, A. (2007), Tunisia as an Arab Woman's Rights Leader. *The Globalist*.

Brynin, M. and Schupp, J. (2000), Education, Employment and Gender Inequality amongst Couples. *European Sociological Review* 16(4): 349–65.

CBC News. *In Depth Lebanon*. Available at: http://www.cbc.ca/news/background/lebanon/ (Retrieved 30 January 2007).

Jamali, D., Sidani, Y. and Safieddine, A. (2005), Constraints Facing Working Women in Lebanon: An Insider View. *Women in Management Review* 20(8): 81–94.

Kerlinger, F.N. (1973), *Foundations of Behavioral Research*. New York: Holt, Rinehart and Winston.

McElwee, G. and Al-Riyami, R. (2003), Women Entrepreneurs in Oman: Some Barriers to Success. *Career Development International* 8(7): 339–46.

Rhode, D.L. (ed.) (2003), *The Difference 'Difference' Makes: Women and Leadership*. Stanford, CA: Stanford University Press.

Russeau, S. (2008), Women, Media and Politics in Lebanon. *International Museum for Women*. Available at: http://www.imow.org/wpp/stories/viewStory?storyId=1495/ (Retrieved 3 May 2015).

United Nations Economic Commission for Europe. (2004), Women's Self-employment and Entrepreneurship in the UNECE Region. Secretariat Note for the Regional Preparatory

Meeting for the 10-Year Review of Implementation of the Beijing Platform for Action (Beijing +10) – ECE/AC.28. Geneva UNECE Publication. Available at: http://www.unece.org/press/pr2004/04gen_n06e.htm/ (Retrieved 28 April 2015).

UNDP. (2005), *Human Arab Development Report. Towards the Rise of Women in the Arab World.* Available at: http://www.undp.org/arabstates/PDF2005/AHDR4_03.pdf/ (Retrieved 2 May 2015).

Varia, N. (2008), Women's Work. *As-safai.* Available at: http://www.hrw.org/english/docs/2008/03/08/lebano18245.htm/ (Retrieved 8 March 2015).

Wadhwa, W. (2006), Fixing Engineering's Gender Gap, Viewpoint. *Business Week.* Available at: http://www.businessweek.com/smallbiz/content/mar2006/sb20060314_760860.htm/ (Retrieved 14 March 2015).

Williams, D. (2007), Lebanon's Muslims, Christians Unite in Quest for Jobs Abroad. *Bloomberg Anywhere.* Available at: http://www.bloomberg.com/apps/news?pid=20601085&sid=aBJEdCZC2AOg&refer=europe/ (Retrieved 7 February 2014).

Woldie, A. and Adersua, A. (2004), Female Entrepreneurs in a Transitional Economy: Business Women in Nigeria. *International Journal of Social Economics* 31(1/2): 78–93.

Chapter 6

Perception of Serbian Women's Status at Work

Snežana Videnović, Vesna Pavlićević and Nevena Jovanović

Introduction

For centuries the predominant view was that men and women are different, and even today that view justifies the discriminative treatment of women in some societies. When we introduce the concept of success to the male/female context, women were allowed to be successful in the family, but not in society or at work.

The concept of business success on a personal level is highly complex and includes, besides the economic dimensions of success (earnings), climbing the social ladder, all of which combines to create a specific lifestyle. Although the number of successful women, especially in middle management, has grown tenfold compared to the end of the twentieth century, in the sphere of higher business their number is still disappointing. On the Fortune 500 list for 2010, there are only 2.4 per cent of women among the executive directors. Some other more extensive studies show lower results on the issue of women at the top in business, and when we approach a deeper analysis of the situation of women in these positions, it can be concluded that even when they reach the top positions, they earn less than men. However, some progress is still taking place, especially in European countries with higher standards – the Netherlands, Sweden, Finland and Norway, where 44.2 per cent of women are on managing boards (Toebel, 2011). The high percentage of women in top positions is not just the case, but a strictly regulated rule. In 2008, Norway enacted a law which requires that company boards consist of at least 40 per cent women. By legislative regulation of the issue of direct discrimination, the state paves the way for solving the problem of indirect discrimination: fathers who do not use the 'father quota', i.e. four weeks of parental leave, which they should devote to the newborn, pay fines. Consequently, it is no longer unusual for a husband to take paternity leave because his wife contributes more to the household budget.

The 1960s opened the door for the consumer society and the entry of women into a world which until then had been largely reserved for men – the world of business. The increasing proportion of women in all spheres of social life was not commensurate with the positive changes in the perception of the role and status of women at work. Rosabeth Moss Kanter, in her study 1977 'Men and Women of the Corporation', began an inquiry into women's behaviour at work, and came to the conclusion that women generally are in an inferior position compared to men. Since then, extensive research has been done in which it was concluded that there are significant stereotypes regarding the role of women's performance, which meant that they have fewer opportunities in their socialization for reaching leadership positions in the companies they work for.

Recent worldwide studies show that prejudice against women is far less pronounced than it was just a few decades ago; however, there are still those that point to the existence of some differences. Some articles highlight the differences in the biological functioning of the two sexes; others focus on finding different patterns of behaviour between men and women; others still are based on the fact that men and women cultivate different leadership styles and management methods. According to some authors, men and women have a different relationship with subordinates and/or superiors, and a different attitude to life in the corporate world and the place of women in it.

Previous studies in Serbia have examined various aspects of gender relations: sociodemographic differences between men and women according to various criteria, attitudes on discrimination against women in society, as well as attitudes about gender roles, stereotypes and patterns of behaviour. Official results of the National Statistics Office show that in 2010 in the Republic of Serbia, about 10 per cent more men than women were employed. The table illustrating employed people by occupation and sex shows that in the area of 'legislators, senior officials and managers' about 70 per cent of men were employed versus 30 per cent women. Experts, associates, technicians, clerks, facility service workers and merchants are mostly women. Only in the basic, simple occupations is there an even percentage of equality in the representation of both sexes. The 'typically male' professions – the military and manual labour – are still reserved for men.

The Institute of Social Sciences published research about the attitudes of citizens in Serbia on many dimensions of gender equality in 2010, and concluded that public opinion in Serbia is still not fully sensitized to the issue of gender equality. If the same deduction is projected onto a narrower segment – the operation and status of women at work – we are forced to conclude that there will be no major deviations in that area. A similar situation exists in neighbouring countries. Totus Opinionmeter's research, conducted on a sample of 400 respondents from Croatia, gives interesting information on how the citizens of Croatia experience women in today's business world (Sikavica and Bahtijarević, 2004: 262). According to the survey, citizens perceive employed women as fair, just, communicative, team-oriented, responsible and educated. The dominant view was that the most common benefits of having women in business are responsibility and ability. When asked to consider the most common shortcomings, the majority of respondents could not list any, although some pointed out excessive care and family responsibilities. It is interesting that as the first attribute to which they link the concept of businesswomen, respondents reported appearance. This means that businesswomen have to look as respondents' stereotypes of businesswomen. According to research conducted by the Centre for Entrepreneurship and Economic Development in Montenegro, more than half of women think that it is easier for men to find employment than for women, primarily because of the prejudice against women.

The Research Project

Formulation of the Problem

The basic issue raised by this study is to obtain answers to the question: How is the position of women at work perceived in today's Serbia? Therefore it is necessary to examine what successful women bring to the job – what are their psychological, working and leadership characteristics? What does a 'prototype' of modern successful businesswomen look like? To what degree are the stereotypes of employed women still present, and can it be expected of women that, if they have the required properties, they will be able to overcome prejudice and become competitive against men in the Serbia of the twenty-first century? The results obtained in this study will be used for comparison with the results obtained in earlier studies of similar themes, both throughout the world and in Serbia.

Goals of Research

The aim of the study is to describe the profile of women leaders in Serbia, based on respondents' evaluations of the checklist, and to determine the influence of sociodemographic (independent) variables in assessing the qualities that successful businesswomen in Serbia should have. Research should also determine to what extent prejudice against women is still present in our society and the impact of sociodemographic (independent) variables in the level of agreement with the prejudice about women. The survey will also be used to determine whether there is a connection and what the structure is between the estimated traits of successful women leaders and prejudice about women.

Finally and most importantly, this study will examine the structure of forming opinions when making judgements about successful businesswomen in Serbia. The aim is to find out if there is an attitude of gender equality in this dimension of human activities.

The Subject of Inquiry

The subject of this research is a thorough analysis of the perception of working women's position in Serbia. It is also important to determine which properties are characteristic for successful women and whether a woman who has them can be considered an equal partner in the fight for each job and position, as well as leadership positions in a culture such as ours.

In accordance with our initial intention to explore public opinion on the status of women at work, this study consists of two sections. The first part of the study discusses the characteristics of a successful businesswoman, while the second deals with the most frequent stereotypes related to the notion of woman at work. We have tried to connect the individual and the characteristics of the national culture for the purpose of consideration of the business environment and the women in it.

Classification and Definition of Variables

The independent variables in the study are the following sociodemographic variables: gender, age, education level, employment status, marital status, years of service, place of residence, children, children's gender, mother's education, father's education and religion.

Dependent variables: the checklist consisted of 30 personality traits, which are evaluated on a 5-point Likert scale, and a questionnaire consisting of 26 statements concerning prejudice against women, which are evaluated by the degree of agreement on a 5-point Likert scale.

Methodology

The survey was conducted in 2013, in larger and smaller cities and all regions of the Republic of Serbia. The sample was random, stratified, and consists of 338 subjects of both genders, aged over 18. The study is explorative in type. Processing analysis of variance techniques and factor analysis were used on the data.

Results and Discussion

Necessary and desirable characteristics that successful women in Serbia should have were evaluated by the respondents on the basis of personal experience, i.e. knowing women who are successful according to their criteria, or classifying features that the 'ideal' hypothetical women at work should have. However, given that they should have evaluated 30 characteristics of successful women, it is assumed that the respondents assessed the desirability of each of these features in a wider context.

The most desirable traits were persistence (4.54) and communication skills (4.53), then resourcefulness (4.49), confidence (4.49), intelligence (4.42), courage (4.33), thoughtfulness (4.33), ambition (4.29), education (4.27), consistency (4.26), emotional stability (4.22) and equity (the quality of being fair and impartial) (4.20), while the least desirable characteristics included recklessness (2.37), vengefulness (2.22) and aggression (2.78).

This research on desirable traits in successful women gave very similar results to previous efforts, and once again proved that the quality and specificity of women leaders who were singled out for effectiveness, and thus formed a typical 'profile', can be clearly defined.

One of the first studies in our country which was conducted at the Institute of Economic Sciences in 2005 shows that the profile of women leaders in Serbia, apart from some socio-personal characteristics that we did not consider in this study, is characterized by the following features and capabilities: intuition, communication, understanding associates and employees; willingness to change quickly; organization; a dominant personality, enthusiasm, activity and working energy, high level of self-discipline, personal charisma, a high degree of self-control and strong will; attention in making decisions, persistence, boldness, awareness of responsibility to others, and teamwork.

Although they are not entirely compatible, when we compare the profile of successful women in this study and Radovic's study, some of the results do coincide. Further, the combination of some characteristics and traits forms a feature profile of a successful woman in the research of the Institute of Economic Sciences. Greater inconsistency was observed while comparing results. Research from 2005 found that successful women 'have emotional stability, i.e. have the ability to tolerate stress and frustration'. This research confirmed that emotional stability is a necessary characteristic of successful women, but in the context of emotional maturity: appropriate, consistent and predictable emotional reactions, rather than in terms of susceptibility to stress.

Analysis of the Properties of the Checklists: Gender and Other Demographic Variables

In line with the research goals, we examined differences in attitudes which respondents with different sociodemographic characteristics have about the extent to what it is necessary for a successful woman in this country to have, according to a checklist.

The respondents assessed characteristics on a five-point scale and ranked how important it was that successful women possessed a given trait; the figure in brackets is the arithmetic mean of the degree to which a trait was desirable, as assessed by the respondents on a scale from 1 to 5.

For each of the properties, the values between which the greatest difference of the arithmetic mean was obtained are shown, that is statistically significant in the subgroup, which is the set of independent variables.[1]

Emotional Stability

Considering emotional stability, the greatest differences were between urban men (3.91) and rural women (4.47); that is, urban men believe that emotional stability is a less desirable characteristic of successful women than rural women. This trend also exists when it comes to the differences between men with secondary education (3.77) and women with doctorates (4.63); further, between unemployed men (3.5) and employed women (4.36), and between single men (3.24) and single women (4.43), men without children (3.49) and women with at least one female child (4.49), men whose mothers have doctorates (3.25) and women whose mothers have undergraduate degrees (4.61), men whose fathers have primary education (3.67) and women whose fathers have undergraduate degrees (4.54). Also, differences in the perception of the desirability of these characteristics are observed between men who are religious (3.85) and women who are either religious or undisclosed (4.38), men with 10 years of service (3.74) and women with 21–30 years of service (4.46), men under 35 (3.55) and women under 35 (4.42), but also men over 55 (4.5).

Sincerity

Men with doctorates (3.13) believe that honesty is a less desirable property for the profile of successful women than women with secondary education (4.08). These differences also exist between unemployed men (3.17) and unemployed women (4.0), also between single men (3.57) and men without children (3.44) and women with partners (4.04) and those who predominantly have male children (4.18), between men with under 10 years of service (3.46) and women with under 30 years of service (4.14), men under 35 (3.26) and women over 55 (4.2).

Deliberation

Considering this dimension, the most noticeable distinctions are between urban men (3.77) and rural women (4.36), men with university degrees (3.75) and women with master's degrees or doctorates (4.5), unemployed men (3.42) and employed women (4.25), single men (3.62) and men without children (3.63), women with partners

(4.27) and children of both genders (4.44), men whose mothers have undergraduate studies (3.67) and/or whose fathers have masters or doctorates (3.67) and women whose parents have undergraduate studies (4.4). Furthermore, the differences are discriminatory too between men who have 10 years of service (3.76) and women with 21 to 30 years of service (4.51), and men who are under 35 (3.68) and women over 55 (4.4).

Honesty

As one of the major differences in this dimension is between rural men (3.69) and rural women (4.31), men who have university degrees (3.56) perceived honesty as a less important characteristic for a successful businesswoman than women who have doctorates (4.44); such a relationship exists between men (3.17) and women (4.44) who are unemployed, men (3.48) and women (4.26) without partners, men without children (3.49) or with at least one female child (3.53) and women who have more than one child, with at least one female child among them (4.34); furthermore, men whose parents have university degrees (3.5 and 3.0) and women whose parents have undergraduate studies (4.43 and 4.28), men (3.51) and women who are religious (4.34), men who have under 10 years of service (3.52) and women with 11 to 20 years of service (4.48), men under 35 (3.32) and women, but also men, over 55 years of age (4.33).

Equality

Considering this quality, the greatest differences are between urban men (3.72) and rural women (4.37), i.e. urban men perceived equality as a less important characteristic for a successful businesswoman, than rural women. This trend also exists when it comes to men with undergraduate and graduate degrees (3.6) and women with doctorates (4.69), unemployed men (3.0) and employed women (3.92); furthermore, single men (3.57) and single women (4.43), men without children (3.49) and women with predominantly female children (4.43), men whose parents have the highest educational level (3.25 and 2.67) and women whose mothers have undergraduate degrees (4.52) and/or fathers have undergraduate/graduate educational level (3.1), men who are religious (3.72) and women who are religious (4.43), men who have under 10 years of service (3.68) and women with 11 to 20 years of service (4.52), and men under 35 (3.32) and women under 45 (4.4).

Self-assuredness

Considering self-confidence as a significant characteristic proved to be the difference between urban men (4.13) and women (4.62), men with undergraduate degrees (4.17) and women with doctorates (4.75), men who are employed (4.29) and women who are not employed (4.66), men who have partners (4.27) and women without partners (4.66), men without children (4.2) or male children (4.29) and women without children (4.66). Also differences in the perception of the importance of these characteristics exist among men whose parents have doctorates (4.0 and 3.67) and women whose parents have undergraduate degrees (4.8 and 4.61), men who did not disclose about their religiosity (4.2) and women who are religious (4.58), men from 11 to 20 years of service (4.19) and women from 31 to 40 years of service (4.7), men who are from 36 to 45 years old (4.25) and women under 35 (4.6).

Vengefulness

Regarding the characteristic of vengefulness, major differences exist between rural men (2.69) and urban women (1.74), i.e. rural men consider this trait more desirable for a successful businesswoman than urban women. Furthermore, this proportion of difference exists between women with at least a bachelor's degree (2.6) and men with undergraduate studies (1.86), unemployed men (3.75) and employed women (1.98), single men (3.14) and women regardless of partnership status (2.0), men (2.95) and women (1.89) without children, men whose mothers/fathers have doctorates (4.0 and 3.65), and women whose mothers/fathers have secondary education (1.9). Also, this trend is notable between women regardless of religiosity (1.98 and 1.83) and men who did not disclose religiosity (2.9), women (1.6) and men (3.14) who are from 31 to 40 years old, and women over 55 (1.67) and men over 55 (3.17).

Tolerance

Regarding tolerance, urban men (3.72) consider this trait less desirable than rural women (4.22). This can also be applied to men with bachelor's degrees (3.44) compared to women who have doctorates (4.56); also unemployed men (3.33) when compared to unemployed women (4.28), men (3.43) and women (4.28) without partners, men without children (3.56) or female children (3.59), and women with female or children of both genders (4.2), men who are religious (3.68) and women who are religious (4.23), men who have between 31 and 40 years of service (3.57) and women with 11 to 20 years of service (4.34), men over 55 (3.5) and women who are 36 to 45 years old (4.3). The following difference is interesting: men whose mothers have bachelor degrees (4.31) appreciate this trait more than men whose mothers have lower degrees (3.75 and 3.25). A similar situation exists in women whose mothers have undergraduate studies (4.52), compared to primary school degrees (3.81). The biggest difference in the desirability of these properties is between men (3.25) and women (4.25) whose mothers have undergraduate degrees. Men whose fathers have doctorates (3.3) believe that tolerance is a less desirable trait than women whose fathers have this level of education (4.29).

The above data suggest that men and women perceive certain personality traits that successful women should have quite differently. However, this research suggests that successful women, especially the socially desirable ones, are exactly those women who are accomplished, as far as business and family is concerned.

Analysis of the Properties of the Checklists: Place of Residence and Other Demographic Variables[2]

Aggressiveness

Respondents from the urban areas with undergraduate degrees (2.31) evaluated aggression as less desirable than respondents from rural areas with doctorates (3.33). This appears for the following groups of subjects too: respondents from urban (2.05) and rural areas (3.79), unemployed, urban without partners (2.41) and rural without partners (3.33), urban with female children (2.41) and rural without children (3.08), urban whose mothers have secondary or undergraduate degrees (2.3) and rural whose mothers have doctorates (4.0), respondents, regardless of place of residence, whose fathers have elementary education (2.33) and rural whose fathers have doctorates (4.0), urban who did not disclose religiosity (2.33) and rural who are not religious (3.42), urban who have 31 to 40 years of service (83, 14), urban who are over 55 (2.8) and rural who are under 35 (3.13).

Recklessness

Urban respondents with undergraduate degrees (3.3) deem recklessness less desirable than respondents from rural areas with doctorates (2.79). The same is true for the following groups of respondents: urban unemployed (1.8) and rural unemployed (3.46), urban with partners (2.02) and rural with partners (3.12), urban with female children (1.91) and rural without children (2.78), rural whose fathers have doctorates (1.0) and urban whose fathers have elementary school (2.94), urban who did not disclose religiosity (1.6) and rural who are not religious (3.17), urban who have 21 to 30 years of service (1.87) and rural who have 11 to 20 years of service (2.85), urban who are over 55 (1.69) and rural who are 46 to 55 years old (2.83). Considering education of mothers the biggest difference is within rural areas, but according to place of residence, urban respondents whose mothers have undergraduate degrees (1.72) estimate this characteristic to be less desirable then the rural ones whose mothers have primary (2.65) or secondary education (2.66).

Dominance

Respondents from urban areas with doctorates (3.3) evaluate this trait as less desirable than the rural respondents with this level of education (4.5). The same is also true for the following groups of respondents: employed urban ones (3.7) compared to rural unemployed (4.42), urban with partners (3.64) and single rural ones (4.23), urban with female children (3.5) and rural without children (4.06), urban whose mothers have doctorates (3.57) and rural whose mothers have doctorates (5.0), rural whose fathers have primary education (3.6) and also rural whose fathers have masters or doctorates (5.0). But compared to the urban areas, that would be respondents whose fathers have primary education, ones who did not disclose religiosity (3.37) and from the villages who did not disclose religiosity (4.04), from the cities who have 31 to 40 years of service (3.6), and rural of the same category (4.14).

Elegance

Respondents from urban areas with doctorates (3.9) evaluate this trait as less desirable than the rural ones with this level of education (4.57). The same is true for the following groups of respondents: employed from the cities (3.99) and unemployed from the villages (4.5), urban with partners (3.96) and rural without partners (4.47), urban with male or female children (3.8) rural with children of both genders (4.43), urban whose mothers have doctorates (3.57) and rural whose mothers have doctorates (5.0), urban whose fathers have doctorates (3.67) and rural whose fathers have doctorates (5.0), urban who are religious (3.86) and rural who are religious (4.38), urban who have 11 to 20 years of service (3.87), from the villages who have 31 to 40 years of service (4.57), and urban who are 36 to 45 years old (3.82), and rural who are 46 to 55 years old (4.49).

Wittiness

Employed respondents from the urban areas (3.79) consider this trait less important for successful women than employed people from rural ones (4.18), urban respondents with partners (3.78) and rural with partners (4.15), urban with male children (3.64) and rural with children of both genders (4.28), urban whose mothers have doctorates (3.57) and rural whose mothers have doctorates (5.0), urban whose fathers have doctorates (3.22) and rural whose fathers have doctorates (5.0), urban who are/are not religious (3.77 and 3.78) and rural who are religious (4.18), urban who have 21 to 30 years of service (3.54), urban who have 31 to 40 years of service (4.3), compared to the respondents from the village who have 11 to 20 years of service (4.28), and rural who are over 55 (3.63) and 36 to 45 years old (4.29), there are no significant differences.

Physical Attractiveness

Respondents from the cities with doctorates (but also with secondary education and university degrees) (3.3) evaluate physical attractiveness as a less desirable trait of successful businesswomen than respondents from the rural areas with doctorates (4.36). The same is true for the following groups of respondents: urban employed (3.31) and rural unemployed (4.17), urban with partners (3.23) and rural without partners (4.12), urban with male children (3.28) and rural with children of both genders (4.14), urban whose mothers have secondary education (3.27) and rural whose mothers have doctorates (5.0), urban whose fathers have graduate or undergraduate degrees (3.33) and rural whose fathers have doctorates (5.0), urban who are religious (3.24) and rural who are religious (4.02), urban who have 11 to 20 years of service (3.3), rural who have 11 to 20 years of service (4.13), urban who are 46 to 55 years old (3.25), rural who are 36 to 45 years old (4.15).

Intrusiveness

Respondents from the cities with university degrees (3.09) believe intrusiveness (intrusiveness is aggressive and dominant behaviour) to be a less desirable trait than respondents from the village with doctorates (3.64). The same is true for the following groups of respondents: urban unemployed (3.05) and rural unemployed (3.83), urban with partners (3.18) and rural with partners (3.55), rural with children of both genders (2.97) and rural with female children (3.67), urban whose mothers have secondary education (3.06) and rural whose mothers have doctorates (5.0), urban whose fathers have secondary education (3.02) and urban whose fathers have masters and doctorates (3.89), compared to the respondents from the villages whose fathers have primary education (3.6) and from the cities who did not disclose their religiosity (3.0) and from the villages who are not religious (3.83), and from the cities who have 31 to 40 years of service (3.0), and from the villages who have 11 to 40 years of service (3.58), and from the cities who are over 55 (2.92), and from the villages who are over 55 (3.63).

Vengefulness

Respondents from the cities with undergraduate degrees (1.78) estimate the characteristic of vengefulness as more undesirable than respondents who have doctorates

(3.0). This trend is notable for the following groups of respondents: urban with partners (1.89) and rural with partners (2.67), urban with male children (1.92) and rural without children (2.61), rural (1.0) and urban (3.57) whose mothers have doctorates, rural whose fathers have doctorates (1.0) compared to the urban respondents whose fathers have only primary education (3.11), rural who are not religious (1.84) and rural who did not disclose religiosity (2.85), and rural who have 31 to 40 years of service (1.86) and urban who have 31 to 40 years of service (2.5).

Charisma

Charisma as a property is less prized by respondents with a partner but without children (3.74) than those who are single and have only female children (4.4).

Considering the data above it is evident that urban and rural areas are different in terms of evaluating certain characteristics of successful women. It is interesting that these are the features that can be said to mark a successful individual in the biological and evolutionary sense, and thus allow her advantage and survival. Simply put, healthy, expansive (extremely extroverted) and attractive women are more valued in the community where, from the historical and biological perspective, survival depends on these qualities.

Perception of Claims

In order to further consider and evaluate factors that influence the position of women in Serbia, we assess the attitudes toward claims and prejudice that are often associated with women. With regard to the attitudes formed in the process of socialization in the family, school and society, the assumption is that a high percentage of agreement with stereotypes and prejudice substantially direct the behaviour of each individual, and thus directly affect the position of each entity, object or social phenomenon.

The results showed the respondents' attitudes regarding the position of women in business, ranging from traditional to modern. The traditional attitude is characterized by the desire to retain a conservative opinion that contains explicit or subtle sexist prejudices, while the modern view is characterized by an individual's tendency to evolve social roles.

The high degree of agreement (3.97) with the statement that women are more susceptible to stress at work than men shows that women are still considered 'weaker' in the physical and emotional sense than men, pointing to a traditionalist stance on women. However, one possible reason for this attitude is the considerable pressure imposed upon women. The only work Serbian women used to perform was at home. Today they have the same responsibilities for the household, but also for the economic survival of the family during the current economic crisis. In these new circumstances of global recession, it is not surprising that respondents evaluate that women are more susceptible to stress than men.

Some attitudes have not changed regardless of the passage of time. Established 'female values', such as the need for maintaining good interpersonal relationships, balance and harmony are confirmed by this inquiry. All previous studies conducted in Serbia proved that harmony and teamwork are very important to women. Thus, of the 26 statements offered in this research, agreement with the statement: 'Harmonious relations and good atmosphere at work are the most important to women', was very high (3.80).

Highly valued (3.72) are the claims: 'attractive women often consciously use their advantages to advance their careers', and 'women are more capable of learning through various forms of training than men'. The first claim related to the use of attractiveness in order to advance in their careers is congruent with research conducted in Croatia, in which respondents to the concept of a businesswoman was tied primarily to their appearance. The claim related to learning and development has an identical result to the first one. Observing two identical results for these two separate claims, the conclusion is that businesswomen in Serbia need to have an extra 'quality'. In fact, if they do not have the same opportunities as men, if they are not equal, then they use the range of potential possibilities available to them.

The claim that 'women are more likely to plot than men' (3.70) is probably the most frequent stereotype associated with women's behaviour at work. The high percentage of agreement with this statement tells us that among the respondents there is still a deeply rooted traditionalist thinking about women. Although plotting is common to both women and men, this prejudice has its roots in a period when women were 'idle', i.e. worked only at home. All other values of agreement with the statement indicate interweaving traditionalist and modern attitudes about women business leaders, and finally the lowest percentage of agreement occurred with the statement that 'woman's place is at home'. On the one hand, this is a positive step forward in understanding of the role and place of women in our society, and on the other, the impression is unavoidable that this attitude places even more pressure on women. Women need to get out of the house and work – this is not disputed, but the level of agreement with offered statements varies depending on the specific sociodemographic variables, as shown in Tables 6.1–6.9.

Male respondents agree less than females with statements about women being more responsible, more motivated, more productive, more innovative, better leaders,

Table 6.1 Prejudice about women in business

Prejudice	Gender	
	Male	Female
Women are more responsible at work than men.	2.94	3.95
Women are more motivated for work than men.	2.92	3.69
Women are better leaders than men.	2.46	3.53
Women are more productive than men.	2.85	3.80
Women make more correct decisions than men.	2.70	3.51
Women are more loyal to the employer than men.	3.10	3.59
Women are more capable of learning through various forms of training than men.	3.34	3.88
Women are more innovative at work than men.	3.00	3.74
To women, harmonious relations and good atmosphere at work are most important.	3.46	3.96
Women are more susceptible to stress at work than men.	3.53	4.17
Managing my business I would trust a woman, rather than a man.	2.47	2.99

Table 6.2 Prejudice about women in business

Prejudice	Gender	
	Male	Female
Women are more likely to plot than men.	4.09	3.52
Women are more prone to conflict at work than men.	3.71	3.21
Ambitious women are unscrupulous, and therefore immoral.	2.99	2.15
A woman's place is at home.	2.33	1.38
Women who do not have offspring progress faster than those who have children.	3.41	2.64
Single women progress faster than married ones.	3.22	2.53
Attractive women rapidly advance their careers.	3.97	3.16
Women who flirt with superiors progress faster in their careers.	3.87	3.22
Women who have 'affairs' with supervisors at work progress faster in their careers.	3.69	3.20
Attractive women often consciously use their 'benefits' in order to progress in their careers.	4.11	3.54
Behind every successful woman is a powerful man.	3.05	2.45

Table 6.3 Educational level

Prejudice	Educational level			
	SE	Under grad.	Bachelor	Master/Doctorates
Ambitious women are unscrupulous, and therefore immoral.	2.80		2.16	
A woman's place is at home.	2.11		1.40	
Single women progress faster than married ones.	3.03			2.25
Attractive women often consciously use their 'benefits' in order to progress in their careers.		4.00		3.33

Table 6.4 Employment status

Prejudice	Employment status	
	Unemployed	Employed
To women, family is more important than work.	2.95	3.47

Table 6.5 Partnership status

Prejudice	Partnership status	
	With partner	Single
Managing my business I would trust a woman, rather than a man.	2.72	3.12

Table 6.6 Years of service

Prejudice	Years of service			
	To 10	11–20	21–30	31–40
To women, harmonious relations and good atmosphere at work are the most important.	3.60			4.12
Women who do not have offspring progress faster than those who have children.		2.60		3.76
Women who flirt with superiors progress faster in their careers.		3.09		4.18

Table 6.7 Children

Prejudice	Children	
	Yes	No
Women make more correct decisions than men.	3.38	3.06
To women, harmonious relations and good atmosphere at work are the most important.	3.94	3.58

Table 6.8 Mother's education

Prejudice	Mother's education				
	PE	SE	US	Bachelor	Master/ Doctorate
Ambitious women are unscrupulous, and therefore immoral.	2.88			1.96	
A woman's place is in the home.	2.03			1.33	
To women, family is more important than work.				3.63	2.25
Single women prosper faster than married ones.	3.06				2.00
Women who flirt with superiors progress faster in their careers.	3.63				2.63
Attractive women often consciously use their 'advantages' in order to progress in their careers.		3.93	3.33		

Table 6.9 Father's education

Prejudice	Father's education				
	PE	SE	US	Bachelor	Master/ Doctorate
Women are better associates/colleagues than men.			3.52		2.10
Women are more productive than men.			3.91		2.70
Ambitious women are unscrupulous, and therefore immoral.	3.04			1.88	
A woman's place is at home.	2.35			1.41	1.40

making more correct decisions, loyal to the employer, and ready for development; for women, harmonious relations and good atmosphere at work are the most important, that they are more susceptible to stress, and in the management of the company they would rather trust a woman.

Female respondents agree less than male respondents with the statements that women are more prone to intrigues and conflicts, that ambitious women are unscrupulous, and therefore immoral, that women's place is at home, that single women and without children advance faster in their careers than married ones with children, that attractive women rapidly advance in their careers and often use their 'advantages' to progress, as well as those who flirt or have affairs with superiors, also that behind every successful woman there is a powerful man.

Respondents who have bachelor's degrees agree less with statements that ambitious women are unscrupulous, and therefore immoral, and that women's place is at home, than respondents with secondary education. Respondents with master's degrees and doctorates agree less with the claim that women without partners prosper faster than single ones than respondents with secondary education, as well as with the statement that attractive women often consciously use their 'advantages' in order to progress in their careers.

Respondents who are unemployed agree less than respondents who are employed with the statement that, to women, family is more important than work.

Respondents who have partners agree less than the respondents who are single with the statement that they would choose a woman for a supervisor.

Respondents who have 31 to 40 years of service agree with the statement that women who do not have offspring progress faster than those who have children, as well as do those who flirt with superiors at work, than respondents who have 11 to 20 years of service. They also agree with the statement that, to women, harmonious relations and good atmosphere at work are the most important thing, than respondents who have under 10 years of service.

Respondents who have children agree more than the respondents without children with statements that women make more correct decisions than men, and that women most value harmonious relations and good atmosphere at work.

Respondents whose mothers only have primary education agree more with the statements that ambitious women are unscrupulous, and therefore immoral, that women's place is at home, that single women prosper faster than married ones, that women who flirt with their superiors progress faster in their careers, than respondents whose mothers have bachelor's degrees, master's degrees or doctorates. Respondents whose mothers have secondary education are more supportive of the opinion that attractive women often consciously use their 'advantages' in order to progress in their careers, than respondents whose mothers have undergraduate degrees.

Respondents whose fathers have master's degrees or doctorates agree less than respondents whose fathers have undergraduate degrees with the statements that women are better associates/colleagues than men and are more productive. Respondents whose fathers have only primary education agree more with the statements that ambitious women are unscrupulous, and therefore immoral, and that women's place is at home, than those whose fathers have bachelor degrees, masters or doctorates. There are no statistically significant differences in the attitudes of the respondents towards religiosity, respondents' age, place of residence, as well as the gender of children. The following factor analysis will show the invisible threads that bind these prejudices.

Factor Analysis

Factor analysis, based on the common characteristics that are dominant, of the 56 dependent variables (personality traits of prejudice against women), has isolated 12 main components – factors that explain 65.5 per cent of the variance. These 12 factors are crucial for the perception of the position of women in business in Serbia.

Factor I Business competence	
Women are more responsible at work than men.	0.803
Women are more motivated for work than men.	0.818
Women are better leaders than men.	0.792
Women are better associates/colleagues than men.	0.595
Women are more productive than men.	0.808
Women make more correct decisions than men.	0.766
Women are more loyal to their employer than men.	0.669
Women are more capable of learning through various forms of training than men.	0.705
Women are more innovative at work than men.	0.743
To women, harmonious relations and good atmosphere at work are the most important.	0.405
Women are more susceptible to stress at work than men.	0.427

The first factor, business competence, consists of variables that essentially contain all the elements necessary for success at work. In fact, if one does not possess sufficient competence, one will not be competitive or successful in any work environment. Responsibility to obligations at work, loyalty, motivation to work, caring and harmonious relationships with colleagues and associates, productivity, proper decision-making, learning and development, and innovation, are the characteristics that every successful leader must possess. However, not all those who possess these qualities become successful. This statement in the context of the status of women at work raises the question of whether this is a possible reason why women are more susceptible to stress than men. Also, this is probably the reason why the variable 'women are more susceptible to stress at work than men', grouped with business competence, still became their indispensable part, although by its nature does not belong and does not fit in this factor.

However, the slight theoretical advantage is on the women's side this time, because modern leadership is based on female attributes and therefore is more suitable for women than men.

Factor II Desirable social traits	
Consistency	0.459
Emotional stability	0.354
Sincerity	0.646
Restraint	0.702
Honesty	0.816
Equity (the quality of being fair)	0.790
Tolerance	0.753
Flexibility	0.659
Analytical skills	0.561

The second factor is determined by the social traits that are desirable for anyone who aspires to be socially accepted. Being successful at work inevitably includes a social component. If leaders are not characterized by consistency, emotional stability, sincerity, restraint, honesty, equity (the quality of being fair), tolerance, flexibility and analytic ability, they will not be perceived as successful at work.

Factor III Alpha qualities	
Aggressiveness	0.727
Uncompromising	0.672
Carelessness	0.761
Dominance	0.671
Cunning	0.719
Intrusiveness (Intrusiveness is aggressive and dominant behaviour)	0.709
Vengefulness	0.604

The third factor, which grouped alpha qualities, consists of the features that are not socially desirable, but to a certain level and conditions which are very important for the survival of the individual in society.

Factor IV Effectiveness	
Intelligence	0.373
Communication	0.440
Education	0.446
Thoughtfulness	0.462
Self-confidence	0.711
Resourcefulness	0.801
Creativity	0.511
Persistence	0.687
Courage	0.353

Effectiveness as the fourth factor is the common denominator of personal characteristics such as intelligence, communication skills, education, thoughtfulness, self-confidence, resourcefulness, creativity, persistence and courage. There is no doubt that all of these traits are, to a greater or lesser extent, of considerable importance for the effectiveness of the individual, and effectiveness is only one of many important characteristics of success at work.

Factor V Transparent sexuality	
Attractive women prosper faster in their careers.	0.684
Women who flirt with superiors faster progress in their careers.	0.901
Women who have 'affairs' with supervisors at work, progress faster in their careers.	0.881
Attractive women often consciously use their 'advantages' in order to progress in their careers.	0.764

The fifth factor counted variables that are based on the transparent sexuality of women at work. Respondents who think that attractive women advance rapidly in their careers also believe that women consciously use their strengths in order to progress. The same is true for women who flirt with superiors and have affairs at work. This use of female attributes for the purpose of career advancement could be called sexual abuse in the workplace.

Factor VI Appearance	
Wittiness	0.670
Elegance	0.722
Emotional stability	0.343
Physical attractiveness	0.830
Charisma	0.653

The sixth factor grouped variables that may be collectively called appearance or impression, as it consists of the following characteristics: wittiness, elegance, emotional stability, physical attractiveness and charisma.

Factor VII Woman as choice	
In my company, I'd rather choose a woman than a man for the vacant position.	0.819
If I could choose I would like a female boss.	0.853
Managing my business I would trust a woman, rather than a man.	0.825

The seventh factor grouped variables related to personal choice. If they could choose, they would trust a woman managing a company, they would choose her for a vacant position, and they would like to have a female boss.

Factor VIII Traditional gender role	
Ambitious women are unscrupulous, and therefore immoral.	0.481
Woman's place is at home.	0.509
To women, families are more important than work.	0.695
Women who do not have offspring progress faster than those who have children.	0.676
Single women prosper faster than married ones.	0.634
Behind every successful woman is powerful man.	0.337

The eighth factor grouped variables that may be collectively called the traditional gender role. Ambitious women are equated with traits such as unscrupulous and immoral because the woman's place is at home. Considering the woman's place, there is a clear correlation with the variable that to women, family is more important than work, that women who do not have offspring and partners advance more quickly in their careers than women who have children and partners. All these variables are somehow derived from each other, and the last in the series that 'behind every successful woman is a powerful man' is grouped within this factor probably as a logical sequence of thinking. If that is true, and yet there are successful women, it must be the case that behind her is a powerful man. She could not succeed on her own, because she is a woman, and woman's place is at home, among children.

Factor IX Undesirable communication channels	
Women are more likely to plot than men.	0.837
Women are more prone to conflict at work than men.	0.841

The ninth factor is called undesirable communication channels because it grouped variables that are not acceptable for successful functioning at work. Those who consider women more likely to plot at work find that women are more prone to conflict than men.

Factor X Universal competence	
Ambition	0.672
Intelligence	0.357
Communication	0.486

Universal competence within the tenth factor grouped ambition, intelligence and communication skills. This factor suggests that universal competence is key to success in any field of human activity. In fact, if among all traits we have to choose three critically significant factors for success, it would probably boil down to these three.

Factor XI Safe house	
To women, harmonious relations and good atmosphere at work are the most important.	0.684
Women are more susceptible to stress at work than men.	0.612

The eleventh factor emphasizes women's need for security and a good atmosphere at work. A variable connected to the idea of harmonious work relations is that women are more susceptible to stress than men. A possible reason for the joint presentation of these two variables in this factor is that the lack of good and harmonious relationships at work causes stress, which reflects more on women than on men. However, this factor suggests that women prefer stable relationships at work, that their relationship to the collective is emotional and ethical and that they are not resistant to pressure. Implicitly we can conclude that women do not have expressive needs for achievement and they are not prone to self-actualization.

Factor XII 'Basic courage'	
Courage	0.427

The twelfth factor is courage. It is self-explanatory. Courage as a personality trait may or may not be related to making business decisions, selection and building a career, family life and so on. There is no doubt that a degree of courage, from choice of occupation and across many business and personal decisions, is necessary in order to be successful in what we do.

Conclusion

This research has described the profile of women leaders in Serbia based on the assessment of the respondents to a checklist of properties. Features that stand out are persistence and communication skills, then resourcefulness, confidence, intelligence, courage, prudence, ambition, education, consistency, emotional stability and equity (the quality of being fair). However, similar or very similar results have been presented in the studies that have described the leaders of Serbia regardless of gender. On the other hand, the characteristics of the leaders in Serbia largely coincide with the data reported in the literature of distinguished scholars of management and leadership. Virtually all studies that have examined the personality characteristics of the people who have become leaders show that these qualities produce a large number of leaders. The question that arises is why are there almost no women in top leadership positions in Serbia?

The answer to this question is likely to be present in the results of the second part of the survey, which is an evaluation of the attitudes of respondents in terms of prejudice against women: attitudes still present in our society and rooted in traditionalist thinking about the position and role of woman in Serbia. Prejudice about the role that women should have, as well as stereotypes about women as executives, is a strong obstacle to the advancement of women at work and is the most difficult to change.

The influence of sociodemographic variables in terms of stereotypes about women is more pronounced than ideas about the qualities that a woman leader should possess. However, the results obtained in this study did not show a correlation between the estimated traits of women leaders and prejudice against women, nor what the structure of forming opinions may be when making judgements of successful women in business in Serbia.

This inquiry proved again the differences in attitudes among sexes, i.e. it confirmed previous studies on a similar subject, but it also provided new data. This research has shown that younger people are more liberal than the older, that more educated people are less informed by prejudice in terms of gender than the less educated, and that there is a big difference in the attitudes of respondents from urban and rural areas. The data suggest that it is necessary to systematize impact (systematization of all this and many other impacts is a method which will improve women's status at work based on critical reflection and interpretation of the research) in improving the status of women at work, especially with regard to the direction of education of employees in line with the development of values that are based on equality of gender. When it comes to career development, or the acceptance of women in a leadership role, it is essential to overcome stereotypes about the typical male/female roles and neutralize gender barriers to progress. In order to ensure an equal starting point for taking a leadership position, i.e. a mature awareness of gender equality in this dimension of human activity, it is necessary to redefine the expectations of gender roles, to modify perceptions of leadership roles and features that are necessary for success at work. This is especially important if we bear in mind that many of the characteristics of modern leadership are considered feminine attributes and therefore more suitable for women than men. This study is characterized by several specifics, although similar traits are already noted in this region and in the world. It covers the entire population, working-age population, regardless of whether they are employed or not. Its second characteristic is that we investigated opinions and attitudes related exclusively to women at work without comparison with men. Opinions and attitudes of men are particularly expressed in the results, but have not determined the differences and similarities between the two sexes in relation to the desirable dominant characteristics and attitudes related to the position in the workplace.

It is also important to note that this is an initial study: in the future similar periodic surveys will be organized for better observation and monitoring of changes occurring in the position of businesswomen in Serbia.

Notes

1 Subcategories which did not determine significant differences were not mentioned in the analysis.
2 Subcategories between which there are no significant differences were not mentioned in the analysis.

References

Sikavica, F. and Bahtijarević, Š. (2004), *Менаџмент: Теорија менаџмента и велико емпиријско истраживање у Хрватској*. Zagreb: Masmedia.
Toebel, G. (2011), *Disappointing Statistics, Positive Outlook*. Available at: http://www.forbes.com/ (Retrieved 6 December 2013).

Chapter 7

Accounting for Women's Labour

Explaining the Present from the Past

Rute Abreu and Fatima David

Introduction

This research investigates women's labour based on accounting research. So, the authors collected bank statistics related with number of working women that pursue managerial careers (Davidson and Burke, 1994; Mirvis and Macy, 1976). Indeed, the Portuguese society is centred on the woman based on the reasons present by Nogueira, Paúl and Amâncio (1995: 209) say,

> there is a long tradition of female work in agriculture, both as wage workers and in subsistence farming, as well as [the] textile industry. . . . In 1994, 13.5% of active women worked in agriculture, 24.3% in industry and 62.2% in the services sector.

Although the economic issues have been discussed, Moen and Yu (2000) defend the view that the entrance of women of all ages into the labour force in the second half of the twentieth century has created another period of structural lag, and discuss the relevance of many other questions. Amâncio (1996: 1,003) argues that 'social thinking still holds several myths about male and female categories that appear both in feminism and in academic research'.

The women's labour based on the accounting research cannot simply be done as an abstraction of human resources (Tomassini, 1976), because there is professional progress of the careers made about them. At the firm level, this is usually concentrated 'on achieving productive work and arranging for the maximum opportunity for expression of the full range of people's abilities and capacities in that productive work' (Bakke, 1961: 24).

Undoubtedly these questions still have to consider other micro-effects of working women. For example, Tilly and Scott (1978) argue that the family economy operated as a cohesive unit; typically all family members, regardless of age or gender, were engaged in productive labour during the Industrial Revolution, but the evolution was essentially associated with married life. In Portugal, the average age of women at first marriage was 29.2 years in 2010, representing an increase of 3.5 years compared to 2000, and the first birth was 28.9 years in 2010, representing a postponement of motherhood for 2.4 years compared to 2000 (INE, 2012a). Also, the number of larger families has fallen in recent decades. In 2011, families with five or more people represented 6.5 per cent of the population but in 2001 was 9.5 per cent and in 1991 was 15.4 per cent (INE, 2012b).

In a further example, Becker (1985) suggests that women traded work effort and income for more time and energy to devote to domestic labour, but recent statistics show that the number of women living alone, regardless of age, grew 26.6 per cent in the decade from 2001 to 2011. These women represent 63.8 per cent of the population living alone and in the age group 65 and over the value rises to 77.1 per cent (INE, 2012b).

Silver and Goldscheider (1994) explain that the more time women spend on housework the greater will be the family demands on a working woman, and the less help she receives from the members of the family; in 2010, 91.3 per cent of women missed work to stay at home taking care of children. These statistics are a matter of concern because of their possible long-term macro-effects: in Portugal in 2010 each woman had on average 1.4 children but in 2000, that average was 1.6 children (INE, 2012a). With the introduction of Law no. 16/2007 of 17 April (AR, 2007), the increase in the number of abortions recorded rose from 4,325 in 2007 to 17,277 in 2010.

Assessment of women´s labour from the perspective of the accounting research enhances the range of discussion of macro-effects and micro-effects. This range is illustrated on several macro-effects in Portugal. One of them is the distribution of unemployment and employment rate, from 2004 to 2011, as illustrated in Table 7.1.

The data in Table 7.1 was obtained from an employment survey promoted by the Portuguese Statistics Institute. It shows that in 2011 the total unemployment rate was 12.7 per cent. The change of women's unemployment has a progressive acceleration from 7.6 per cent in 2004 to 13.1 per cent in 2011, especially for less-educated women, poor and low-income families and families with sick, disabled and elderly parents (OECD, 2012b). The youth unemployment rate increased to a maximum value of 30.1 per cent in 2011 from 15.3 per cent in 2004. In a scenario in which job losses are common, young people will need to be able to learn other skills to prevent social exclusion due to long-term unemployment. This requires government intervention to prevent the increasing marginalization of young people and a substantial increase in poverty among those who cannot call on parental support (OECD, 2012b).

This evolution in the employment rate has occurred due to the dynamics of job creation and destruction that are closely linked to the flexibility of working contracts, and fixed contracts are more prevalent for younger people and women. In the third

Table 7.1 Distribution of unemployment and employment rate, 2004–2011

	2004	2005	2006	2007	2008	2009	2010	2011
Unemployment rate (% of labour rate)	**6.7**	**7.6**	**7.7**	**8.0**	**7.6**	**9.5**	**10.8**	**12.7**
Men	5.8	6.7	6.5	6.6	6.5	8.9	9.8	12.4
Women	7.6	8.7	9.0	9.6	8.8	10.1	11.9	13.1
Young (15–24)	15.3	16.1	16.3	16.6	16.4	20.1	22.4	30.1
Employment rate 15–64 years (% of population)	**72.9**	**73.4**	**73.9**	**74.1**	**74.2**	**73.7**	**74.0**	**74.1**
Men	79.0	79.0	79.5	79.4	79.5	78.5	78.2	78.5
Women	67.0	67.9	68.4	68.8	68.9	69.0	69.9	69.8

Source: adapted from BP (2012a).

quarter of 2012, 45.6 per cent of the women of working age (between 15 and 64 years old) had a formal job or were self-employed. However, the employment rate was only 23.5 per cent for women of working age compared with the total population, and for men the rate was 25.8 per cent (INE, 2012b).

Difficulties and risks deriving from the institutional reforms promoted by the Portuguese Government as a result of the framework of the Economic and Financial Assistance Programme for Portugal are having the same effect:

> During the second half of the 1960s, and continuing through the 1970s, the Swedish labour market changed substantially. Structural changes in society, a greater concentration of employment in certain densely populated areas, a high level of immigration, increasing labour obsolescence and a higher percentage of women on the labour market were a few of the changes that occurred during this period.
>
> (Jonson, Jonsson and Svensson, 1978: 261)

In reality, Portugal in general, and the poor areas of the interior of the country in particular, face a lack of economic development, the loss of jobs and the total decline of expectations. The key to economic success will be a change of strategy and women playing a central role. The educational profile of women in Portugal has two different tendencies: 11 per cent (1,143,432) of women have not completed their education. Second, there are 7 per cent (764,469) of women who have been through the higher education system (INE, 2012b).

The strong contraction and recessionary evidence shows the deterioration of the labour market (OECD, 2012a) and the need to implement better working conditions and offer well-being to all citizens. Indeed, the OECD (2009: 1) Better Life Index shows that:

> In Portugal, the average person earns $18,689 per year, less than the OECD average of $22,387 per year. But there is a considerable gap between the richest ($40,174) and poorest ($6,632) – the top 20% of the population earn six times as much as the bottom 20%.

In this context, there is a need for a new dynamic that increases employment levels and enhances labour productivity which will benefit women and men. In the literature review, Connell (2009: 10) says that gender

> is, above all, a pattern of social relations in which the positions of women and men are defined, the cultural meanings of being a man and a woman is negotiated, and their trajectories through life are mapped out.

Beyond this concept, the influence is aggravated with workers' behaviour. The challenge must be aligned with a reward system in the organization, because this has a high impact on the firm's long-term success (Whitman, Van Rooy and Viswesvaran, 2010) and may place their long-term viability at risk when reward is only for short-term task performance (Felton and Fritz, 2005). However, Bergeron et al. (2012: 3) argue different micro-effects and consider whether 'what is good for the organization may not always be good for the worker'.

These cyclical and structural evolutions of the economy, based on the limitations above, still remain restrictive and are coupled with disturbances in the transmission of monetary policy in the euro area and in the economy's structural adjustment.

The structure of this research is organized as follows. According to the various empirical methodologies, our second section, Method, will develop an empirical analysis that will promote an overall assessment of a sample from the Portuguese banking system to enhance the influence of women on labour market. The next section, Results, will explore the results of this sample and provide a contrast of the economy's structural characteristics, as well as the cyclical developments of women on the labour market. Conclusions presents the discussion, but it does not allow for conclusions on the future evolution of the economy in a context of structural transformation and the macro and micro-effects of accounting for working women in Portugal.

Method

In this section we consider diverse empirical methodologies, such as field studies and case studies, to provide insights that are desirable to produce long-run consequences at macro-effect and micro-effect levels. This is consistent with the proposal of Haller et al. (2012) and Trombetta, Wagenhofer and Wysocki (2012: 128) that use effect analysis

> in a broad sense to encompass the many possible costs and benefits realized by a wide range of stakeholders from the regulation or standardization of firm's financial reporting and disclosure activities.

With regard to the research's theoretical implications, the empirical analysis based on field studies will be supported by the public data available on the Portuguese Banking Association. This association is a group of monetary financial institutions that is responsible for 96 per cent of the Portuguese banking system, which as at 31 December of 2011, had 33 members that represented 56 per cent of the total number of banks (59) in the Portuguese banking system (BP, 2012c). The empirical analysis based on case studies will collect the disclosure and published information of these banks, for example, the 2001 Annual Report (Yin, 2003). Through a content analysis (Krippendorff, 2004), the plan is to promote the legitimacy and transparency of research in this sector. Furthermore, the research is focused on banks, so in Table 7.2, we use the banks registered between 2004 to 2011 with the Bank of Portugal.

Table 7.2 Distribution of banks registered on the Bank of Portugal, 2004–2011

	2004	2005	2006	2007	2008	2009	2010	2011
Total number of Banks	**68**	**61**	**63**	**64**	**67**	**64**	**63**	**59**
Branches of banks of other EU member states	24	22	23	23	23	22	23	21
Branches of banks of non-EU member states	1	1	1	2	3	2	2	2

Source: adapted from BP (2012a).

In this sense, the Bank of Portugal provides the description of the activities of these entities on the Legal Framework of Credit Institutions and Financial Companies (MF, 1992: 6056 [25]) that detail:

a) Acceptance of deposits or other repayable funds; b) Lending, including the granting of guarantees and other commitments, financial leasing, and factoring; c) Money transmission services; d) Insurance and administration of means of payment, e.g. credit cards, traveller cheques and bank drafts; e) Trading for own account or for account of clients in money market instruments, foreign exchange, financial futures and options, exchange or interest-rate instruments, goods and transferable securities; f) Participation in securities issues and placement and provision of related services; g) Money broking; h) Portfolio management and advice, safekeeping and administration of securities; i) Management and management consultancy in relation to other assets; j) Advice to undertakings on capital structure, industrial strategy and related questions as well as advice and services relating to mergers and purchase of undertakings; k) Dealings in precious metals and stones; l) Acquisition of holdings in companies; m) Trading in insurance policies; n) Credit reference services; o) Safe custody services; p) Leasing of movable property, under the terms allowed to financial leasing companies; q) Provision of the investment services referred to in Article 199-A, not covered by the preceding subparagraphs; r) Other similar transactions not forbidden by law.

Table 7.2 shows two different tendencies. The first is the precipitous drop in 2011 on the number of banks observed in the period. The second tendency expresses a very small number of branches of banks of non-EU member states that operating in Portugal. Using Portuguese laws and regulations, the Bank of Portugal obliges each bank to fulfil authorization rules and, in particular, several requirements, such as control of qualifying shareholdings, minimum initial capital, feasibility of the business plan and the adequacy of financial, technical and human resources (BP, 2012a).

This last requirement demands from banks an attractive strategy for human resources to pursue the labour code law. The obligation of each bank is to establish fundamental principles of non-discrimination and integrated policies articulating education and training, employment and conciliation between work and family (Friedman and Johnson, 1997) and equality of opportunities (Rodgers, 1992).

However, outcomes in banks are unlikely to be quite so straightforward and we will develop empirical evidence on this subject, because there is less research and, as Riley et al. (2001: 20) says, 'facts, research methods and research data do not speak for themselves; they are interpreted by researchers and others'.

Clearly it is better to have less evidence that could be improved on of the knowledge of the reality of Portuguese working women, than not to know that reality at all.

Results

The main objective of this section is to highlight the importance and role of women on the labour market using the sample of the 33 banks registered, between 2004 and

2011, with the Bank of Portugal. The results of the empirical analysis are significantly affected because

> In the sphere of the Economic and Financial Stability Programme and taking into account the proposed measures for ensuring the medium term adjustment of the financial system, it is to be expected that the banks will maintain moderately negative rates of balance sheet growth.
>
> (BP, 2012b: 76)

However, with a view to comparing the economic performance of each banks' sample and then analysing the influence of working women, it is more appropriate to use accounting data in accordance with the International Financial Reporting Standards. The financial statements for 2011 were prepared in accordance with the Adjusted Accounting Standards, within the terms of Bank of Portugal – Notice no. 1/2005 (BP, 2005).

Table 7.3 presents the number of workers in the human resources department for each bank.

The total number of human resources fell by about 2.2 per cent in 2011 to 57,130 at the end of the year. This was essentially due to cost-cutting policies. In 2012, banking system profitability depended on the resilience of the structural elements of net interest income and commissions, as the Bank of Portugal justifies (BP, 2012b: 7): 'in a context of low level of interbank interest rates and of a decline in economic activity, as a new increase in provisions and impairments for credit is expected'.

Table 7.4 presents the distribution of several income statement accounts in detail: net interest income, net operating income, personnel costs and net income of the human resources department for each bank.

The net interest income of the full sample of the banking system deteriorated significantly in 2011, and €159.736 million and €273.136 million were, respectively, the

Table 7.3 Distribution of people working in the human resources department

	Banif Mais	Barclays	Banco BPI	CGD	BNP SS	Sant Consumer	BII	Invest
Human Resources	200	2,375	6,502	9,509	490	190	1	115

	CBI	BPI	BIG	Fortis	BAC	Banif	Besi	BPN
Human Resources	154	168	160	30	95	2,529	245	1,584

	BNP WM	Banif inv	Activobank	Finantia	Montepio	Best	Santander Totta	CCCAM	BES
Human Resources	5	125	133	142	3,910	157	5,663	3,845	6,116

	Deutsche Bank	Banco BIC	BNP	Itaú	BB	BBVA	Popular	Millennium bcp
Human Resources	454	84	79	108	82	776	1,329	9,714

Source: adapted from APB (2012).

Table 7.4 Distribution of the income statement accounts, 2011

	Banif Mais	Barclays	Banco BPI	CGD	BNP SS	Sant Consumer	BII	Invest
Net interest income	35,003	283,358	460,776	1,126,592	−28	35,558	23,365	12,543
Net operating income	48,204	467,751	818,823	1,892,231	18,038	49,413	24,209	10,895
Personnel costs	8,676	125,034	342,577	555,868	11,994	9,361	644	4,802
Net income	7,553	(74,757)	(216,770)	(316,255)	1,001	7,062	(42,023)	(5,095)

	CBI	BPI	BIG	Fortis	BAC	Banif	Besi	BPN
Net interest income	28,456	4,907	19,773	11,815	5,433	197,437	9,050	56,705
Net operating income	50,352	25,617	33,038	24,395	12,918	340,025	101,075	79,620
Personnel costs	13,627	3,458	8,760	2,570	4,214	115,336	47,522	65,371
Net income	1,465	−69	2,464	190	876	(15,699)	(9,377)	(95,450)

	BNP WM	Banif inv	Activobank	Finantia	Montepio	Best	Santander Totta	CCCAM	BES
Net interest income	776	9,408	(2,913)	33,596	303,473	4,155	376,989	343,039	653,938
Net operating income	749	22,613	7,580	36,596	559,566	25,990	779,118	471,722	1,585,451
Personnel costs	1,007	7,398	4,582	3,506	217,319	6,387	292,579	161,264	372,815
Net income	(2,520)	3,063	(3,994)	16,256	32,823	7,059	22,289	53,328	(133,089)

	Deutsche Bank	Banco BIC	BNP	Itaú	BB	BBVA	Popular	Millennium bcp
Net interest income	48,660	19,923	17,867	32,494	3,994	83,151	131,087	900,896
Net operating income	75,889	25,343	17,013	73,666	11,310	139,745	166,857	1,421,546
Personnel costs	26,266	6,217	6,907	20,285	4,550	80,736	59,890	661,628
Net income	4,652	5,115	836	(111,989)	2,470	(17,646)	13,432	(468,527)

Source: adapted from APB (2012).

average and standard deviation. Also, the maximum value has €1.126.592 million in CGD and the minimum value has -€2.913 million in Activobank. For example, CGD (2012) have a financial product called 'Caixa Woman' for working women that is the official sponsor of the Portuguese Women's Business Forum, that aims to support incentives for female entrepreneurialism and continues to strengthen its position in the market in the form of an upgrade of its offer and commercial initiatives associated with events.

Due to this specific product, the authors observe that if the sample was spread between the banks with more than 50 per cent women of the total of the human resources, then the average and standard deviation increases to €280.661 million and €410.986 million, respectively, and to the banks with more than 50 per cent men of the total of the human resources, then the average and standard deviation decreases to €127.179 million and €226.063 million correspondingly. Of course, the size of the group is very different, because the first has seven banks and the second 26: this is due to comparing different entities with their relative financial position, performance and changes in financial position.

The disparity in performance of the net interest income and net operating income, especially in 2011, explains the profound change in the banking sector's cost structure. Between 2008 and 2010 operating costs represented almost twice the provisions and impairments and were the only item accounting for more than 50 per cent of net operating income. In 2011, the situation was radically different: both items reached very similar amounts and weights and exceeded net operating income by 21.7 per cent (APB, 2012).

Personnel costs fell in 2011, with the average and the standard deviation, respectively, €98.580 million and €166.656 million. Also, the Millennium BCP has €662.868 million with the maximum value and in BII has €644 million with the minimum value. In terms of cost structure, operating costs were important, accounting for 60.8 per cent of net operating income. Within these, personnel costs, with a weight of 56.1 per cent in total costs, demonstrate the intensity with which the banking sector employs labour (APB, 2012).

The net income of the full sample of the banking system, in 2011, deteriorated significantly with an average of €40.343 million and a standard deviation €106.847 million because of considerable strengthening of provisions due to the deterioration of risk within a deepening economic recession. Also, in the corporate annual report, the maximum value has €53.328 million in CCCAM and the minimum value has €468.527 million in Millennium BCP (2012: 65). The reasons are 'exceptional negative factors related to the reinforcement of loan impairment charges, [and] the recognition of impairment relative to the goodwill of Millennium bank in Greece'.

Table 7.5 presents the distribution of human resources by gender for each bank in Portugal.

In Table 7.5, the authors see a trend of seven banks that have more women than men (a range from 50 to 100 per cent) and the other 26 banks have more men than women (a range from 50 per cent to 73 per cent). The trend in Table 7.5 is similar to previous years, but with a small increase of the percentage of women in the sector. Men constitute the majority of the bank workers, though their proportion fell by around 0.3 per cent in 2011 as a result of a 3.2 per cent decrease as opposed to 2.0 per cent in the number of women (APB, 2012). In 2011, the biggest bank in terms of number of workers is Millennium BCP with 9,714 full-time workers of which only

Table 7.5 Distribution of human resources by gender, 2011

	Banif Mais	Barclays	Banco BPI	CGD	BNP SS	Sant Consumer	BII	Invest
Men	100	1,174	3,042	4,188	213	72	–	84
% Men of Total HR	50.0%	49.4%	46.8%	44.0%	43.5%	37.9%	0.0%	73.0%
Women	100	1,201	3,460	5,321	277	118	1	31
% Women of Total HR	**50.0%**	**50.6%**	**53.2%**	**56.0%**	**56.5%**	**62.1%**	**100.0%**	27.0%

	CBI	BPI	BIG	Fortis	BAC	Banif	Besi	BPN
Me	103	111	102	19	59	1,557	151	973
% Men of Total HR	66.9%	66.1%	63.8%	63.3%	62.1%	61.6%	61.6%	61.4%
Women	51	57	58	11	36	972	94	611
% Women of Total HR	33.1%	33.9%	36.3%	36.7%	37.9%	38.4%	38.4%	38.6%

	BNP WM	Banif Inv	Activobank	Finantia	Montepio	Best	Santander Totta	CCCAM	BES
Men	3	74	77	80	2,190	87	3,125	2,097	3,329
% Men of Total HR	60.0%	59.2%	57.9%	56.3%	56.0%	55.4%	55.2%	54.5%	54.4%
Women	2	51	56	62	1,720	70	2,538	1,748	2,787
% Women of Total HR	40.0%	40.8%	42.1%	43.7%	44.0%	44.6%	44.8%	45.5%	45.6%

	Deutsche Bank	Banco BIC	BNP	Itaú	BB	BBVA	Popular	Millennium bcp
Men	245	45	42	57	42	391	945	5,903
% Men of Total HR	54.0%	53.6%	53.2%	52.8%	51.2%	50.4%	71.1%	60.8%
Women.	209	39	37	51	40	385	384	3,811
% Women of Total HR	46.0%	46.4%	46.8%	47.2%	48.8%	49.6%	28.9%	39.2%

Source: adapted from APB (2012).

39 per cent are women. The second-biggest bank in number of workers is CGD with 9,509 full-time workers of which more than 56 per cent are women. These are two opposite cases that promote equal opportunity in hiring, career development, growth and reconciliation of the working life with the personal life of men and women using completely different strategies. Unequivocally, the authors observe these tendencies based on the disclosure of the corporate annual report 2011. For example, the chairman of Banco Popular (2012: 5) says: 'The progress made in all these areas could not have been achieved had it not been for the professional and responsible attitude and collaboration of all the women and men in the Group.' Such a message is an example amongst several others that provides a basis on which banks are proceeding, based on men and women working together to promote economic activity. Table 7.6 presents the distribution of human resources by activity for each bank in Portugal.

Table 7.6 Distribution of human resources by activity, 2011

	Banif Mais	Barclays	Banco BPI	CGD	BNP SS	Sant Consumer	BII	Invest
By Activity	200	2,375	6,502	9,509	490	190	1	115
Commercial	23	1,119	3,711	7,405	–	88	–	55
Other	177	1,256	2,791	2,104	490	102	1	60

	CBI	BPI	BIG	Fortis	BAC	Banif	Besi	BPN
By Activity	154	168	160	30	95	2,529	245	1,584
Commercial	154	9	64	4	72	1,754	–	1,028
Other	–	159	96	26	23	775	245	556

	BNP WM	Banif Inv	Activobank	Finantia	Montepio	Best	Santander Totta	CCCAM	BES
By Activity	5	125	133	142	3,910	157	5,663	3,845	6,116
Commercial	1	60	127	31	2,913	89	3,551	2,720	3,726
Other	4	65	6	111	997	68	2,112	1,125	2,390

	Deutsche Bank	Banco BIC	BNP	Itaú	BB	BBVA	Popular	Millennium bcp
By Activity	454	84	79	108	82	776	1,329	9,714
Commercial	230	41	8	1	24	480	992	6,726
Other	224	43	71	107	58	296	337	2,988

Source: adapted from APB (2012).

In general, the table divides the activity into commercial and other areas. The first group may be based on workers who, directly or indirectly, provide services or establish significant commercial relations with clients. The second group might be supported by other activities and it is important to notice that higher levels of internal mobility allow the balance between branches of each bank to converge and support divisions, and 79 per cent of the total number of full-time employees are engaged in a commercial activity (APB, 2012).

Table 7.7 presents the distribution of human resources by age for each bank in Portugal.

Table 7.7 shows that 5,904 workers are aged up to 30 years, or 10 per cent of the total of workers; 31,376 workers are aged between 30 and 40 years, or 55 per cent of the total of workers; and 19,789 workers are aged over 45 years, or 35 per cent of the total of workers. In relation to age, usually non-discrimination and equal opportunity for men and women is a basic and essential principle applied in all cases. The CGD (2012) stated in its corporate annual report 2011 that gets the maximum value of workers aged up to 30 years (1,287):

> During the course of 2011, CGD on the basis of its placements programme gave 302 young people an opportunity to make contact with the banking world. Most

Table 7.7 Distribution of human resources by age, 2011

	Banif Mais	Barclays	Banco BPI	CGD	BNP SS	Sant Consumer	BII	Invest
Up to 30 years	30	466	629	1,287	217	11	0	24
30 to 40 years	147	1,678	3,845	4,479	266	153	1	74
45 years or over	23	231	2,028	3,743	7	26	0	17

	CBI	BPI	BIG	Fortis	BAC	Banif	Besi	BPN
Up to 30 years	20	25	57	2	15	327	50	59
30 to 40 years	80	102	93	9	36	1,383	139	1,145
45 years or over	54	41	10	19	44	819	56	380

	BNP WM	Banif Inv	Activobank	Finantia	Montepio	Best	Santander Totta	CCCAM	BES
Up to 30 years	–	12	19	16	306	39	424	250	626
30 to 40 years	3	98	96	89	2,588	113	3,147	1,929	3,378
45 years or over	2	15	18	37	1,016	5	2,092	1,666	2,112

	Deutsche Bank	Banco BIC	BNP	Itaú	BB	BBVA	Popular	Millennium bcp
Up to 30 years	55	13	4	26	15	119	223	538
30 to 40 years	327	59	39	65	51	388	861	4,515
45 years or over	72	12	36	17	16	269	245	4,661

Source: adapted from APB (2012).

of them were recent graduates or finalists on courses considered to be of interest in terms of a commercial banking activity.

(CGD, 2012: 48)

Another bank that places a higher value on women workers over 45 years (approximately 68 per cent) is BES, which put into practice a programme of 'equal career opportunities' and in its Annual Report 2011 argues that:

The Group continues to make an effort to rejuvenate and qualify its staff as it works hard to build loyalty among its junior, high-potential employees. In this regard, career management is particularly relevant as a decisive strategic tool for motivating and retaining human resources.

(BES, 2012: 30)

Table 7.8 presents the distribution of human resources by years of service for each bank. In the following analysis, the authors identify 22,507 workers have more than 15 years of service that represent 39 per cent of the total of workers, 12,401 workers have between 11 and 15 years of service that represent 22 per cent of the total of workers, 12,010 workers have between 1 and 5 years of service that represent 21 per cent of the total of workers, 9,033 workers have between 6 and 10 years of service that

Table 7.8 Distribution of human resources by years of service and type of employment contract, 2011

	Banif Mais	Barclays	Banco BPI	CGD	BNP SS	Sant Consumer	BII	Invest
Up to 1 year	2	109	170	219	37	42	–	17
1 to 5 years	60	1,795	1,433	1,474	443	40	–	63
6 to 10 years	50	230	1,208	761	3	7	–	11
11 to 15 years	49	47	1,445	1,347	6	73	1	24
over 15 years	39	194	2,246	5,708	1	28	–	–
Contract Permanent	184	2,096	6,433	9,131	490	188	1	79
Contract – Fixed term	16	279	69	378	–	2	–	36

	CBI	BPI	BIG	Fortis	BAC	Banif	Besi	BPN
Up to 1 year	13	21	23	1	5	9	6	1
1 to 5 years	31	52	90	3	19	685	100	270
6 to 10 years	55	21	14	6	70	502	36	779
11 to 15 years	21	29	33	2	–	422	51	499
over 15 years	34	45	–	18	1	911	52	35
Contract Permanent	154	165	121	30	89	2,498	229	1,575
Contract – Fixed term	–	3	39	–	6	31	16	9

	BNP WM	Banif Inv	Activobank	Finantia	Montepio	Best	Santander Totta	CCCAM	BES
Up to 1 year	1	6	2	4	30	22	59	50	111
1 to 5 years	1	62	26	34	956	88	944	547	1,012
6 to 10 years	–	32	16	33	1,003	43	1,128	526	1,240
11 to 15 years	–	21	47	34	1,257	4	879	2,075	1,025
over 15 years	3	4	42	37	664	–	2,653	647	2,728
Contract Permanent	4	113	127	125	3,890	127	5,582	3,672	5,879
Contract – Fixed term	1	12	6	17	20	30	81	173	237

	Deutsche Bank	Banco BIC	BNP	Itaú	BB	BBVA	Popular	Millennium bcp
Up to 1 year	31	10	1	9	21	23	36	27
1 to 5 years	282	74	7	54	37	164	392	772
6 to 10 years	57	–	3	24	9	104	330	732
11 to 15 years	59	–	13	9	2	254	361	2,312
over 15 years	25	–	55	12	13	231	210	5,871
Contract Permanent	434	80	79	101	48	748	1,261	9,698
Contract – Fixed term	20	4	–	7	34	28	68	16

Source: adapted from APB (2012).

represent 16 per cent of the total of workers, and 1,118 workers have up to 1 year of service that represent 2 per cent of the total of workers.

Table 7.8 shows two separate groups by type of employment contract. First, 1,638 workers or 2.9 per cent of the total of workers have fixed-term contracts; and second, 55,431 workers or 97.1 per cent of the total of workers have permanent contracts.

In this sense, looking to what banks are already doing to better integrate male and female employment, the Annual Report 2011 of BES argues that:

> Attracting and retaining the best professionals, a training plan, internal mobility and evaluating and rewarding merit – these are the key pillars for the development and career advancement of BES Group employees.
>
> (2012: 31)

Moreover, Banco Popular (2012: 40) says:

> Most senior managers are employees whose professional careers have taken place within the Group and who have gradually been promoted on merit, as a result of on-the-job training and the teamwork experience they have gained, having risen in the ranks in the course of their career.

The Millennium Declaration aims to achieve eight Millennium Development Goals (UN, 2009). In this research, the authors focus on the third goal: 'promote gender equality and empower women' and the target: 'eliminate gender disparity in primary and secondary education, preferably by 2005, and in all levels of education no later than 2015'.

Table 7.9 presents the distribution of human resources by academic qualifications for each bank in Portugal and their relationship with gender. The Portuguese

Table 7.9 Distribution of human resources by academic qualifications, 2011

	Banif Mais	Barclays	Banco BPI	CGD	BNP SS	Sant Consumer	BII	Invest
9th grade	20	–	99	1,365	–	1	–	1
12th grade	109	522	2,434	3,623	47	96	–	43
Higher education	71	1,853	3,969	4,521	443	93	1	71

	CBI	BPI	BIG	Fortis	BAC	Banif	Besi	BPN
9th grade	5	–	2	–	22	268	8	180
12th grade	43	34	29	14	32	1,006	42	673
Higher education	106	134	129	16	41	1,255	195	731

	BNP WM	Banif Inv	Activobank	Finantia	Montepio	Best	Santander Totta	CCCAM	BES
9th grade	–	–	–	7	206	–	254	508	686
12th grade	3	15	51	52	1,889	28	2,956	2,064	1,884
Higher education	2	110	82	83	1,815	129	2,453	1,273	3,546

	Deutsche Bank	Banco BIC	BNP	Itaú	BB	BBVA	Popular	Millennium bcp
9th grade	7	–	–	3	3	1	21	907
12th grade	190	23	38	25	23	365	503	4,210
Higher education	257	61	41	80	56	410	805	4,597

Source: adapted from APB (2012).

education system is organized in three sequential levels: pre-primary education (from 3 to 5 years), primary education (from 6 to 14 years) and secondary education (from 15 to 19). Since the school year of 2009/10 schooling is compulsory 12 years of school for any student. In the last decade, there has been a reduction of the illiteracy rate (GEPE, 2012). In 2011, Portugal recorded a figure of 5.2 per cent (499,936 people) who were illiterate, but the figure was 9.0 per cent in 2001 and 11.0 per cent in 1991. The illiteracy rate among women (6.8 per cent) was about twice that of men (3.5 per cent) and the regional approach shows large asymmetries. The illiteracy rate in Lisbon (3.2 per cent) shows the lowest value, while in Alentejo (9.6 per cent) it is higher at 9.6 per cent (INE, 2012b).

Table 7.9 allows us to conclude that the majority of workers have higher education with a total of 29,429 workers, 12th grade with a total of 23,066 workers and till the 9th grade with a total of 4,574 workers. On the other hand, the average of workers with higher education is 892 workers, 12th grade is 699 workers and till the 9th grade is 139 workers.

Due to the evidence that more women have a higher education, the authors observe that if the sample was spread between the banks with more than 50 per cent women of the total of the human resources then the average and standard deviation increase to 1,564 and 1,945 workers and to the banks with more than 50 per cent men of the total of the human resources then the average and standard deviation decrease to 711 and 1,177 workers. Furthermore, the maximum value happens in Millennium BCP with 4,597 and the minimum value in BII with only one worker.

Table 7.10 presents the distribution of human resources by position for each bank. The authors strongly believe that to reach a specific position in the bank sector requires a combination of competence and determination, merit and hard work. It can be challenging for most workers to have the specific position, which allows top managers to draw correct inferences and gives visibility to the right work. Another example is the European Union Central Banks that as the European Commission (2010: 19) reports:

> Across Europe in 2009, every central bank has a male governor and more than four out of every five members of key decision-making bodies are men. The central banks of Germany, Cyprus, Luxembourg, Austria and Slovenia do not have a single female representative on the main decision-making bodies.

This research identifies another macro-effect, because the economic crisis is also a social crises that raises awareness of the gender inequalities that still exist in the banking sector and so creates an exceptional occasion for promoting change.

Table 7.10 allows us to conclude, on the one hand, that men are heads of most departments and specific jobs and, on the other hand, that women hold the majority of administrative and ancillary jobs. Numbers of the former rose (+0.4 percentage points) but fell sharply in the latter (−13.4 percentage points). Because of a net increase in the number of heads of department and specific jobs in 2011, small institutions and branch offices were more egalitarian in terms of gender and presented a human resource structure that is more stable. Indeed, almost half of the new head of department jobs created in net terms were occupied by women. This was even more notable in specific jobs, where around 60 per cent of new workers were women (APB, 2012).

Table 7.10 Distribution of human resources by position, 2011

	Banif Mais	Barclays	Banco BPI	CGD	BNP SS	Sant Consumer	BII	Invest
Heads of department	27	805	2,041	1,832	69	57	–	19
Specific	54	1,379	2,386	2,385	415	104	I	91
Administrative	78	191	1,973	5,145	6	29	–	5
Auxiliary	41	–	102	147	–	–	–	–

	CBI	BPI	BIG	Fortis	BAC	Banif	Besi	BPN
Heads of department	76	61	53	4	24	559	123	314
Specific	57	94	100	13	26	413	98	583
Administrative	16	12	5	13	45	1,542	16	673
Auxiliary	5	1	2	–	–	15	8	14

	BNP WM	Banif Inv	Activobank	Finantia	Montepio	Best	Santander Totta	CCCAM	BES
Heads of department	2	27	47	24	951	17	1,263	925	1,282
Specific	–	88	47	70	1,211	113	3,230	2,020	2,394
Administrative	3	10	37	48	1,682	27	1,153	673	2,389
Auxiliary	–	–	2	–	66	–	17	227	51

	Deutsche Bank	Banco BIC	BNP	Itaú	BB	BBVA	Popular	Millennium bcp
Heads of department	175	9	25	24	18	179	564	2,651
Specific	208	48	37	8	14	450	456	3,871
Administrative	70	27	17	76	50	147	307	3,061
Auxiliary	1	–	–	–	–	–	2	131

Source: adapted from APB (2012).

The APB (2012) report that the branch offices had the largest proportion of women as heads of department (37 per cent) and in specific jobs (54 per cent) compared to subsidiaries, respectively, with heads of department (25 per cent) and in specific jobs (47 per cent) at the end of 2011. In medium-sized institutions, fewer women are heads of department (22 per cent) and a large percentage of women are ancillary (80 per cent), so this group presents the greatest inequality between genders in these categories.

The evidence of this research suggests that 'women and men should have the same opportunities and be given the same possibilities to take leadership positions'. Due to the importance of this micro-effect, the European Commission released the Strategy for Equality Between Women and Men (European Commission, 2010) with the commitment to implementing gender mainstreaming as an integral part of its policy-making during the years 2010–15. Also, the EU Multiannual Financial Framework will provide the necessary support to implement several actions foreseen in the Strategy after 2014–2020.

Some countries (e.g. Finland, Latvia and Sweden) show 25 per cent of women are board members of the large listed companies. Others (Portugal, Greece, Ireland,

Italy, Hungary, Luxembourg and Estonia) confirm near 10.0 per cent of the total members (European Commission, 2012). In the EU in the major publicly listed companies women make up 13.7 per cent of the board members. The European Commission encourages women and men to enter professions where they are under-represented, such as in the leadership positions in general, and board positions in particular. Currently, in Portugal, as a result of personal choices made by women and men, boards are dominated by one gender: the non-executive board members are 94.6 per cent of men and 5.4 per cent of women and executive board members are 92.4 per cent of men and 7.6 per cent of women. All these gender inequalities are persistent in the labour market, and there are several initiatives to give priority to the underrepresented sex.

The European Commission proposed a Directive with an objective of a 40 per cent presence of the underrepresented sex among non-executive directors in around 5,000 listed companies in the European Union. It does not apply to small- and medium-sized enterprises or non-listed companies. When comparing wages per hour of week, sector and occupation are the most important factors driving the gender wage gap.

Conclusion

Finally, considering the alignment of past data to explain the present in the strategy of accounting for working women, the authors are concerned about all of the possible changes, particularly in gender inequalities. However, when a society needs to reinforce strategies to maintain the courage to face the future, then the citizen feels safer and trusts more on the bank system. The recession strongly affects the recovery of the economic activity that is derived from the financial and banking crises. The Bank of Portugal (BP, 2012a: 7) argues that:

> In 2011, the Portuguese banking system activity was performed in a particularly adverse and demanding environment, deriving from the scarcity of market funding, intensification of the sovereign debt crisis in the euro area and increased materialisation of credit risk in domestic activity.

At the end of 2011, most banks had fewer workers than on the same date of the previous year, mainly because the economic situation was not encouraging for significant investments. This necessitates a rigorous implementation of the human resources strategy and, at the same time, leads the banks to hire temporary workers. This was accompanied by a significant level of workers who left the bank due to an increase in early retirement and end of fixed-term contracts coupled with the subsequent rise of public spending (in retirement pensions and unemployment subsidies).

The combination of macro- and micro-effects shows that the successive reductions of workers have promoted greater balance between genders, however the achievement of this equality should not be seen as the end of the process, but rather as the starting point. Since 1979 the Portuguese Constitutional Law implements the principle of non-discrimination based on gender and, at the same time, promotes gender equality in the workplace, employment and training. As a consequence, since 1999, the award 'Equality is Quality' distinguishes organizations which have introduced outstanding gender equality initiatives in the labour market or measures designed to balance work life with family/personal life.

Effectively, the sample of this research shows more women in higher positions due to more admissions and fewer departures than among men. In 2011, the reorganization of banks mainly took an increase in the average age of the banking sample and a slight reversal of the upward trend in years of service in the sector (APB, 2012). The authors propose that solutions must be found to increase the equality of the proportion of women in banks, because it will be more cost-effective in the near future. One of the proposals could be the involvement of well-organized and joined-up teams to enable these women access to appropriate opportunities for employment and afterwards to manage their careers.

The authors agree with Waddock (2005), who suggests that the systematic change that is needed requires citizens to care more about working women, because they understand that sustainability and welfare are necessarily based on social values. In essence, the ability to reflect actions, decisions, attitudes and behaviours of working women has strong implications in society and success will be seen in a near future.

Acknowledgements

The authors wish to thank José Ángel Pérez López of Universidad de Seville (Spain). Also, the current version is a publication supported by the Project PEst-OE/EGE/ UI4056/2014 UDI/IPG based on the Unidade de Investigação para o Desenvolvimento do Interior do Instituto Politécnico da Guarda, financed by the Fundação para a Ciência e Tecnologia. The authors are members of the Centro de Investigação de Contabilidade e Fiscalidade.

References

Amâncio, L. (1996), Gender Representations and the Representation of Person. *The European Legacy* 1(3): 999–1003.

APB (Associação Portuguesa de Bancos). (2012), *Activity Report. Annual 2011.* Lisbon: APB.

AR (Assembleia da Republica). (2007), Lei no. 16/2007. *Diário da República*, 75, Série I-A, 2417–18. Lisboa: Imprensa Nacional da Casa da Moeda

Bakke, E.W. (1961), The Human Resources Function. *Management International Review* 1(2): 16–24.

Banco Popular. (2012), *Annual Report 2011.* Lisbon: CGD.Becker, G. (1985), Human Capital, Effort, and the Sexual Division of Labor. *Journal of Labor Economics* 3(1): 33–58.

Becker, G. S. (1985). "Human Capital, Effort, and the Sexual Division Labor." *Journal of Labor Economics.* 3:1 Supp., pp. S33–S58.

Bergeron, D., Shipp. A., Rosen, B. and Furst, S. (2012), Organizational Citizenship Behavior and Career Outcomes: The Cost of Being a Good Citizen. *Journal of Management* 39(4): 1–29.

BES (Banco Espirito Santo). (2012), *Annual Report 2011.* Lisbon: CGD.

BP (Bank of Portugal). (2005), *Notice no. 1/2005-Adjusted Accounting Standards.* Lisbon: BP.

———. (2012a), *Annual Report. The Portuguese Economy in 2011.* Lisbon: BP.

———. (2012b), *Financial Stability Report. May.* Lisbon: BP.

———. (2012c), *SIBAP.* Lisbon: BP.

CGD (Caixa Geral de Depósitos). (2012), *Annual Report 2011.* Lisbon: CGD.

Connell, R.W. (2009), *Gender.* Malden, MA: Polity Press.

Davidson, M. and Burke, R. (1994), *Women in Management: Current Research Issues*, vol. 1. London: Chapman Publishing.

European Commission. (2010), *Strategy for Equality between Women and Men (2010–2015)*. COM (2010) 491 final, 21 September. Brussels: Official publications of the European Commission.

———. (2012), *Gender Balance in Business Leadership: A Contribution to Smart, Sustainable and Inclusive Growth*. COM (2012) 615 final, 14 November. Brussels: Official publications of the European Commission.

Felton, R.F. and Fritz, P.K. (2005), The View from the Boardroom. *The McKinsey Quarterly* 1: 48–65.

Friedman, D.E. and Johnson, A.A. (1997), 'Moving from programs to culture change: The next stage for the corporate work–family Agenda', in S. Parasuraman and J.H. Greenhaus (eds), *Integrating Work and Family: Challenges and Choices for a Changing World*. Westport, CT: Quorum Books, pp. 192–208.

GEPE (Gabinete de Estatística e Planeamento da Educação). (2012), *Educação em Números – Portugal 2011*. Lisbon: GEPE.

Haller, A., Nobes, C., Cairns, D., Hjelstrom, A., Moya, S., Page, M. and Walton, P. (2012), The Effects of Accounting Standards: A Comment. *Accounting in Europe* 9(2): 113–26.

INE (Instituto Nacional de Estatística. (2012a), *Estatísticas no Feminino: Ser Mulher em Portugal, 2001–2011*. Lisbon: INE

———. (2012b), *Censos 2011 – Resultados Provisórios*. Lisbon: INE.

Jonson, L., Jonsson, B. and Svensson, G. (1978), The Application of Social Accounting to Absenteeism and Personnel Turnover. *Accounting, Organization and Society* 3(3/4): 261–8.

Krippendorff, K. (2004), *Content Analysis: An Introduction to This Methodology*. Thousand Oaks, CA: Sage Publications.

MF (Ministério das Finanças). (1992), Decreto-Lei no. 298/92, aprova o Regime Geral das Instituições de Crédito e Sociedades Financeiras. Diário da República, 301, I Série-A, 6° Suplemento, 31 Dezembro, 6056 (24)–6056 (51). Lisboa: Imprensa Nacional da Casa da Moeda

Millennium BCP. (2012), *Annual Report 2011*. Lisbon: BCP.

Mirvis, P.H. and Macy, B.A. (1976), Accounting for the Costs and Benefits of Human Resource Development Programs: An Interdisciplinary Approach. *Accounting, Organizations and Society* 1(2–3): 179–93.

Moen, P. and Yu, Y. (2000), Effective Work/Life Strategies: Working Couples, Work Conditions, Gender, and Life Quality. *Social Problems* 47(3): 291–326.

Nogueira, C., Paúl, C. and Amâncio, L. (1995), 'Women in management in Portugal: A demographic overview', in L. Amâncio and C. Nogueira (ed), *Gender, Management and Science*. Braga: Universidade do Minho, pp. 207–18.

OECD (Organisation for Economic Cooperation and Development). (2009), *Better Life Index: Data by Country-Portugal*. Paris: OECD Publishing.

———. (2012a), *OECD Economic Surveys: Portugal 2012*. Paris: OECD Publishing.

———. (2012b), *The Future of Families to 2030*. Paris: OECD Publishing.

Riley, M., Wood, R., Clark, M., Wilkie, E. and Szivas, E. (2001), *Researching and Writing Dissertations in Business and Management*. London: Thomson Learning.

Rodgers, C.S. (1992), The Flexible Workplace: What Have we Learned? *Human Resource Management* 31: 183–99.

Silver, H. and Goldscheider, F. (1994), Flexible Work and Housework: Work and Family Constraints on Women's Domestic Labor. *Social Forces* 72(4): 1103–19.

Tilly, L. and Scott, J. (1978), *Women, Work, and Family*. New York: Holt, Reinhart & Winston.

Tomassini, L. (1976), Behavioral Research on Human Resource Accounting: A Contingency Framework. *Accounting, Organizations and Society* 1(2–3): 239–50.

Trombetta, M., Wagenhofer, A. and Wysocki, P. (2012), The Usefulness of Academic Research in Understanding the Effects of Accounting Standards. *Accounting in Europe* 9: 127–46.

UN (United Nations). (2009), *The Millennium Development Goals Report*. New York: UN.

Waddock, S. (2005), Hollow Men and Women at the Helm . . . Hollow Accounting Ethics? *Issues in Accounting Education* 20(2): 145–50.

Whitman, D.S., Van Rooy, D.L. and Viswesvaran, C. (2010), Satisfaction, Citizenship Behaviors, and Performance in Work Units: A Meta-analysis of Collective Construct Relations. *Personnel Psychology* 63(1): 41–81.

Yin, R. (2003), *Case Study Research: Design and Methods*. Thousand Oaks, CA: Sage Publications.

Chapter 8

Women on Boards

The Polish Experience within the Context of EU Recommendations

Maria Aluchna

Introduction

The financial crisis and the economic slowdown which started with the credit crunch on the American subprime mortgage led to the sovereign debt crisis and the severe uncertainty on stock markets in the majority of developed economies. The growing economic challenges triggered the formulation and adoption of many codes of best practice and a set of recommendations which are intended to improve the performance of companies and countries. The adoption of more restricted regulations, the discipline of national budgets, and the supervision over public debt policies as well as the stock market belong to the most debated recommendations. The additional set of recommendations is provided by the codes of corporate governance which refer to the structure and size of executive compensation, board work, composition and structure, shareholder activism and rights execution and risk management. The answers to the economic slowdown are also to be found in the social policy which addresses the issues of social mobility, innovation and creativity.

The recommendations on the increase of female participation in business and their presence on corporate boards remains one of the guidelines. The recent European Communication to the Parliament known as the 'Strategy for gender equality between women and men 2010–2015' is viewed as a tool for assuring greater female involvement in business and one of the EU's responses to the financial crisis. Females are expected to enrich the leadership style, deliver new values and, as a result, contribute to the better performance and firm value increase. Although gender equality and female presence in business belong to one of the most highly debated issues in business and regulations and the main assumption of gender strategy are well-known, the main theme of the discussion refers to the strategies for the participation of female directors as well as the issues of introducing quotas for increasing female presence on corporate boards.

This chapter discusses the issue of female presence on corporate boards with respect to the latest recommendations on gender management. Corporate boards are essential bodies for governance and management and their efficiency determines company performance. From the perspective of influence, power and prestige as well as organizational hierarchy corporate boards are the top corporate bodies. Hence the discussion on women's participation in business inevitably and essentially needs to refer to their presence on corporate boards. It is also a reliable indicator of gender equality advancement and policy adopted by countries and companies. The remainder of the chapter is organized as follows. The first section presents the literature and regulatory review on female participation on boards addressing the provisions provided in the EC Communication to the European Parliament known as 'The strategy of gender equality between women and men: 2010–2015'. The second section delivers the practical dimensions of female directors and women's role in business and addresses the recommendation on introducing quotas providing for women's presence on boards. Particular attention will be devoted to the Polish case with the illustration of females on the boards of the largest companies listed on the Warsaw Stock Exchange. Many countries across the EU, including Poland, remain reluctant to the introduction of formal regulations on women's presence on boards and therefore the arguments of opponents and proponents of quotas for women's presence on boards are discussed in the third section. The final remarks are presented in the conclusion.

Female Directors and the Strategy for Gender Equality

Strategy for Gender Equality in the EU

The recommendations for the increase of a female presence on corporate boards are heavily rooted in the policies which stress gender equality with reference to the opportunities and chances, anti-discrimination laws and the programme for improving the living standards of all social groups. These initiatives were also reinforced by the recommendations delivered by international organizations (UN, OECD, the World Bank), regional best practice (EU) as well as national and local associations. Equalities, including gender equality, belong to the five fundamental assumptions upon which the EU is based. The first policies on gender equality were adopted in 1975 and then elaborated in the directives introduced in the 1980s and 1990s, and in the twenty-first century. The crucial EU documents on gender equality include:

- '100 words for equality: a glossary of terms on the equality between women and men' (European Commission, 1998).
- 'Roadmap for equality between women and men 2006–2010' (Communication of the European Commission to the Parliament [COM 92], 2006).
- 'Tackling the multiple discriminations, practices, policies and laws' (European Commission, 2007).
- 'Communication on the gender pay gap' (Communication of the European Commission to the Parliament [COM 424], 2007).
- 'Study to assess the feasibility and options for the introduction of elements of gender budgeting into the EU budgetary process' (European Commission, 2007).
- 'Mid-term progress report on the roadmap for equality between women and men' (Communication of the European Commission to the Parliament [COM 760], 2008.
- 'Communication on improving work-life balance' (Communication of the European Commission to the Parliament [COM 635], 2008).
- 'Report on the implementation of the Barcelona targets in the field of childcare' (Communication of the European Commission to the Parliament [COM 638], 2008).

- 'Evaluation on policy: promotion of women innovators and entrepreneurship–Final Report' *Directore General Enterprise and Industry* (European Commission, 2008a).
- 'Mapping the maze: getting more women to the top in research' *Directorate-General for Research* (European Commission, 2008b).
- 'Women in science and technology: creating sustainable careers' *Directorate-General for Research Science, Economy and Society* (European Commission, 2009).
- 'Roadmap for equality between women and men' (2006–10), Work Programme 2009–10.

In September 2010 the European Commission issued the Communication called 'Strategy for gender equality between women and men 2010–2015'. According to the Communication the lack of gender equality remains a violation of fundamental rights. The document emphasizes the following fundamental rules (European Commission, 2010):

- achieving equal economic independence for women and men;
- better reconciliation of work and private family life;
- promoting equal participation of women and men in decision-making;
- eradicating gender-based violence;
- promoting gender equality outside the EU.

The European Commission emphasizes the necessity for practical action and tools for increasing women's participation in the economy as females still encounter cultural and structural hindrances with regards to their professional development. Although women constitute half of society and over 50 per cent of university graduates, they are underrepresented on the labour market and at the highest levels of corporate structure in particular. The unwritten rule known as the glass ceiling states that the higher in the organizational structure, the lower the percentage of women (Powell, 2000: 236–49; Sanders, 2002: 62–4). For instance, in the EU on average one in four members of the National Parliament and one in four ministers is female. Women make up 10 per cent of executive boards and only 3 per cent of CEO positions (Davidson and Burke, 2004: 6–10). This data has remained stable over a longer period of time (Davidson and Cooper, 1992: 2–4; Haigh, 2008: 5–6). Only slightly better statistics are found among academics and small and medium enterprises (SMEs) – females constitute 19 per cent of full professors and make up for 33 per cent of entrepreneurs. The other issue refers to the difference in pay for the same job which is estimated in the EU at an average of 17.8 per cent and ranges from 4.9 per cent in Italy, 8.5 per cent in Slovenia, 9 per cent in each Belgium and Romania, and 25.5 per cent in Austria, 26.2 per cent in the Czech Republic and 30.9 per cent in Estonia (Davidson and Burke, 2004).

According to the European Commission the activities undertaken so far have proved to be efficient and assured for many positive changes. For instance, recent years have shown the increase in the employment rate for women from 52 per cent in 1998 to 62.5 per cent in 2009, being still however lower by 21 per cent for women as compared with men. Out of over 12.5 million newly created jobs between the years 2000–2009 women took 9.8 million jobs. However, women still work in less attractive professions and 32 per cent of them are employed in part-time jobs as compared with only 8 per cent of men (European Commission (2010). Finally, women are found to be more affected by poverty and social exclusion and experience lower pension payments.

The European Commission's analyses indicate that the low employment of females is negative from the perspective of talent management and mainly affect the policy of fighting the economic crisis. The increase of women's participation in economic life may also balance the negative aspects of the ageing population and lower the threat of insufficient labour supply. Thus, the 'Strategy for gender equality between women and men 2010–2015' delivers a set of guidelines and recommendations to increase the female presence on the labour market, in particular at the decision-making level. As the chapter focuses on females participation on corporate boards attention is paid to the EC recommendations which suggest:

- the increase of female presence on corporate boards to 30 per cent by 2015;
- the increase of female presence on corporate boards to 40 per cent by 2020.

These recommendations address all public listed companies regardless of the ownership structure or the identity of the shareholders and refer to corporate boards understood as the supervisory board and management board in the case of a two-tier model and board of directors in the case of a unitary model. Introducing legally binding quotas provided by regulations is perceived by the European Commission as the best option for increasing the presence of women on boards. As a result, these solutions are targeted to enhance the productivity and efficiency of listed companies and to become an important tool in fighting the financial crisis.

The Policy for Gender Equality in the Economy

The EU member states differ significantly with respect to the policy for gender equality in the economy. Taking into account two criteria of female participation in economic life (presence on corporate boards and differences in pay and working hours) and the work–family life balance (raising children, percentage of working mothers), McKinsey & Company in its report 'Women matter: gender diversity, a corporate performance driver' provided the following four models of gender equality:

1   the non-interventionist model (characterized by the high participation of women in the economy combined with the low level of work and family life balance) which is found in the UK;
2   the traditionally conservative model (characterized the low participation of women in the economy combined with the low level of work and family life balance) which includes the Italian and Spanish solutions;
3   the egalitarian model (characterized the high participation of women in the economy combined with the high level of work and family life balance) introduced in Sweden, Finland and Norway;
4   the pro-family model (characterized the low participation of women in the economy combined with the high level of work and family life balance) which is found in France and Belgium.

The typology of countries in the EU with respect to the policy of gender equality in the economic and social systems is presented in Figure 8.1.

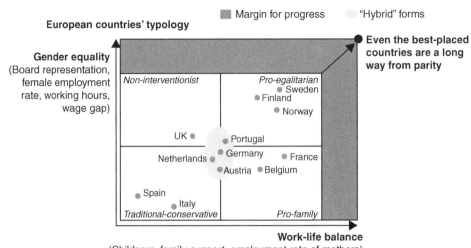

Figure 8.1 Typology of diversity in the economic and social systems

Source: McKinsey & Company (2007). 'Women matter: gender diversity, a corporate performance driver', p. 18.

As shown in Figure 8.1 the member states differ significantly with respect to the policy on gender equality and women's participation on corporate boards. Additionally, McKinsey & Company identified the hybrid model (in the centre of the matrix in Figure 8.1) which represents the solution adopted in Holland, Austria, Germany and Portugal. The main conclusion derived from the presented typology is the notion that even those out-of-member states which introduced the egalitarian model did not manage to provide for full gender equality in the economy which is an interpretation that even extensively adopted instruments do not prove effective in increasing female involvement in economic life. These results cast doubts on the recent EU recommendations to introduce quotas to the level of 40 per cent for members of corporate boards.

The reasons for the EU policy supporting the active participation of women in enterprises are heavily rooted in the structural hindrances which females face while pursuing their career. The most important reasons for the low presence of women at higher levels of organizational structure are referred to by McKinsey & Company (2009, 2010) and Davidson and Burke (2004: 2–4):

- The unequal dedication to household work and responsibilities – the analyses show that women devote much more time to household work compared to men. The divergence is estimated at 73 minutes in Sweden (making a total of 3 hours and 42 minutes), 110 minutes in Germany (a total of 4:11), 143 minutes in Poland (a total of 4:45), 198 minutes in Spain (a total of 4:55) and 225 minutes in Italy (a total of 5:20). The EU average in the case of household work accounts for women to 4 hours and 29 minutes as compared to 2 hours and 18 minutes for men (which is 131 minutes less).
- The corporate career model known as 'anytime, anywhere' which demands significant geographical mobility (business trips, visits, meetings, expatriations) and time

availability standing in conflict with raising a family. As a result, 65 per cent of American women and 96 per cent of graduates of prestigious French universities perceived family and maternity as a main hindrance for developing their personal careers.

- The modesty and underestimation of themselves by women, the tendency not to promote themselves – for instance, 70 per cent of MBA programmes' female graduates assess their achievements at the level comparable to the achievements of other participants of the courses. Seventy per cent of male graduates perceive their performance as much better compared to their peers. This turns out to be problematic at the stage of professional development and promotion which is based on the masculine model of aggressive competition, rivalry and confrontation.
- The lack of leaders, mentors and coaches for women who would support them in their careers – only 33 per cent of female graduates of MBA programmes (as compared to 42 per cent of male graduates) claim that finding a mentor at work is an easy task. Simultaneously, the dominance of the masculine pattern career is viewed as the main obstacle for a professional career and development by 64 per cent of American women.
- The lower activity of women with respect to networking, building connections, searching for professional alliances and coalitions (Haigh, 2008: 110–23).
- The lack of social policy encouraging the activism of women who have children, the lack of systemic and institutional solutions.
- The lower ambitions and determination of women as compared to men – only 15 per cent of females are determined to get promoted to a position characterized by power and influence.

Women on Corporate Boards

Women on Corporate Boards Worldwide

Corporate boards are essential bodies for governance and management, and their efficiency determines the company's performance. The board is a crucial element of the corporate governance structure, and its efficiency and performance determines the success of monitoring and the operation of the company. As noted by Monks and Minow (2004: 252), boards 'are the link between people who provide capital (the shareholders) and the people who use that capital to create value (the managers)'. The board is also seen as a liaison between concentrated or dispersed shareholders of different identities (individuals, funds, companies, banks and so on) who exert the residual rights, and executives, who as a matter of fact constitute the powerful group that runs and controls the company (Mallin, 2004; Roe, 1994). The board responds to challenges of separation of ownership and control and acts towards mitigating agency problems, aligning the goals of managers with the interest of shareholders. Its main task is to represent, formulate and realize the interests and expectations of shareholders as the owners of the companies (see also Hambrick and Jackson, 2000). It is the board which holds the ultimate accountability and bears the final responsibility for corporate success or failure (Ibrahim and Angelidis, 1994). Therefore, from the perspective of influence, power, responsibilities and prestige as well as organizational hierarchy, corporate boards are the top corporate bodies. The discussion on women's participation in business inevitably needs to refer to their presence on corporate boards. It is also a reliable indicator of gender equality advancement and policy adopted by countries and companies.

The analysis of gender policy and gender equality very often focuses on the proportion of women at the top levels of companies either on supervisory boards, executive committees or boards of directors. The greater presence of female directors is viewed as a case of gender equality, and a corporation's understanding of a woman's role and importance for the efficient management and contribution to corporate performance. The presence of women on boards is a theme gaining growing interest and being studied worldwide. Research indicates the significant regional and national differences in the level of female participation among board members ranging from 0 per cent up to 32 per cent (McKinsey & Company, 2010). Figure 8.2 presents the data on female presence on boards and executive committees in selected countries.

As shown in Figure 8.2 the relatively low participation of women on boards is revealed in the case of emerging markets such as India, China, Brazil and Russia. Interestingly, a low number of female executives is depicted in Germany. The higher presence of female directors is noted in Anglo-Saxon countries such as the UK and the US, reaching the level of 12–14 per cent. The EU average of female presence on corporate boards is estimated at 12 per cent, differing significantly across member states (Vinnicombe, 2000: 9–25). The high presence of women on corporate boards in Norway is a result of the regulations introducing quotas to provide female participation to the level of 40 per cent (Huse, 2007: 90–91). The quotas were implemented in 2008 making Norway the essential benchmark for the policy of gender equality and delivering many arguments for the proponents of such an institutionalization of female presence on corporate boards. Similar regulations providing quotas to the level of 40 per cent have been already adopted in Spain and France and are expected to start at the beginning of 2017, respectively.

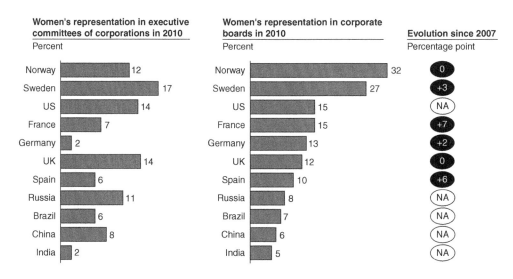

Figure 8.2 Female participation on corporate boards in 2010

Source: based on McKinsey & Company (2010). 'Women Matter 2010. Women at the top of corporations: making it happen', pp. 2 and 3.

Women on Corporate Boards in Poland

Women's participation on boards in Poland accounts for 11 per cent (Sieminska, 2004: 128–44). Women are present only in 25 per cent of management boards of listed companies (Domagalski, 2011) and only in the case of 26 companies (6.5 per cent) are they CEOs. The statistics slightly improve in the case of a larger sample (not only public listed companies) – in nearly 41 per cent of companies women are present on the management board, although in most cases only one woman sits on the executive committee (30.5 per cent). Moreover, 49.4 per cent of supervisory boards have no females, and 32.9 per cent supervisory boards have only one female (Bohdanowicz, 2011). This data places Poland among the countries which have a relatively low presence of women on boards.

A good illustration of women's presence on corporate boards in Poland delivers the analysis of the companies covered by the WIG20, the main index of the Warsaw Stock Exchange, which includes the largest and the most liquid (in terms of free float) companies. The list of the WIG20 companies with their short characteristics referring to the sector of operation and ownership structure is presented in Table 8.1.

As shown in Table 8.1, although the WIG20 covers the largest and the most liquid companies listed on the Warsaw Stock Exchange, the majority of them are

Table 8.1 Main characteristics of WIG20 companies

Company	Industry	Main shareholder
Asseco Poland	IT sector	Private investor (A.Góral) 10.42% Pension funds: OFE Aviva – 12.10%, OFE PZU – 6.45%
Bogdanka	Coal mining	Pension funds: OFE Aviva – 14.74%; OFE PZU – 9.76%; ING OFE – 9.63%; AMPLICO OFE – 5.10%
BRE	Banking	Commerzbank – 70%
Getin	Banking	Founder (L. Czarnecki) – 55.65% via LC Corp – 44.16%
GTC	Construction/ real estate	GTC Real Estate Holding B.V. 27.75%
Handlowy	Banking	Citibank – 75%
JSW	Coal mining	State – 58.20%
Kernel	Commodity transport	Namsen Limited – 37.59%; Comgest SA – 5.96%
KGHM	Copper mining	State – 31.79%
Lotos	Petrochemicals	State – 53.19%
PBG	Construction	Founder (J.Wiśniewski) – 41,48%; Pension fund (ING) – 10.24%; Investment funds (PIONEER PEKAO) – 14.99%
PGE	Energy	State – 69.29%
PEKAO	Banking	Unicredit Group – 59.24%; Aberdeen Asset Management – 5.03%
PGNiG	Oil and Gas	State – 72.40%
PKN Orlen	Petroleum	State – 27.52%; Pension fund (OFE Avila) – 5.08%
PKOBP	Banking	State – 40.99%; Bank (BGK) – 10.25%
PZU	Insurance	State – 35.18%; Pension fund (ING) – 5.02%
TAURON	Energy	State – 30.06%; KGHM S.A. – 10.39%; Pension funds (ING) – 5.06%
TPSA	Telecommunication	France Telecom S.A. – 49.79%; Capital Group International, Inc. – 5.06%
TVN	Media	ITI Group – 55.64%; Cadazin Trading & Investment – 2.02%; N-Vision B.V. – 1.15%

Source: own compilation based on corporate websites.

characterized by the ownership concentration and reveals a strong involvement by the state. Interestingly, among the largest 20 companies, many originate from the banking sector as well as operating in mining, energy or the construction sectors. As the Polish corporate governance system is based on the two-tier board model the analysis refers to female presence on the supervisory and management boards. The number of female directors as well as their proportion with the reference to the overall size of the two boards is presented in Table 8.2.

As shown in Table 8.2, Polish supervisory and management boards of the WIG20 index companies differ significantly with respect to the presence of women. The presence of female directors on supervisory boards ranges from a minimum of 0 per cent to a maximum of 33 per cent. Interestingly, the highest presence of women on a supervisory board at the level of 33 per cent is revealed in the case of the mining company Bogdanka operating in the mining sector traditionally dominated by male directors. Relatively good results are also observed in the case of the energy and petroleum sector, while surprisingly poor results are noted in the case of banks, controlled by foreign financial conglomerates in particular (0 per cent in the majority of analysed cases). The average presence of women on the supervisory board of the WIG20 companies accounts for 10.75 per cent (or 18 female directors for 20 supervisory boards). As far as the management board is concerned the participation of women ranges from a minimum of 0 per cent to a maximum of 36 per cent. The highest presence of

Table 8.2 Women on corporate boards in the WIG20 companies

Company	Supervisory board			Management board		
	Size of the board	No of female directors	% of female directors	Size of the board	No of female directors	% of female directors
Asseco Poland	5	0	0	7	1	14%
Bogdanka	6	2	33%	5	1	20%
BRE	10	1	10%	7	1	14%
Getin	5	0	0	3	1	33%
GTC	7	0	0	7	0	0
Handlowy	12	0	0	6	2	33%
JSW	12	0	0	4	0	0
Kernel	NA – one tier model			11	4	36%
KGHM	10	1	10%	3	0	0
Lotos	5	1	20%	4	0	0
PBG	4	0	0	5	1	20%
PGE	9	2	22%	3	0	0
PEKAO	9	1	11%	6	0	0
PGNiG	7	2	28%	4	0	0
PKN Orlen	9	1	11%	5	1	20%
PKOBP	9	1	11%	7	0	0
PZU	7	1	14%	6	0	0
TAURON	7	1	14%	5	1	20%
TPSA	13	2	15%	5	0	0
TVN	11	1	9%	4	0	0
Average	11	1	9%	4	0	0

Source: own compilation based on corporate websites.

female executives at the level of 36 per cent is revealed in Kernel, the Ukrainian food processing company while the lowest presence of 0 per cent is noted in 12 WIG20 companies, which represents more than half of the sample. The average presence of women on the management board of WIG20 companies accounts for 10.5 per cent (13 females for 20 executive boards).

Quotas for Women on Corporate Boards: Discussion

Quotas for Women on Corporate Boards: Arguments for

The discussion on female presence on corporate boards is rooted in the fundamental postulates of diversity management pointing at the benefits and improved corporate performance resulting from the presence of different gender, ethnic, national and religious representatives at a top corporate level. The notion of diversity management indicates that a more heterogeneous board is more responsive to the needs and expectations of a diverse group of customers and shareholders (Ibrahim and Angelidis, 1994; Sheridan, 2001). Moreover, diversified groups lower the tendency of group syndrome or homogeneous culture inefficiencies as different members enrich decision-making, communication and strategic analysis contributing to higher efficiency (Dalton and Daily, 1993; Westphall, 1998).

The proponents of a higher presence of women on boards indicate the following arguments (Bilimoria and Wheeler, 2000; European Commission [COM 164], 2011; McKinsey & Company, 2009, 2010):

• Increased diversity of the supervisory and management boards' composition leads to a better experience and enriches the board discussion as more aspects are taken into consideration (Hamill et al., 2011; McInerney-Lacombe, Bilimoria and Salipante, 2008). Greater heterogeneity contributes to higher efficiency.

• Greater heterogeneity leads to a better understanding of expectations of a wide range of stakeholders (customers, employees, local communities) which assures the essential importance of reading the needs of the market participants. Female presence on the board is supported by the evidence which shows that on average 70 per cent of purchasing decisions are made by women. This finding refers to various product groups, as in Japan women decide on car purchases in 60 per cent of cases. Thus the female presence on corporate boards should contribute to better sales results.

• Companies characterized by greater female presence on corporate boards turn out to be more socially responsible as the evidence shows that women more often than men incorporate ethical aspects into business decisions. Therefore companies with more females on the board are expected to show greater dedication to corporate social responsibility (CSR) initiatives and be more involved in sustainable business activities. Such a strategy should result in improving corporate reputation and lead to better financial results.

• The labour force and talent management will be allocated better – the total number of women in the EU ready to undertake work is estimated at 21 million (COM 164). As the number of female university graduates is comparable to the number of male graduates, women are ready to play similar roles and positions in business as men. This finding appears as a crucial solution to the rising problems of the ageing population and the noted lack of qualified employees.

- Introducing new leadership styles of women participating in business and particularly on corporate boards is expected to enrich leadership style by introducing new values such as better communication, cooperation instead of confrontation and openness to new ideas. These values would be incorporated in business as long as females truly develop a female leadership style and do not copy typically masculine behaviour patterns (Vinkenburg, Jansen and Koopman, 2000; Vinnicombe and Bank, 2003: 273–80).

The analysis of the efficiency of female presence on a board notes positive results. The studies investigate the profitability and shareholder value referred to the number of women on a board. The research by McKinsey & Company on the sample of companies originating from five EU countries (UK, France, Germany, Spain, Sweden) and Norway reveal a better performance of companies which are placed in the first quartile with respect to the female presence on boards as compared to the boards where no women are present. More precisely, the performance measured by ROE was higher by 7 percentage points (41 per cent) for companies from the first quartile of female presence on boards as compared to companies with no women on their boards (ROE = 22 per cent versus ROE = 15 per cent based on the sample of 279 companies). The performance measured by EBIT was better by 6 percentage points (56 per cent) for companies from the first quartile of female presence on boards as compared to companies with no women on their boards (EBIT = 17 per cent versus EBIT = 11 per cent based on a sample of 231 companies; McKinsey & Company, 2010). The study by McKinsey & Company and the Amazone Euro Fund on a sample of 89 European companies of market capitalization of more than €150 million and characterized by the highest gender diversity of executive boards indicates that these companies outperform their industry-based peers (McKinsey & Company, 2009). For the period of 2005–2007 the companies with a larger heterogeneity of executive boards revealed higher ROE indicators accounted for 11.4 per cent (as compared to the industry average of 10.3 per cent), higher EBIT indicators estimated at 11.1 per cent (as compared to the industry average of 5.8 per cent) and a share price increase by 64 per cent (as compared to the industry average of 47 per cent). The research on the sample of Finnish companies managed by a female CEO showed a 10 per cent increase of profit as compared to the situation when the CEO function was fulfilled by a man (Kotiranta, Kovalainen and Rouvinen, 2007). The positive correlation was also noted in the case of Danish firms (Smith, Smith and Verner, 2006). Similar results were found in American companies – the research on the sample of Standard & Poor's 500, S&P Midcaps and S&P SmallCap companies for the period of 1996–2003 revealed a positive correlation between female presence on boards and the corporate governance standards (attendance of board members, CEO fluctuation, performance-related pay) and financial performance (shareholder value) (Adams and Ferreira, 2009). The studies on Fortune 500 companies for the period of 1999–2000 and 1998–2002 also noted positive relations between women's presence on boards of directors and shareholder value.

These results provide arguments for women's presence on corporate boards. Additionally, due to the constant gender imbalance and significant homogeneity

Table 8.3 Education level of women versus their presence on corporate boards

Country	Year, analysed criteria	Women's presence	Year, analysed criteria	Women's presence
Sweden	1978 % of women in the university graduates population	61%	2008 % women in the university graduates population	64%
	2010 % of women among top executives	17%	2040 % of women among top executives	18%
France	1975 % women in the university graduates population	41%	2008 % women in the university graduates population	55%
	2010 % of women among top executives	7%	2040 % of women among top executives	9%
Spain	1976 % women in the university graduates population	32%	2008 % women in the university graduates population	60%
	2010 % of women among top executives	6%	2040 % of women among top executives	11%
Germany	1975 % women in the university graduates population	32%	2008 % women in the university graduates population	55%
	2010 % of women among top executives	2%	2040 % of women among top executives	4%

Source: McKinsey & Company (2010). 'Women Matter 2010. Women at the top of corporations: making it happen', p. 5.

of boards, the proposal of adopting quotas is raised. As experience shows, female involvement at the top organizational level would not improve unless institutional support is provided. As presented in Table 8.3, although women account for a significant proportion of university graduates, their presence on corporate boards remains at a relatively unchanged level.

As shown in Table 8.3 graduating from university does not necessarily lead to the development of female careers and has no impact on their presence on corporate boards 25–30 years later of their career. This finding is interpreted as the dominance of masculine patterns for a corporate career which significantly limit the possibility for 'joining the club' by females. Moreover, the hindrances to a woman's career development in business and in corporations particularly indicated above (Haigh, 2008) appear to create dramatic structural limitations for the increase of women's presence on boards without any regulatory intervention.

Quotas for Women on Corporate Boards: Arguments Against

Quotas are the central instrument for increasing female participation on corporate boards recommended by the European Commission. However, this guideline of instrumental and formal regulation on women's participation on boards remains one

Table 8.4 The list of arguments criticizing quotas for females on boards

Argument	Explanation
Excessive interference with company management	Limitation for investors' decision on appointing the (educated and experienced) director to the board
Shortage of women with adequate experience and knowledge	Statistical effect, no fundamental changes
Questionable efficiency of female leadership style	Compromise and cooperation while confrontation and aggressive competition create value
Instrumental treatment of women to fulfil the recommendation	Favouring women on boards due to the recommendation on gender equality, threat of discriminating against men
Questionable sustainability of female leadership	Successful women follow masculine pattern of behaviour since it is more effective
Role of informal aspects	'Natural' environment for doing business

Source: own compilation.

of the hottest and most-debated topics, raising many controversies and strong criticism. Many countries across the EU, including Poland, remain reluctant to introduce the formal regulation on women's presence on boards. The opponents of quotas for women's presence on corporate boards submit a wide range of arguments criticizing this recommendation. Table 8.4 presents the list of arguments criticizing quotas for females on boards.

As presented in Table 8.4 the first argument criticizing the introduction of quotas for women on corporate boards refers to the excessive intervention of the regulatory authorities in business life and internal affairs of a company's management. The guideline of 40 per cent of mandates for corporate directors guaranteed for women is perceived as a limitation of freedom of choice for investors who wish to appoint the best director to the board regardless of gender (Domagalski, 2011). The essential role of corporate boards for company management and governance indicates that shareholders should have full autonomy to decide whom they intend to appoint to the board and who would represent their interest and possess adequate experience and knowledge. Appointing a different person on the basis of gender, not knowledge and experience, may be detrimental to shareholders and destroy shareholder value. Although the regulatory authorities are encouraged to provide equal chances for professional development and education and assure for the active participation of females in social and political lives, the recommendation interfering with an investor's sovereign decision remains highly controversial. Moreover, the recommendation of female presence on the board can be placed in the best practice of corporate governance. This solution is already adopted in several documents, for instance in the best practice of corporate governance for companies listed on the Warsaw Stock Exchange (2010) or the Green Paper, the EU framework of corporate governance (European Commission, 2011).

The second argument usually raised in the criticism of quotas for females on corporate boards refers to the shortage of women who possess an adequate level of knowledge, experience and skills as well as time required to fulfil a board director function. The small number of women who would be able to sit on a board combined with quota requirements may result in a pathological outcome when the same females are appointed to serve on several boards. It would thus improve the situation statistically without providing for any fundamental and structural changes.

The third argument criticizing the adoption of quotas for females on corporate boards raises questions on the real efficiency of female leadership or management style. The female tendency to incorporate stakeholders' expectations and to pay more attention to social problems and environmental damage prove to be useful in international organizations but not necessarily in the case of business corporations. Corporate performance depends on the adopted strategies and results from aggressive competition, confrontation and the focus on results. The quotas opponents indicate that such an aggressive attitude increases competition and is a fundamental requirement for growth and development. A more collaborative approach and compromise instead of competition and rivalry may affect performance and financial results. This notion may be seen as an explanation for a series of studies which did not find statistically significant relationships between the female presence on boards and corporate performance. As revealed in the research on American banks (Richard, Ford and Ismail, 2006) and Danish companies (Rose, 2007) the larger participation of women on boards neither improves nor otherwise affects financial results. Moreover, several studies show that females are worse at dealing with work stress and their presence on corporate boards may not lead to better performance (Davidson and Cooper, 1992).

The next issue raised by critics of adopting quotas for females on corporate boards refers to the sustainability of a female leadership style as many successful women follow masculine behaviour patterns as being more efficient and for assuring better results (Ruderman and Ohlott, 2002: 21–3; Sanders, 2002: 31–3). Thus introducing quotas would not provide any change in the quality of leadership on corporate boards.

The opponents of introducing quotas for women on corporate boards also indicate that formal regulations on quotas may lead to instrumental treatment of women to fulfil the recommendation and that the gender may prove to be a more important criterion for board appointment as opposed to experience and knowledge. Thus the regulation on quotas may result in a hypothetical situation that women will be appointed to the board because they are women but not necessarily better candidates. Thus such a policy may lead to wrong practices of lowering the importance of women in business (Bilimoria and Wheeler, 2000). Moreover, the strategy of eliminating discrimination against women may turn into discrimination against men.

Finally, the critics of introducing quotas for females on corporate boards point to the informal aspects of doing business and effective leadership. According to proponents of quotas, the masculine patterns of behaviour and the alpha male leadership style are perceived as the main hindrances to the development of careers for females. The importance of discussions at golf clubs or at fitness centres are supposed to discourage women who lack these informal contacts. However, opponents of quotas criticized changing the 'natural' environment of doing business or decision-making as quotas would force the increased presence of women.

Conclusion

The issues of women's participation on boards remain at the centre of corporate governance debates as one of the elements of fighting a crisis and undoubtedly require more debate and study. The guidelines for increasing women's involvement in business and greater presence on boards are widely accepted as studies reveal the direct and indirect positive impact of female participation on corporate boards upon performance. As research indicates, the heterogeneity of corporate boards enhances the quality of discussions and communication, increases the number of issues discussed and lowers the risk of group syndrome. Diversity management indicates the value of understanding the expectations and needs of various stakeholder groups, which may improve a company's performance on the market.

Finally, the female presence on boards is also seen as an element of anti-crisis strategy as additional human resources are used. However, the tools and legal provisions to achieve the goals of greater female activity at top corporate levels are intensively debated. The idea of introducing formally binding quotas remains both fundamentally controversial as well as effectively questionable. Thus the latest European Commission recommendation known as the 'Strategy for gender equality between women and men 2010–2015' to introduce quotas to increase female presence on corporate boards to the level of a minimum of 40 per cent casts many doubts and faces far different reactions from member states ranging from enthusiasm to reluctance and resistance. The fundamental arguments of proponents of quotas refer to the notion that the market itself proves not to be able to increase the active participation of women on corporate boards as social, cultural and institutional aspects tend to favour a masculine leadership style. Therefore without regulatory intervention no structural changes are expected. However, the severe shortcomings of introducing quotas and the questionable results of imposing these provisions upon listed companies indicate that the problems are far from being solved. Therefore the issues of women's presence on boards leaves us with further research and analysis.

References

Adams, R. and Ferreira, D. (2009), Women in the Boardroom and their Impact on Governance and Performance. *Journal of Financial Economics* 94: 291–309.

Bilimoria, D. and Wheeler, J. (2000), 'Women corporate directors: Current research and future directions', in M. Davidson and R. Burke (eds), *Women in Management: Current Research Issues*, Vol. 2. London: SAGE, pp. 138–63.

Bohdanowicz, L. (2011), 'Kobiety w organach statutowych polskich spółek publicznych [Women on statutory bodies of Polish listed companies', Współczesne problemy nadzoru korporacyjnego, nr 2/1, Prace i Materiału Wydziału Zarządzania Uniwersytetu Gdańskiego, pp. 227–38.

Dalton, D.R. and Daily, C.M. (1993), Board of Directors Leadership and Structure: Control and Performance Implications. *Entrepreneurship: Theory and Practive* 17: 65–81.

Davidson, M. and Burke, R. (2004), 'Women in management worldwide: Facts, figures and analysis – an overview', in M. Davidson and R. Burke (eds), *Women in Management Worldwide: Facts, Figures and Analysis*. Aldershot: Ashgate, pp. 1–20.

Davidson, M. and Cooper, C. (1992), *Shattering the Glass Ceiling: The Woman Manager*. London: Paul Chapman Publishing.

Domagalski, M. (2011), 'Czy więcej kobiet będzie zarządzać biznesem?' [Will more Women Manage Business?], *Rzeczpospolita*, 12 August, p. C1.

European Commission. (1998), *100 Words for Equality: A Glossary of Terms on Equality Between Women and Men*. Available at: http://ec.europa.eu/europeaid/sp/gender-toolkit/en/pdf/section3.pdf/

———. (2006), Roadmap for Equality Between Women and Men 2006–2010, Communication of the European Commission to the Parliament, COM: 92. Available at: http://europa.eu/legislation_summaries/employment_and_social_policy/equality_between_men_and_women/c10404_en.htm/

———. (2007a), Communication on the Gender Pay Gap, Communication of the European Commission to the Parliament, COM: 424.

———. (2008a), Evaluation on Policy: Promotion of Women Innovators and Entrepreneurship-Final Report. *DG Enterprise and Industry*. Available at: http://ec.europa.eu/enterprise/newsroom/cf./_getdocument.cfm?doc_id=3815/

———. (2008b), Mapping the Maze: Getting more Women to the Top in Research. *Directorate-General for Research*. Available at: http://ec.europa.eu/research/science-society/document_library/pdf_06/mapping-the-maze-getting-more-women-to-the-top-in-research_en.pdf/

———. (2009), Women in Science and Technology: Creating Sustainable Careers. *Directorate-General for Research Science, Economy and Society*. Available at: http://ec.europa.eu/research/science-society/document_library/pdf_06/wist2_sustainable-careers-report_en.pdf/

———. (2011), Green Paper. The EU Corporate Governance Framework, COM: 164.

Haigh, J. (2008), *Tales from the Glass Ceiling*. London: Piatkus Books.

Hambrick, D.C. and Jackson, E.M. (2000), Outside Directors with a Stake: The Linchpin in Improving Governance. *California Management Review* 42(4): 108–27.

Hamill, P., Ward, A. and Wylie, J. (2011), Stronger Boards – are Women the Answer? *Chartered Accountants Ireland*. Available at: http://www.gaaaccounting.com/gaa_issues.aspx?q=October%202011\\CAI_issue5_article2&t=GAA%20Issue%20-%20October%202011/

Huse, M. (2007), *Boards, Governance and Value Creation: The Side of Corporate Governance*. Cambridge: Cambridge University Press.

Ibrahim, N.A. and Angelidis, J.P. (1994), Effect of Board Members' Gender on Corporate Social Responsiveness. *The Journal of Applied Business Research* 10(1): 35–42.

Kotiranta, A., Kovalainen, A. and Rouvinen, P. (2007), Female Leadership and Firm Profitability. *EVA Analysis* 3. Available at: http://www.europeanpwn.net/files/eva_analysis_english.pdf/

Mallin, C.A. (2004), *Corporate Governance*. Oxford: Oxford University Press.

McInerney-Lacombe, N., Bilimoria, D. and Salipante, P.F. (2008), 'Women on corporate boards of directors: International research and practice', in S. Vinnicombe, V. Singh, R.J. Burke, D. Bilimoria and M. Huse (eds), *Championing the Discussion of Tough Issues: How Women Corporate Directors Contribute to Board Deliberations*. Northhampton, MA: Edward Elgar, pp. 123–39.

McKinsey & Company. (2009), Women Leaders, a Competitive Edge in and After the Crisis. *Women Matter 3*. Available at: http://www.mckinsey.de/sites/mck_files/files/women_matter_3_brochure.pdf.

McKinsey & Company. (2010), Women at the Top of Corporations: Making it Happen. Available at: www.mckinsey.com.

Monks, R.A. and Minow, N. (2004), *Corporate Governance*. Oxford: Blackwell.

Powell, G. (2000), 'The glass ceiling: Explaining the good and bad news', in M. Davidson and R. Burke (eds), *Women in Management: Current Research Issues*, Vol. 2. London: SAGE, pp. 236–50.

Richard, O.C., Ford, D. and Ismail, K. (2006), Exploring the Performance Effects of Visible Attribute Diversity: The Moderating Role of Span of Control and Organizational Life Cycle. *International Journal of Human Resource Management* 17(12): 2091–109.

Roe, M. (1994), *Weak Owners, Strong Managers*. Princeton, NJ: Princeton University Press.

Rose, C. (2007), Does Female Board Representation Influence Firm Performance? The Danish Evidence. *Corporate Governance: An International Review* 152(2): 404–13.

Ruderman, M. and Ohlott, P. (2002), *Standing at the Crossroads: Next Step for High-Achieving Women*. London: Wiley & Sons.

Sanders, E. (2002), *Talking about Success: Conversations with High-Flying Women*. London: Pro Bono Books.

Sheridan, A. (2001), A View from the Top: Women on the Boards of Public Companies. *Corporate Governance* 1(1): 8–14.

Sieminska, R. (2004), 'Women in management in Poland', in M. Davidson and R. Burke (eds), *Women in Management Worldwide: Figures and Analysis*. Aldershot: Ashgate, pp. 128–44.

Smith, N., Smith, V. and Verner, M. (2006), Do Women in Top Management Firms Affect Firm Performance? A Panel Study of 2 500 Danish Firms. *International Journal of Productivity and Performance Management* 55(7): 569–93.

Vinkenburg, C., Jansen, P. and Koopman, P. (2000), 'Feminine leadership: A review of gender differences in managerial behavior and effectiveness', in M. Davidson and R. Burke (eds), *Women in Management: Current Research Issues*, Vol. 2. London: SAGE, pp. 120–37.

Vinnicombe, S. (2000), 'The position of women in management in Europe', in M. Davidson and R. Burke (eds), *Women in Management: Current Research Issues*, Vol. 2. London: SAGE, pp. 9–25.

Vinnicombe, S. and Bank, J. (2003), *Women with Attitude: Lessons for Career Management*. London: Routledge.

Westphall, J.D. (1998), Board Games: How CEOs Adapt to Increases in Structural Board Independence from Management. *Administrative Science Quarterly* 43(3): 511–37.

Chapter 9

The Influence of Women on Earnings Management

Public Companies in Brazil

Liliane Segura, Henrique Formigoni,
Fatima David and Rute Abreu

Introduction

In recent decades, earnings management has been part of discussions in accounting and financial literature (Niskanen et al., 2011). The disclosure of information and the quality of the information that is disclosed has also received a lot of attention. Investors must be concerned that the quality of information supplied by firms means, according to Healy and Whalen (1999), that the firm can manage their results in such a way as to confuse investors about their performance or to influence their contracts, based on the accounting numbers. Rafik (2002) states that earnings management is a strategy for the management of the firm and, although it is not illegal, it is considered unethical by the users of financial statements (Johari et al., 2008; Rafik, 2002).

Research on women in power has, on the one hand, gained great importance in recent years: e.g. Adams and Ferreira (2009), Campbell and Minguez-Vera (2008), Carter, Sinkins and Simpson (2003), Farrell and Hersch (2005), Peni and Vähäma (2010) and Rose (2007). All have examined the effect of female executives on the firm's performance. On the other hand, much research about the presence of women on the board still shows no consensus about its relationship with earnings management. Some researchers found a positive relationship (Scapin, Garcia-Lara and Penalval-Zuasti, 2013), others a negative one (Gulzar and Wang, 2011), and others still found no relationship at all between the presence of women on the board and earnings management (Moradi et al., 2012).

The search and review of the literature has defined the theoretical and conceptual framework of this research and suggested the question to investigate, which is:

Does the Presence of Women on the Board of the Firm Influence Earnings Management?

In parallel, the methodological aspects justify the most appropriate processes for the treatment of the non-probability sample (Balakrishnan and Penno, 2013). Thus the longitudinal exploratory analysis relies on an analysis of variables that the literature indicates have a relationship with earnings management: firm size, industry and leverage. Additionally, the literature shows that some variables should have a relationship with earnings management and these will be tested: the number of independent directors, level of transparency of accounting information and the size of the board.

The aim of this research is to identify whether the presence of women on the board tends to lead to lower earnings management than occurs in a firm where there are only men on the board. This chapter is divided into five parts. Besides this introduction, the authors study the theoretical framework, followed by the methodology, results and, finally, the conclusion.

Participation of Women on the Board and Earnings Management

The participation of women on the board and their effect has motivated several studies in the social sciences. Adams and Ferreira (2009), Campbell and Minguez-Vera (2008), Carter, Simkins and Simpson (2003), Farrell and Hersch (2005), Peni and Vähäma (2010) and Rose (2007) have examined the effects of female executive directors on financial performance and the market value of firms. However, although there have been several studies, there is no unanimity in the findings on women's participation as board members and its impact on firm performance and the reduction of earnings management. Cohn (2013) argues that several recent studies suggest that women are more qualified than men to assess a firm's finances, although the results of their board membership are not yet clear.

Moradi et al. (2012) underscore the inconclusiveness of the research into the participation of women on the board and its effect on firm performance, based on the results of surveys. Bathula (2008) and Carter, Simkins and Simpson (2003) conclude from their research that there is a positive relationship between gender diversity and firm performance. However, Ding and Charoenwong (2004) and Farrell and Hersch (2005) affirm that there is still no conclusive evidence of a significant relationship between the presence of women on the board and shareholder return.

In relation to this, Shukeri, Shin and Shaari (2012) analysed the relationship between the characteristics of board members and the performance of listed firms in Malaysia, and found no significant relationship between gender diversity and firm performance. According to Gulzar and Wang (2011), some studies suggest that there is no significant relationship between performance and the gender of the board members. Watson (2002) found no significant differences between businesses controlled by men and those controlled by women. Rose (2007) showed that there was no statistically significant association between female representation on the board and firm performance. Another study indicated a negative effect between the presence of women on the board and firm performance (Adams and Ferreira, 2009). Peni and Vähäma (2010) found no significant differences between earnings management and the gender of the chief executive officer.

Earnings management is defined as a purposeful intervention in the preparation of reports in the accounting process, arising from the judgement of the directors on the financial and/or operational activities in structuring the firm's choices, in order to influence the analysis of the business's performance by external users, and hence to get a particular benefit (Healy and Whalen, 1999; Schipper, 1989).

McNichols and Wilson (1988) claim that revenue and expenditure in net income have some components that are discretionary and some that are non-discretionary in terms of disclosure, so that administrators can exercise their judgement by choosing the accounting methods of the firm. Jones (1991) corroborates this understanding and states that earnings management can be carried out in several ways, using such things as accruals, changes in accounting methods and changes in capital structure.

In obedience to the accrual basis, the accounting recognition of economic events and transactions that do not generate cash inflows or outflows (i.e. that do not generate cash flows) uses accruals. These can be classified into non-discretionary accruals, which are those inherent to the activities of the firm, and discretionary accruals, which are artificial accruals and are aimed only at manipulating the accounting results (Dechow, Sloan and Sweeney, 1995; Martinez, 2001).

Xiong (2006) explains that the management of financial results cannot be measured directly; the literature therefore provides several operational models for the detection of this practice. In relation to this, Dechow, Sloan and Sweeney (1995) claim that the analysis of management accounting results is usually done by the measurement of the non-discretionary and discretionary accruals. Operational models for detecting earnings management consider discretionary accruals to be proxies of earnings management.

Mohamad et al. (2010) studied the relationship between various aspects of corporate governance and earnings management using panel data for Malaysian firms in the period 2005–2007, and found no important effect of the presence of women on the board on the management accounting results. Gulzar and Wang (2011) investigated the efficiency of the characteristics of corporate governance in reducing earnings management in Chinese firms listed on the Shanghai and Shenzhen stock exchanges. These authors identified abnormal working capital accruals as a proxy for management and used the results to calculate the modified Jones discretionary accruals. They found a positive and significant relationship between earnings management and the presence of women on the board. They argue, therefore, that women tend to assist in the reduction of discretionary accruals, because they are less involved in corruption and fraud.

Wei and Xie (2011) studied the relationship between the gender of the chief financial officer (CFO) and earnings management in China's listed firms from 1999 to 2006. They found that firms whose CFO is a woman have a low value of discretionary accruals, and a low total cost of abnormal production. Moradi et al. (2012) developed a survey of firms listed on the Tehran stock market between 2006 and 2009, and analysed the relationship between the characteristics of the board of directors and earnings management in Iranian accounts. One of the variables relating to the characteristics of the board was the presence of women on the board. Thus they tried to identify whether there was a correlation between the presence of women on the board and the management of results, but this relationship proved to be insignificant.

Additionally, Moradi et al. (2012) noted that the presence of women is still very small in firms: their survey was based on 636 observations and in only 24 cases (approximately 4 per cent) was there were a woman on the board. This study also shows that an increasing number of male directors results in their opinions prevailing over those of the women, even if the female members of the board have different opinions about earnings management.

Hili and Affes (2012) tested the impact of gender diversity on boards of directors on earnings equality. They used a sample of 70 French firms listed on the Société des Bourses Françaises (SBF) 120 index, and they found that the persistent enhancement of earnings could not be attributed to gender diversity. The results do not show significant differences between firms with female directors and firms with male directors. The researchers also concluded that these results may be traced back to the sociopsychological attitude adopted by female directors, and to the existence of barriers that tried to put them in a hierarchical progression. Man, Seng and Wong (2013) conducted a survey of the literature on corporate governance, and found that female directors can develop leadership based on trust, which requires information, and that they are generally more averse to the risk of fraud and/or the management of opportunistic results.

Methodology

The set of firms in the sample was obtained from those who were active in 2008 on the list of the Brazilian Stock Exchange (hereafter BM&FBovespa). The companies without accounting that presented missing data, those missing information, or peculiar characteristics, were excluded. After the depuration process, the final sample was 81 firms for the years 2008–11, with a total of 324 observations. The information about the board of directors and supervision were taken from the External Disclosure of the Securities Commission (DIVEXT report). A further process of confirmation was made for the data collected and the verification of consistency during the years 2008–11. It was possible to corroborate that some firms did not have data for all the years observed, then the authors used an unbalanced panel.

Definitions of Variables in the Study

Dependent Variable

Earnings Management (Ger_Res) is the numeric variable which is determined by Equation 1:

$$TA_{it} = \frac{\left\{ \begin{array}{l} \left[\left(AC_{it} - AC_{it-1} \right) - \left(Disp_{it} - Disp_{it-1} \right) \right] - \\ \left[\left(PC_{it} - PC_{it-1} \right) - \left(FinPC_{it} - FinPC_{it-1} \right) \right] - Depr_{it} \end{array} \right\}}{AT_{it-1}}$$

(Equation 1)

$$\delta_3 = D_{it-1} / FA_{it-1}$$

$$\delta_1 = CR_{it-1} / R_{it-1}$$

$$TA_{it} = \emptyset_0 + \emptyset_1 \left(\delta_1 \frac{R_{it}}{AT_{t-1}} \right) + \emptyset_2 \left(\delta_2 \frac{D_{it}}{AT_{t-1}} \right) + \emptyset_3 \left(\delta_3 \frac{FA_{it}}{AT_{t-1}} \right) + \varepsilon_{it}$$

Equation 1 applies the regression method with R that is equal to net operating income of the period t, weighted by total assets from the previous year (t – 1) and excluding the tax on turnover; D is the value of costs and expenses of the period t, excluding depreciation and amortization, weighted by total assets of the previous year (t – 1); and FA is the total of fixed assets and deferred assets (gross) of the period t, weighted by total assets from the previous year (t – 1) and ε_{it} as the error of the regression equation. Another step of mathematical treatment is determination of the total accruals according to Equation 2:

$$TA_{it} = \varnothing_0 + \varnothing_1 \left(\delta_1 \frac{R_{it}}{AT_{t-1}} \right) + \varnothing_2 \left(\delta_2 \frac{D_{it}}{AT_{t-1}} \right) + \varnothing_3 \left(\delta_3 \frac{FA_{it}}{AT_{t-1}} \right) + \varepsilon_{it}$$ (Equation 2)

Knowing that δ were calculated from the Kang and Sivaramakrishnan (1995) model using CR: Receivables of firm i from the previous period (t – 1); INV: Inventories of firm i from the previous period (t – 1); DespAntec: Prepaid Expenses of firm i from the previous period (t – 1); CP: Current Payables of firm i from the previous period (t – 1), in period; and FA: Fixed assets and deferred assets (gross) of firm i from the previous period (t – 1) that are represented in Equations 3, 4 and 5:

$$\delta_1 = CR_{it-1} / R_{it-1}$$ (Equation 3)

$$\delta_2 = \left(INV_{it-1} + DespAntec_{it-1} + CP_{it-1} \right) / D_{it-1}$$ (Equation 4)

$$\delta_3 = D_{it-1} / FA_{it-1}$$ (Equation 5)

Total accruals (TA) are determined by the equation 6 and knowing that:

$$TA_{it} = \frac{\begin{Bmatrix} \left[\left(AC_{it} - AC_{it-1} \right) - \left(Disp_{it} - Disp_{it-1} \right) \right] - \\ \left[\left(PC_{it} - PC_{it-1} \right) - \left(FinPC_{it} - FinPC_{it-1} \right) \right] - Depr_{it} \end{Bmatrix}}{AT_{it-1}}$$ (Equation 6)

Knowing AC_{it}: Current assets of firm i on period t; AC_{it}–1: Current assets of firm i from the previous period (t – 1); $Disp_{it}$: Cash and cash equivalents of firm i on period t; $Disp_{it}$–1: Cash and cash equivalents from the previous period (t – 1); PC_{it}: Current liabilities of firm i on period t; PC_{it}–1: Current liabilities of firm i from the previous period (t – 1); $FinCP_{it}$: Short-term liabilities of firm i on period t; $FinCP_{it}$: Short-term liabilities of firm i from the previous period (t – 1); and $Depr_{it}$: Depreciation of firm i on period t and AT_{it}: Total of assets of firm i on period t. The error generated in the regression by the total of accruals in the Kang and Sivaramakrishnan (KS) (1995) model was saved with the name *Ger_Res*.

Independent and Control Variables

The research by Barako and Brown (2008), Frías-Aceituno et al. (2012), Ibrahim and Angelidis (1991) and Prado-Lorenzo and García-Sánchez (2010) indicates that women tend to provide greater transparency and higher ethical standards to a business. The authors used WOMAN as a categorical variable representing as a dummy variable indicating if there is a woman on the board (WOMAN = 1) or not (WOMAN = 0). It is the percentage of women on the board of directors of all firms of the sample, which is the same as the percentage of women in the total BD. WOMAN was used to represent the diversity of the board of directors, and it is an independent variable of this study.

In addition, the control variables used to avoid bias in the analysis of the relationship between earnings management and the representation of women on the board were:

- GRI is a numeric variable that represents transparency taking the Global Reporting Initiative (GRI) guidelines as the reference. With this variable, the authors represent the standard of the disclosed information about sustainability practices published by the firm. The GRI reports were obtained from the firms' websites. The level of usefulness and comparability of corporate social responsibility information is determined according to the level of the indicators and the supplementary information included in the sustainability report. Concretely, there are three levels of application of the GRI guidelines: C, B and A (from low to high level of usefulness and comparability). The authors have transformed the levels into 3, 2 and 1, respectively, from level C with number 3 and level A with number 1.

- BSIZE is a numeric variable that represents the size of the board as the total number of directors on the board. In general, research shows that a large board can bring agency problems (Gallego-Álvarez, García-Sánchez and Rodríguez-Domínguez, 2009) and thus disrupt the management outcome. The authors expect to find a relationship between BSIZE and earnings management.

- INDEPENDENCE is a numeric variable that represents the percentage of the number of board members who are external to the firm and are therefore non-executive, which is a proxy for the level of independence of the board as in other studies of the literature (Andres, Azofra and López, 2005).

- SIZE is a numeric variable that represents the firm size and is measured by the logarithm of total assets. According to agency theory, larger firms have greater visibility in the market and society and tend to be more compliant in the production of information (Bonsón and Escobar, 2004; Craven and Marston, 1999; Giner Inchausti et al., 2003; Gul and Leung, 2004; Marston and Polei, 2004; Oyelere, Laswad and Fisher, 2003; Prencipe, 2004). This variable relates to earnings management, because managers of larger firms tend to use earnings management to make the results appear better to the market. Therefore a positive relationship between this variable and earnings management is expected.

- ROA is a numeric variable that represents the annual return on assets. Some studies show a positive relationship between return on assets and disclosure of information, while others find no significant relationship between these variables (Giner et al., 2003; Larrán and Giner, 2002; Marston and Polei, 2004; Oyelere, Laswad and Fisher, 2003; Prencipe, 2004).

- LEVERAGE is a numeric variable that represents the leverage of the firm through the ratio of debt to total assets. It is a major cause of earnings management, because of the need to comply with the covenants imposed by the firm's creditors. Therefore, it is expected that there is a positive relationship between this variable and earnings management.

- SECTOR is a categorical variable that represents the major economic sector activity. It takes values between 1 and 6, and has often been used in studies to eliminate from the expected results the effect of the economic sector activity in which the firm operates.

Model and Analysis Techniques

The relationship between earnings management and the presence of women on the board was evaluated using a panel data regression with a random effects analysis and fixed effects analysis. To decide on the best regression method to apply to the panel data, the authors used the Hausman test. This test is used to check which of the two models (random and fixed effects) is appropriate to the sample. This test gives the result for Prob > $\chi2$ of 0.8391, which means that there are no differences between the two estimation tests applied. So, the authors choose the random effects model.

The authors used the Arellano and Bond (1991) and Arellano and Bover (1995) method called the Generalized Method of Moments (GMM). The GMM is indicated for cases in which the time variable (T) is small and the number of variables (N) is great. This method is also suitable when there are independent variables that are not strictly exogenous and are possibly also correlated with the error. This panel uses fixed effects and assumes that there is heteroskedasticity and autocorrelation among individuals.

Hypothesis

The literature shows, in many respects, that the presence of women in the firm should be of benefit to its shareholders. Thus, the first research hypothesis of this article is:

H_1: The presence of women on the board has a negative influence on earnings management by the firm.

The presence of women on the board was studied by Erhardt, Werbel and Shrader (2003). These authors identified a positive relationship between the presence of women and profitability for American firms. Women can also influence the quality of disclosures by the firm; according to the studies of Ruegger and King (1992), women may have higher ethical standards, and they may make the firm more transparent (Barako and Brown, 2008; Frías-Aceituno et al., 2012; Prado-Lorenzo and García-Sánchez, 2010).

According to Scapin et al. (2013), the presence of women on the board in response to quotas that have been imposed in Europe can be seen to result in an increase in firms' accruals. They suggest this may have occurred because of the inexperience of the newly inducted women on the board and thus the greater manoeuvrability of the existing members. Brazil is still very conservative regarding the presence of women as executives. In line with the study of Scapin et al. (2013), the second research hypothesis is:

H_2: The reduced presence of women on the board has a positive influence *on earnings management by the firm.*

The search by Bruschini and Puppin (2004) shows that the corporate culture still influences the presence of women in firms, and that more traditional firms do not usually accept women on their boards. Madalozzo's (2011) research describes how difficult it is for a woman to take a position on the board of a Brazilian firm. This difficulty may influence decisions made by women who are on the board of directors of these firms.

Results

Univariate Analysis

Table 9.1 presents the univariate statistics of variables: earnings management (Ger_Res), the presence of women on the board (WOMAN), transparency (GRI), size of the board (BSIZE), independence of the board (INDEPENDENCE), firm size (SIZE), return on assets (ROA), leverage (LEVERAGE), economic sector activity (SECTOR), and earnings management winsorized by 2.5 per cent (WGer).

Table 9.1 shows that in the sample of this research, the board of the firm has on average five members and that they may have up to seven members. The percentage of independent members is 18 per cent. The percentage of board members who are women is 9 per cent across all the firms in the sample. The results of earnings management variable has a mean of 0.034, i.e. has a positive accrual on the analysed firms, and if it is winsorized by 2.5 per cent near 0.03. The level of the GRI is close to 27 per cent, meaning that there is little or no transparency in relation to corporate social responsibility practices. Table 9.2 contains a comparison of means for firms that do

Table 9.1 Univariate statistics of the study

Variable	Mean	SD
Ger_RES	0.034	0.351
WOMAN	0.085	0.121
GRI	0.268	0.737
BSIZE	4.660	2.840
INDEPENDENCE	0.182	0.272
SIZE	6.050	1.070
ROA	−10.900	359.000
LEVERAGE	9.180	226.000
SECTOR	2.660	1.850
WGer	0.03	0.14

Table 9.2 Univariate statistics of the study with sample comparison: firms that do and do not have women on the board

Variable	Woman = 0		Woman = 1		Total	
	Mean	SD	Mean	SD	Mean	SD
Ger_Res	0.03	0.53	−0.02	0.44	0.01	0.49
WOMAN	0.00	0.00	0.21	0.1	0.08	0.12
GRI	0.33	0.79	0.35	0.81	0.34	0.8
BSIZE	5.37	2.84	6.02	2.92	5.64	2.89
INDEPENDENCE	0.18	0.27	0.14	0.22	0.17	0.25
SIZE	6.34	0.79	6.46	0.78	6.39	0.79
ROA	0.03	0.31	0.05	0.12	0.04	0.25
LEVERAGE	0.82	1.74	0.62	0.54	0.74	1.38
SECTOR	2.66	1.80	2.68	1.88	2.67	1.83
WGer	0.03	0.13	0.02	0.16	0.02	0.14

not have presence of women on the board (Woman = 0) and with presence of women on the board (Woman = 1).

Table 9.2 shows that in the sample of this research, the firm with women on the board is a larger size with six members whereas other firms that have five members (on average). Also, the higher firm size (6.46 vs. 6.34), and the result for Ger_Res was negative (−0.02), while for firms without a presence of woman on the board has 0.03. The earnings management winsorized variable was included because it was winsorized, taking into account the effects of a possible distortion by numbers that were not within the normal distribution. When using the winsorization, it was noted that the earnings management variable was positive for both the group with a female presence and the group without women on the board.

Multivariate Analysis

The authors performed a regression with the data and random effects analysis, which is presented in Table 9.3, with the variable measuring the presence of women on the board (WOMAN) and the variables that represent the transparency (GRI), size of the board (BSIZE), independence of the board (INDEPENDENCE), firm size (SIZE), leverage (LEVERAGE), economic sector activity (SECTOR) and the year (2008, 2009 or 2010).

Table 9.3 shows that in the sample of this research, it is not possible to identify a significant relationship (R^2 = 47.16) between the presence of women on the board (WOMAN) and the earnings management (WGer) of the firm. However, there was a negative relationship between firm size (SIZE), economic sector activity (SECTOR), the year 2010 (year 2010) and earnings management for the firm. Additionally, the regression was calculated by the GMM method and the results are presented in Table 9.4, with the variable measuring the presence of women on the board (WOMAN) and the variables that represent transparency (GRI), independence of

Table 9.3 Model from the regression analysis with random effects method

Variables	Coefficient	Standard Error	P>z
WOMAN	−0.06	0.06	0.30
GRI	0.00	0.01	0.72
BSIZE	0.00	0.00	0.38
INDEPENDENCE	0.04	0.03	0.28
SIZE	−0.07***	0.01	0.00
LEVERAGE	0.00	0.02	0.97
SECTOR	−0.01**	0.00	0.04
Year 2008	0.02	0.02	0.37
Year 2009	−0.01	0.02	0.68
Year 2010	−0.08***	0.02	0.00
Constant	0.55	0.07	0.00
Wald chi²(10)	97.79		
Prob > chi²	0.0000		

Key: *Statistically significant at the level of 1%; ** Statistically significant at the level of 5%; *** Statistically significant at the level of 10%.

Table 9.4 Model from the regression analysis with GMM method

Variables	Coefficient	Std. Err.	Sig.
WOMAN	7.758**	3.581	0.032
GRI	−0.013	0.024	0.590
INDEPENDENCE	0.006	0.351	0.986
SIZE	1.106**	0.415	0.008
ROA	−0.060	0.132	0.651
LEVERAGE	−0.049	0.063	0.438
Year 2008	0.289**	0.060	0.000
Year 2009	0.190**	0.047	0.000
Year 2011	0.030	0.032	0.345
Wald chi²(10)	43.32		
Prob > chi²	0.0000		

Key: *Statistically significant at the level of 1%; ** Statistically significant at the level of 5%; *** Statistically significant at the level of 10%.

the board (INDEPENDENCE), firm size (SIZE), return on assets (ROA), leverage (LEVERAGE) and the years 2008, 2009 and 2011.

Table 9.4 shows that in the sample of this research, there is a positive and significant relationship at the 5 per cent level of significance between the presence of women on the board and earnings management of the firm in the sample. This result leads us to reject hypothesis H1, that the presence of women on the board would bring a more transparent approach to the firm's bottom line, which is what many authors have stated: Erhardt, Werbel and Shrader (2003), who identify a positive relationship between the presence of women and profitability for US firms; Ruegger and King (1992), who argue that women may be more ethical; and Barako and Brown (2008), Frías-Aceituno et al. (2012) and Prado-Lorenzo and García-Sánchez (2010), who indicate that women have a more transparent attitude than men.

However, the study confirms hypothesis H2, following the research of Scapin et al. (2013), that the presence of women on the board of the firm is not used to have women in power that can make the manipulation of results greater. The authors also found a positive and significant relationship with the years 2008 and 2009 and firm size (SIZE), indicating that larger firms tend to engage in greater manipulation of their results, because of their need to be accountable to the financial market. However, the authors did not find a relationship between earnings management (Ger_Res) and the variables that represent transparency (GRI), return on assets (ROA), leverage (LEVERAGE) and independence of the board (INDEPENDENCE).

Conclusions

The presence of women on the board of a firm has already been investigated in the accounting and financial literature. It is known from some studies detailed that gender diversity can make a good contribution towards performance, transparency and ethics, and thereby increase the value of a firm's shares (Barako and Brown, 2008; Frías-Aceituno et al., 2012; Gulzar and Wang, 2011; Prado-Lorenzo and García-Sánchez, 2010; Ruegger and King, 1992).

On the issue of earnings management, the authors could not find very much in the way of literature about the presence of women. The results, however, are still unclear. Some authors claim that the presence of women on the board makes discretionary accruals decrease, and thus decreases the firm's results (Gulzar and Wang, 2011; Wei and Xie, 2011). Other authors, such as Mohamad et al. (2010), argue that this relationship is insignificant. And still other results have shown that the presence of women on the board can increase earnings management in firms where their presence is still small or recent (Scapin et al., 2013).

This longitudinal exploratory study observed 81 firms using Brazilian accounting data available for the years 2008 to 2011, with a total of 324 observations. This showed the small participation of women on the board of the firm, with only 9 per cent of the total number of directors being women. To assess the data, the authors used two different analytical techniques for panel data: random effects and GMM. First, the random effects analysis showed no significant relationship between earnings management and the presence of women on the board. Second, the GMM analysis, which is more appropriate for capturing the relationship between variables when observing over a small time period and many firms, showed a significant positive relationship between earnings management and the presence of women on the board, confirming Hypothesis H2 and rejecting Hypothesis H1. These results are consistent with the study of Scapin et al. (2013) and they suggest that even a small number of women on the board can increase the possibility of earnings management by firms.

The limitation of this research was that it used data available from reports for the years of the observations (2008–11). Future research should use a base with a greater temporal range and include all publicly traded Brazilian firms. Also, the authors considered the presence of women on the board, rather than in the firm: their presence in the business may have another theoretical contribution, but such studies are not found in the Brazilian literature. The contribution of this work to the study of women is very important because it brings new information about a Latin American country, and even though there are few women in the administration of public firms, there are great possibilities for this in the market.

Acknowledgements

L. Segura and H. Formigoni wish to thank the MackPesquisa for their support for the project and research presented in this paper. R. Abreu and F. David wish to acknowledge the support of the Project PEst-OE/EGE/UI4056/2014a UDI/IPG, financed by the Fundação para a Ciência e Tecnologia.

References

Adams, R. and Ferreira, D. (2009), Women in the Boardroom and Their Impact on Governance and Performance. *Journal of Financial Economics* 94: 291–309.

Andres, P., Azofra, V. and López, F.J. (2005), Corporate Boards in OECD Countries: Size, Composition, Compensation, Functioning and Effectiveness. *Corporate Governance: An International Review* 13: 197–210.

Arellano, M. and Bond, S. (1991), Some Tests of Specification for Panel Data: Monte Carlo Evidence and an Application to Employment Equations. *Review of Economic Studies* 58: 277–97.

Arellano, M. and Bover, O. (1995), Another Look at the Instrumental-variable Estimation of Error-components Models. *Journal of Econometrics* 68: 29–52.

Balakrishnan, R. and Penno, M. (2013), Causality in the Context of Analytical Models and Numerical Experiments. *Accounting, Organizations and Society* 39: 531–4.

Barako, D.G. and Brown, M.A. (2008), HIV/AIDS Disclosures by Oil and Gas Companies. *Social and Environmental Accountability Journal* 28(1): 4–20.

Bathula, H. (2008), *Board Characteristics and Firm Performance: Evidence from New Zealand.* Unpublished Ph.D. thesis, Auckland University of Technology.

Bonsón, E. and Escobar, B. (2004), Voluntary Disclose of Financial Reporting on the Internet. A Comparative Worldwide Analysis. *Spanish Journal of Finance and Accounting* 33(123): 1063–1101.

Bruschini, C. and Puppin, A.B. (2004), Trabalho de mulheres executivas no Brasil no final do século XX. *Cadernos de Pesquisa* 34(121): 105–38.

Campbell, K. and Minguez-Vera, A. (2008), Gender Diversity in the Boardroom and Firm Financial Performance. *Journal of Business Ethics* 83: 435–51.

Carter, D., Simkins, B. and Simpson, W. (2003), Corporate Governance, Board Diversity, and Firm Value. *The Financial Review* 38: 33–53.

Cohn, M. (2013), Studies find Mixed Impact of Women on Corporate Boards. *Accounting Today – Debits & Credits.* Available at: http://www.accountingtoday.com/debits_credits/Studies-Find-Mixed-Impact-Women-Corporate-Boards-67497–1.html/ (Retrieved 09 May 2013).

Craven, B.M. and Marston, C.L. (1999), Financial Reporting on the Internet by Leading UK Companies. *The European Accounting Review* 8(2): 321–33.

Dechow, P.M., Sloan, R.G. and Sweeney, A.P. (1995), Detecting Earnings Management. *The Accounting Review* 70(2): 193–225.

Ding, D.K. and Charoenwong, C. (2004), Women on Board: Is it Boon or Bane?. *FMA European Conference: Research Collection Lee Kong Chian School of Business.* Available at: http://ink.library.smu.edu.sg/lkcsb_research/737/ (Retrieved 11 April 2013).

Erhardt, N., Werbel, J. and Shrader, C. (2003), Board of Director Diversity and Firm Financial Performance. *Corporate Governance: An International Review* 11: 102–10.

Farrell, K.A. and Hersch, P.L. (2005), Additions to Corporate Boards: The Effect of Gender. *Journal of Corporate Finance* 11(1–2): 85–106.

Frías-Aceituno, J.V., Rodríguez-Ariza, L. and García-Sánchez, I.M. (2012), The Role of the Board in the Dissemination of Integrated Corporate Social Reporting. *Corporate Social Responsibility and Environmental Management* 20(4): 219–33.

Gallego-Álvarez, I., García-Sánchez, I.M. and Rodríguez-Domínguez, L. (2009), Universities' Websites: Disclosure Practices and the Revelation of Financial Information. *International Journal of Digital Accounting Research* 9: 153–92.

Giner Inchausti, B., Arce Gisbert, M., Cervera Millán, N. and Ruiz llopis, A. (2003), Incentivos para la divulgación voluntaria de información: evidencia empírica sobre la información segmentada. *Revista Europea de Dirección y Economía de la Empresa* 12(4): 69–86.

Gul, F.A. and Leung, S. (2004), Board Leadership, Outside Directors' Expertise and Voluntary Corporate Disclosures. *Journal of Accounting and Public Policy* 23(5): 351–79.

Gulzar, M.A. and Wang, Z. (2011), Corporate Governance Characteristics and Earnings Management: Empirical Evidence from Chinese Listed Firms. *International Journal of Accounting and Financial Reporting* 1(1): 133–51.

Healy, P.M. and Whalen, J.M. (1999), A Review of the Earnings Management Literature and its Implications for Standard Setting. *Accounting Horizons. Sarasota* 13: 365–83.

Hili, W. and Affes, H. (2012), Corporate Boards, Gender Diversity and Earnings Persistence: The Case of French Listed Firms. *Global Journal of Management and Business Research* 12(22): 51–9.

Ibrahim, N. and Angelidis, J. (1991), Effects of Board Members' Gender on Level of Involvement in Strategic Management and Corporate Social Responsiveness Orientation. *Proceedings of the Northeast Decision Sciences Institute*, 208–10. Available at: http://bas.sagepub.com/content/40/3/266.refs (Retrieved 20 June 2013).

Johari, N.H., Mohd, S.N., Jaffar, R. and Sabri, H.M. (2008), The Influence of Board Independence, Competency and Ownership on Earnings Management in Malaysia. *Journal of Economics and Management* 2(2): 281–306.

Jones, J.J. (1991), Earnings Management During Import Relief Investigations. *Journal of Accounting Research* 29(2): 193–228.

Kang, S.H. and Sivaramakrishnan, K. (1995), Issues in Testing Earnings Management and an Instrumental Variable Approach. *Journal of Accounting Research* 33: 353–67.

Larrán, M. and Giner, B. (2002), The Use of the Internet for Corporate Reporting by Spanish Companies. *The International Journal of Digital Accounting Research* 2(1): 53–82.

Madalozzo, R. (2011), CEOs e Composição do Conselho de Administração: a falta de identificação pode ser motivo para existência de teto de vidro para mulheres no Brasil? *RAC, Curitiba* 15(1): 126–37.

Man, C., Seng, H. and Wong, B. (2013), Corporate Governance and Earnings Management: A Survey of Literature. *The Journal of Applied Business Research* 29(2): 391–418.

Marston, C. and Polei, A. (2004), Corporate Reporting on the Internet by German Companies. *International Journal of Accounting Information Systems* 5(3): 285–311.

Martinez, A.L. (2001), Gerenciamento dos resultados contábeis: estudo empírico das companhias abertas brasileiras. Doctoral dissertation, São Paulo, FEA/USP.

McNichols, M. and Wilson, G.P. (1988), Evidence of Earnings Management from the Provision for Bad Debts. *Journal of Accounting Research* 26(supplement): 1–31.

Mohamad, N.R., Abdullah, S.N., Mokhtar, M.Z. and Kamil, N.F.N. (2010), *The Effects of Board Independence, Board Diversity and Corporate Social Responsibility on Earnings Management*. Available at: http://scholar.google.com.br/scholar?hl=pt-BR&q=The+Effects+Of+Board+Independence%2C+Board+Diversity+and+Corporate+Social+Responsibility+On+Earnings+Management&btnG=&lr=/ (Retrieved 28 October 2013).

Moradi, M., Salehi, M., Bighi, S.J.H. and Najari, M. (2012), A Study of Relationship Between Board Characteristics and Earning Management: Iranian Scenario. *Universal Journal of Management and Social Sciences* 2(3): 12–29.

Niskanen, J., Karjalainen, J., Niskanen, M. and Karjalainen, J. (2011), Auditor Gender and Corporate Earning Management Behavior in Private Finnish Firms. *Managerial Auditing Journal* 26(9): 778–93.

Oyelere, P., Laswad, F. and Fisher, R. (2003), Determinants of Internet Financial Reporting by New Zealand Companies. *Journal of International Financial Management and Accounting* 14(1): 26–63.

Peni, E. and Vähäma, S. (2010), Female Executives and Earnings Management. *Managerial Finance* 36(7): 629–45. Available at: http://ssrn.com/abstract=1740665/ (Retrieved 28 October 2013).

Prado-Lorenzo, J.M. and García-Sánchez, I.M. (2010), The Role of the Board of Directors in Disseminating Relevant Information on Greenhouse Gases. *Journal of Business Ethics* 97: 391–424.

Prencipe, A. (2004), Proprietary Costs and Determinants of Voluntary Segment Disclosure: Evidence from Italian Listed Companies. *European Accounting Review* 13(2): 319–40.

Rafik, Z.A. (2002), Determinants of Earnings Management Ethics among Accountants. *Journal of Business Ethics* 40: 33–45.

Rose, C. (2007), Does Female Board Representation Influence Firm Performance? The Danish Evidence. *Corporate Governance: An International Review* 15(2): 404–13.

Ruegger, D. and King, E.W. (1992), A Study of the Effect of Age and Gender upon Student Business Ethics. *Journal of Business Ethics* 11(3): 179–86.

Scapin, M.P., García-Lara, J.M. and Penalval-Zuasti, J. (2013), *Accounting Quality Effects of Imposing Quotas on Board of Directors*. Working paper. Available at: https://aaahq.org/AM2013/abstract.cfm?submissionID=1437 (Retrieved 15 September 2013).

Schipper, K. (1989), Commentary on Earnings Management. *Accounting Horizons* December: 91–102.

Shukeri, S.N., Shin, O.W. and Shaari, M.S. (2012), Does Board of Director's Characteristics Affect Firm Performance? Evidence from Malaysian Public Listed Companies. *International Business Research* 5(9): 120–7.

Watson, J. (2002), Comparing the Performance of Male- and Female-controlled Businesses: Relating Outputs to Inputs. *Entrepreneurship Theory and Practice* 26(3): 91–100.

Wei, Z. and Xie, F.F. (2011), *CFO Gender and Earnings Management: Evidence from China*. Available at: http://www.fma.org/Hamburg/Papers/wei_xie_efma2010.pdf/ (Retrieved 10 February 2013).

Xiong, Y. (2006), Earnings Management and its Measurement: A Theoretical Perspective. *The Journal of American Academy of Business* 9(1): 214–19.

Chapter 10

Women in Top Management

Zorka Grandov, Verica Jovanović and Maja Đokić

Introduction

Nowadays we face dynamic and diffuse changes that cannot be stopped and that profoundly alter all spheres of social life: economic, social, ecological, political and many others, and they influence almost every individual. If we want to fit into these new trends we must change our approach, i.e. we must apply a wide range of new ideas and solutions to deal with new, uncertain conditions effectively and rationally. In such conditions, it is easier for women, who tend to have the natural instinct of self-preservation, to find more adequate answers to the problems that the world is facing today. The characteristics typical for women, such as, on the one hand, enthusiasm, determination and openness to innovation and, on the other, rationality, devotion and responsibility, make women suitable for the role of leaders in a crisis. However, their abilities are underutilized, although it is obvious that countries that have noticed the potential of women's capital as a growing resource of social fortune, have a competitive advantage compared to those countries that have failed to exploit this potential. Generally, the position of women worldwide has been improving rapidly in the last few decades. They are more educated and can be found in many social, political and economic positions, but advances in the occupation of top management positions are the slowest as far as the number of women is concerned. There are different opinions about this, and in this chapter we try to solve this problem and to help women, who now have a better education, are more active and evidently very successful in many roles which used to be reserved only for men, get the chance to prove themselves even in the most responsible functions.

Tendencies in Changing the Position of Women in the World

For decades a huge number of scientists and research institutions have been interested in the position of women in the world from different viewpoints: there are many articles on this topic and many published reports. However, when we want to find concrete conclusions from a vast amount of data available as far as the number and position of women in the world are concerned, we find only huge numbers of statistical data which can, sometimes, be contradictory. The problem is caused by scientific and professional institutions who conduct research using different methodologies and analysing data which they source from heterogeneous research samples, and it is very difficult to make generalized conclusions from such a diversity (Hausman, 2011).[1] On the one hand, it is indisputable that the data show that the gap between men and women is decreasing; on the other hand, there are many fields with huge workplace disparities between the genders.

According to the methodology of the World Economic Forum, chosen as a referential for collecting secondary data in this article, the gap between the genders is observed taking into consideration four factors: political influence, economic participation, education and accessibility to health maintenance. The results of the last research presented at this Forum in 2011 showed that almost all the countries analysed, approximately 200 of them, had in the last six years made an advance as far as the gap between genders is concerned in all four observed fields. The greatest progress was achieved in health and educational fields, where very high levels of equality have been gained, although there are huge differences in the economic and, especially, in the political field.

As can be seen from the above, it is obvious that the political field is the least accessible to women. If we take into account the women in the highest state positions as being presidents and ministers and their number in national parliaments, we can conclude that there are not many countries in which women have an important political role. According to this criterion, only three countries have an index higher than 0.5: Iceland (0.69), Finland (0.61) and Norway (0.56); many developed countries, amongst which are the US (0.18), France (0.17), Luxembourg (0.17), Italy (0.15), and others, have less than 20 per cent of women in high state positions in comparison to men, and in Japan this index is 0.07. It is obvious that this field is not easily given to women by men, so women should, at the beginning alone or with the help of the non-governmental sector (since the state sector is in the hands of men), fight energetically if they want to have a greater role in deciding the destiny of their own countries. Thanks to this initiative there are new regulations in some European countries[2] which oblige those countries to have proportional representation of women in national parliaments.

Apart from politics, in the field of health care many countries have achieved equality of both genders: in 40 countries there is 100 per cent equality, and almost all of the countries had an index higher than 0.95,[3] i.e. more than 95 per cent equality. The parameters examined in this field are the equality of genders at birth, the length of their 'healthy' life, and accessibility to health care. Even countries with evident economic, political and social problems succeeded in making all their inhabitants equal in this field.

Education is the field in which the gender gap is insignificant, and if there were any huge differences, they were resolved quickly. If all educational levels from primary to tertiary are observed statistically we see that many countries gained complete or almost complete equality in education of both genders, and that over 95 per cent of countries have an index higher than 0.8 in this field: 23 countries have an index of 1. Today more women than men from many developed countries enrol at university. In some mostly Scandinavian countries the ratio of students at the tertiary level of education is 1.5 for women and 1 for men. More women choose to be educated in technical studies or other sciences that used to be the sole province of men. There are more and more women in university education and they are becoming more a competent working class with an important role in economic and social development in their countries.[4]

Economic participation and opportunity is very important and will be analysed in detail later: certainly it is a field in which men are more dominant than women. There are more men employed in this field, with higher wages, it is easier for them to get a job and to advance and there are more men in managerial positions. It is true that nowadays women take over many areas in which men used to be dominant and there are more women in many prestigious professions as a result of the many changes in their educational structure. However, in all countries (apart from Slovenia) they still have lower wages than men (House of Commons Treasury Committee, 2010: 9) and face many obstacles when they want to advance in their career.

When economic inequality is examined, we see, contrary to expectations, that the most developed countries are not the leading countries in equality: the top four positions are for the Bahamas (0.91), Lesotho (0.87), Mongolia (0.85) and Burundi (0.84), and of the most developed countries only Norway has an index slightly higher than 0.8, while Japan is on the lower third of the list with an index of 0.56. It is also characteristic that there is a steady wage gap between genders and the gap is increasing in many developed countries, while in those countries that are still developing there is a tendency for inequality to lessen. However, it should be emphasized that although they do not have the leading position in an overall score, the Nordic countries, according to many variables that compose sub indexes of economic equality and in the field of economic equality, surpass most other countries. It is because the Nordic countries have a high women labour force participation rate, relatively low disparity in wages, higher possibilities for advancement and the availability of logistic services which allow women who are also mothers to work.

To fully understand the economic role of women in the world, it is important to analyse how many of them work in the sphere of the economy as the carriers of business, i.e. the owners of economy subjects. There are no precise data considering the number of women in the world who own their own firms, because this category can be easily changed and there are no systematic records of the number of those firms or the changes in their number. According to data given by GEM Consortium, as the institution which for many years has analysed the tendencies in the field of the entrepreneur in the world through a chosen group of approximately 60 countries, the number of women business owners has risen from 1.4 per cent to 45.4 per cent, depending on the observed country, and that number is steadily growing (Kelley et al., 2010).

The ratio between male and female entrepreneurs differs throughout the world, from 1:5 in Korea and Japan to 6:5 in Ghana. This means that general macro conditions have nothing to do with the decisions of women to become entrepreneurs, since in economically strong South Korea for each firm opened by a woman there are five opened by men, while in Ghana the tendency is the opposite: for five firms opened by men there are six opened by women. However, on average in most countries there are more men than women entrepreneurs. The exceptions are Australia and the US, where both genders are almost equal, then Mexico, Malaysia, China and others, while in Norway only one-quarter of entrepreneurs are women, and in Denmark even fewer.

However, there is a growing number of female entrepreneurs in the world and they have more courage to enter the market struggle, especially in countries with intensive economic prosperity. The problems that they often face are barriers which are given, in entrepreneur theory, in the numbers 100 and 1,000,000 (100 employed people and 1 million dollars of income). Recently, women entrepreneurs cannot reach the threshold of money/staff but there are examples, mostly from China, Russia and others, showing that women can be in bigger businesses.

If we want to analyse the global economic influence and importance on both the national and the world's economy of the number of women entrepreneurs, we should consider the example of the US. In 2011 there were 8.1 million private firms owned by women in the US (29 per cent of the overall number of all private subjects). The incomes of these firms were almost US$1.3 billion, and the number of employed people was about 7.7 million. These figures are very impressive as far as less developed countries are concerned, but if the data are compared with the whole American economy, the women entrepreneurs earned only 4.1 per cent of the national income and they employed only 6 per cent of working people (American Express, 2011). This is not because women are not successful as the firms' owners, but rather that most incomes are made by huge public and multinational companies. Their number is not more than 3 per cent of all firms, but they employ 53 per cent of workers and make 64 per cent of all state income.

According to these data it is logical to conclude that encouraging entrepreneurs is useful for the growth of a national economy, although the huge incomes are made by the biggest companies. It can also be concluded that if we want to give women more space in the economy, it would be logical to give those who are most talented and competent the opportunity to demonstrate their knowledge in leading positions in big firms.

The Presence of Women in Top Management

We said earlier that although there is a great deal of inequality, the presence of women in all fields of social life is constantly growing. The main reasons for this are the growth of general educational and working competence of women, and governments' awareness that treating women as equal to men will strengthen their economic and political powers. Because of this, there are more women present in many well-paid and professionally challenging professions. Today there are more women working in finance, medicine and education, and there are a growing number of women in sectors that used to be reserved only for men: informatics and energy. However, although nowadays there are more highly qualified working women, the percentage of women in the highest positions in the largest companies is very low (Governance Metrics International, 2010: 3). Even here, as in many fields of gender equality, the most successful are the Nordic countries: Norway, Finland and Sweden, although according to geographical regions, there are the best results in North America, then Europe, and after that the Near East and Asia (Table 10.1). It is certain that women are not equally present in all business sectors. Most of them are on the boards of firms dealing with services, i.e. those that are closest to their customers (health care, finances, commerce), and the lowest numbers are in energy and informatics technologies.

In this chapter we are trying to find out if companies with women as their leaders work better economically. Numerous institutions research the effect of women being on the leading boards of big companies, but the research results vary. Positive results came from McKinsey, Catalyst, the World Bank and many other institutions.

Table 10.1 Number of women in leading boards of companies in percentages

Regions	Number of women on boards				Total
	0	1	2	3	
North America	15.8	32.4	33.1	18.7	100
Europe	16.3	27.4	28.7	27.6	100
EMEA[5]	34.7	26	20	19.3	100
Latin America	60.8	28	8.8	2.4	100
Developed Asia	68	19.8	9.4	2.8	100
Emerging Asia	72.1	15.8	7.3	4.8	100
Average	44.62	24.9	17.8	12.6	100.00

Source: Curtis, Schmid and Struber, 2011: 9.

In opposition to this view, Adams and Ferreira and Hersch (2009) claim that there is no connection between more women in leading positions and better results for their companies, and that their companies worked economically better because their success was predetermined. The reason for the opposing results is that the research and analysis involved only a small number of firms chosen as the representative research sample.

They also observed firms only in one country (for example, the UK) or in a specific geographical region (Europe, North America). To overcome these differences in results, as stated before, the most important facts as far as economic work of firms with the women in leading structures is concerned, will be the results from the gender gap report presented at the World Economic Forum in 2011. This report gives economic results for around 2,400 companies from different regions of the world that are rated on the stock market. The firms are divided into two groups: in the first there are companies with a market cap more than US$10 billion dollars, while in the second group there are companies with the market cap that is lower than that of the first group. The key result from this research is that companies with at least one woman in their leading structure had greater growth in their stock prices than those who did not have women in high positions. The bigger growth rate had companies with a market cap higher than US$10 billion dollars – 26 per cent – while the growth of stock prices of the companies with market capitalization[6] was lower at 17 per cent.

If we examine Table 10.1 carefully, we can conclude that there are different trends in the stock price movements of selected firms in the period from 2005 to 2007, i.e. in the period before the world economic crisis of 2008 and afterwards from 2008 to 2011. When the general economic situation was stable, there was only a slight difference in stock prices and/or the firms with only men leading them had better results. In the period of crisis, the firms with both men and women leading them had better results. The detailed analysis of these firms showed that they had better balance in their cycles, with stable growth of income and less debt, so the market trusted them and their stock prices grew.

While examining the causes for the success of these companies, it was possible to draw some assumptions which should additionally be checked in practice. One of these assumptions is that the main reason for the success of these companies is not only in the contribution of women as individuals, but in the presence of both genders and their different approaches and thoughts which create an environment in which decisions are made more effectively and creatively. This statement is based on the assumption that people in different groups think more actively and critically about problems that they should solve, making it easier for them to create new ideas (Watson, Kumar and Michaelsen, 1993). There is also the flip side to this because of potential conflicts and tension, but it is proven that this is a problem at the beginning of the working relationship that can be overcome in time and that the people in groups consisting of both genders become very constructive and successful associates.

The necessity to create non-homogeneous leading structures was recognized by many countries a long time ago, and some have tried to oblige companies by law to employ more women in high positions. For example, in Norway 40 per cent of staff in leading boards in companies must be women. The governments of many other countries have passed a law, or are about to pass one, which obliges firms to employ more women than they used to. However, this law is often violated because many companies do not want to organize their leading teams by quota. They claim that a successful leader should have huge work experience and proven positive results on previous leading positions in order to obtain the highest position in their boards. Women with such references and extensive working experience in leading positions are hard to find, because they have only recently started to gain the highest leading positions, and could not have that level of experience.

There are many talented women who are capable of being successful leaders, but they do not fit into stereotypes by which successful top managers are selected. We can only hope that companies will more carefully analyse the signs that are apparent in the previous period of crisis when many thus far successful leaders brought their firms to bankruptcy, while women were mostly successful as the leaders of some companies. Perhaps those signs will make companies think carefully when choosing their leaders in future.

Conclusion

If our starting point is that women are scientifically proven to be as skilful as men as far as the professional and quality performance of the most complex leading jobs are concerned, and bearing in mind that women are rapidly enlarging their educational competence, it is a fact that there is a vast amount of unused human capital. If this is not used in economic and social flows, especially today when the world is in economic crisis, it is a huge loss for society. Countries with wise national politicians try to use their social capital to maximum effect. In some countries there are legal obligations for the state institutions and economic organizations to have requisite proportions in gender structure on leading positions.

Such solutions show in practice changeable effectiveness as far as the growth in the number of women in leadership is concerned; however, it is also proven that countries which have more women in top positions have better economic results. Since the majority of these countries are the most developed ones, there is a dilemma as to whether economic effectiveness is better in these countries because women are better leaders than men in high position or because, as all wise leaders would do, they simply used the favourable general macroeconomic conditions in their environment to lead their organizations successfully and improve their effectiveness and competing position.

No matter which of the two previous answers is correct, women in top positions have proven that they can deal with the most responsible tasks and problems, and that in the most complex conditions they can make effective decisions to save the position of their organizations. It is also proven by scientific research that after 2008 in a period of crisis, companies with female leaders had better economic results and secured a better position for their firms in the market. The reason for this success could lie in women's intuition, as well as in their inventiveness. These features, together with women's hostility towards unreasonable risk, make it possible for women to make the right decisions in critical situations. It is logical to conclude that those countries that do not want to use their capital, i.e. the growing number of women who are competent to perform the most responsible roles, are behaving irresponsibly, and allowing an asset to be wasted irretrievably.

Notes

1 For the concrete review of the position of women in the world, data used most in this article are from the World Economic Forum and publication Global Report *Women's Report 2010*, published by Global Entrepreneurship Monitor (Kelley et al., 2011), as well as a few additional research reports of renowned world research and consultative institutes. The reports used are chosen as referential mainly because of the wide range of population researched and consistent use of methodological principles in analysing and showing the gained results.
2 It is important to emphasize that some Scandinavian countries in the 1970s introduced voluntary gender quotas as far as the number of women in parliament was concerned, with the result that there are more than 45 per cent of women representatives in the parliaments of these countries. Some countries, such as Denmark, cancelled this recommendation as they felt it was unnecessary. Canada and the Philippines set themselves a goal of 40 per cent of women in administrative committees.
3 The index score can have a value from 0.00 to 1.00. An index of 1.00 means the equality of genders in the observed field, while the index 0.00 means the complete domination of men, i.e. no women participants.
4 Modern research on human intelligence shows that both genders made some improvements in brain functions, but women have developed more than men and now women's intelligence is equal to men's or even more developed. The causes for this are the obligations imposed on women in modern of life where they have to solve few problems from different fields simultaneously. Kathy Matsui in Bloomberg Business Week, "The Economic Benefits of Educating Women." *Bloomberg Business Week*, 7 March 2013, www.bloomberg.com/.../the-economic-benefits-of-educating-
5 This is a comprehensive list of East Europe, Middle East and African countries.
6 Market capitalization refers to the value of a company's outstanding shares. Market Capitalization = Current Stock Price × Shares Outstanding.

References

Adams, B. Renee and Ferreira, D. (2009), Women in the Boardroom and Their Impact on Governance and Performance. *Journal of Financial Economics* 94: 291–309.

American Express. (2011), The American Express OPEN, State of Women-Owned Businesses Report. *A Summary of Important Trends, 1997–2011*. Available at: https://c401345.ssl.cf1.rackcdn.com/ (Retrieved 31 December 2011).

Curtis, M., Schmid, C. and Struber, M. (2011), *Gender Diversity and Corporate Performance*. Geneva: Credit Suisse.

GovernanceMetrics International. (2010), *Women on Boards, A Statistical Review by Country, Supersector and Sector.* Available at: http://www.gmiratings.com/hp/Women_on_Boards_March_2010.pdf (Retrieved 10 December 2011).

Hausman, R., Tyson, L. and Zahidi, S. (2011), *The Global Gender Gap Report 2011.* Zurich: World Economic Forum.

House of Commons Treasury Committee (UK). (2010), *Women in the City: Tenth Report of Session 2009–10.* London: HMSO.

Kelley, D., Brush, C., Greene, P. and Litovsky, Y. (2010), *Report: Women Entrepreneurs Worldwide 2010.* Wellesley, MA: Babson College and the Global Entrepreneurship Research Association (GERA).

———. (2011), *Global Entrepreneurship Monitor, 2010 Women's Report, Women Entrepreneurs Worldwide.* Wellesley, MA: Babson College, Babson Park. Available at: http://www.gemconsortium. org/docs/download/768 (Retrieved 18 October 2011).

Watson, W.E., Kumar, K. and Michaelsen, L.K. (1993), Cultural Diversity's Impact on Interaction Process and Performance: Comparing Homogeneous and Diverse Task Groups. *Academy of Management Journal* 36: 590–602.

Chapter 11

Sexual Harassment in the Workplace

New Forms of Discrimination Based on Sex in EU Law

Biljana Chavkoska

Introduction: An Overview of Gender Equality Legislation in the European Union

The European Union (EU) was created as an economic union, but through the years it has expanded its competences in the area of human rights law. This area is covered by the founding treaties and os treaties that amend existing legislation, such as the case law by the European Court of Justice. The European Union has created minimum standard procedures for protecting human rights.

From the first the EU adopted important primary and secondary law for gender equality. The European Court of Justice played an important role in promoting gender equality and equal opportunities among all EU citizens. In recent years the European Court of Justice has issued over 50 judgments further consolidating the legal framework on equal opportunities of women and men.

The treaty for creating the European Economic Community had only one article, 119, as a legal base for the member states to implement equal pay for equal work. In the EU context the greatest achievement for protecting human rights was the adoption of the Treaty of Amsterdam. Gender equality particularly is important: article 2 states that 'gender equality is one of the goals of the European Union' and article 3 has a new paragraph 2 which specifies that '[in] all EU activities, the Community has to eliminate inequalities between women and men and to promote gender equality' (OJ C350 10/11/1997).[1] Article 141 regulates equal opportunities in matters of employment and occupation, including the principle of equal pay for equal work or work of equal value.

New article 13 of the Amsterdam Treaty extends the list for prohibiting discrimination: in addition to gender, new legal bases are race or ethnic origin, religion or belief, invalidity, age and sexual orientation. The Treaty of Amsterdam significantly enhanced the primary law by giving the Community's legislative body a specific legal basis to take action in the area of equal opportunities and equal treatment for women and men.

Regarding secondary law, the Council of Ministers adopted Directives for equal treatment between women and men in the workplace. The most important Directives for gender equality are those for equal pay (European Commission [1975], OJ L45/19) (75/117/EEC), Directive 76/207/EEC on the implementation of the principle of equal treatment for men and women as regards access to employment, vocation training, and promotion and working conditions, (European Commission

[1976], OJ L39/40) Directive 2002/73/EC (European Commission [2002], OJ L269, 5 October) amending Council Directive 76/207/EEC, Directive 86/613/EEC on the application of the principle of equal treatment between women and men engaged in activity, including agriculture in a self-employed capacity, and on the protection of self-employed women during pregnancy and motherhood, (OJ L359, 11 December 1986) and Directive 2006/54/EC on the implementation of the principle of equal opportunities and equal treatment of men and women in matters of employment and occupation (European Commission [2006], OJ L204/23, 26 July 2006).

Council Directive 76/207/EEC is the foundation of EU law and policy in the area of gender equality in employment. As amended in 2002, the Equal Treatment Directive states that

> the principle of equal treatment means that there shall be no direct or indirect discrimination on the grounds of sex in the public or private sectors, including public bodies, in relation to conditions for access to employment, vocational guidance and training, employment and working conditions, including dismissal and membership in organizations of workers or employers.
>
> (European Commission, 1976)

In the area of social security, Council Directive 96/97/EC amends Directive 86/378/EEC on the implementation of the principle of equal treatment for men and women in occupational social security schemes, Council Directive 92/85/EEC deals with the introduction of measures to encourage improvements in the safety and health at work of pregnant workers and workers who have recently given birth or are breastfeeding, Directive 79/7/EEC introduces the progressive implementation of the principle of equal treatment for men and women in matters of social security were adopted.

For the very first time the 2002 amendment to the Equal Treatment Directive, Directive 2002/73/EC (European Commission, 2002), introduces the concepts of harassment related to sex and sexual harassment and states that they are forms of discrimination in violation of the equal treatment principle.

EU Directive 2006/54/EC is a recast Directive that puts previous Directives and case law on equal treatment for women and men in employment into one single text. The Directive characterizes sexual harassment as both a form of sex discrimination and a violation of the dignity of workers in the workplace.

The EU Directives are legally binding for member states, but they require the adoption of implementing measures on a national level. EU member states were required to adopt implementing legislation meeting the objectives described in Directive 2002/73/EC by 5 October 2005. Member states were obligated to adopt national legislation in accordance with EU Directive 2006/54/EC definition of sexual harassment by August 2008.

There are no Treaty provisions specifically addressing violence against women and trafficking of women within the EU. The European Commission has indicated that the prevention of and fight against domestic violence falls mainly under local and national competencies and member states should follow up developments by using the set of indicators on violence agreed by the Council of Ministers.[2]

This chapter aims to analyse the effect of Directive 2002/73/EC in the national law of member states as the first binding EU law against sexual harassment, to consider what constitutes good practice, and to point out the weaknesses of the Directive and to make future recommendations for member states.

EU Sexual Harassment Definitions

Public awareness of the issue of sexual harassment was raised in the United States and the term *sexual harassment* was brought to the world in 1990. Although Europeans were often sceptical about the relevance of the issue to their lives, surveys report that about the same percentage of women in EU member states and in the United States have experienced sexual harassment at work.

It took years for the EU to adopt a legal framework for the prevention of gender-based harassment, even though the research taken in the member states showed that this was a serious problem for women workers. The European Commission reports that almost 30 to 50 per cent of women workers are facing sexual harassment, compared with 10 per cent of the male population who are usually sexually abused by other men. Women workers who experienced sexual harassment in the workplace testified to the psychological and physical pain for the victims which can also result in the loss of jobs.

There have been several scandals involving men accused of harassment. The British Crown has been in the news twice regarding allegations of sexual harassment among the staff. Most recently, Elaine Day, 45 years old and a former personal assistant who worked in Prince Charles's household for four years, resigned and filed a sexual harassment and unfair dismissal suit, testifying that her dismissal was a retaliation for her complaint of 'inappropriate touching' by the Prince's assistant private secretary Paul Kefford. She said that she felt threatened by Kefford and that he had sexually harassed two other staff members.

The EU has been a major force in putting sexual harassment on the agenda of its member states and has created a new way of addressing sexual harassment in the workplace due to the historical tradition of workers' rights and protection of vulnerable groups. This time harassment and sexual harassment is addressed in the broader context of violations against workers' dignity. Before the Directive 2002/73/EC was adopted the EU introduced several important soft law instruments. The European Parliament Resolution of 1986 on violence against women, the 1990 Council Resolution on the protection of the dignity of women and men at work, the 1991 Commission Recommendation on protecting the dignity of women and men at work with its annexed Code of Practice, the 1991 Council Declaration on the implementation of the Commission's recommendation and Code of Practice, the 1993 Guide to implementing the Commission's Code of Practice, the European Parliament Resolution of 1994 on a new post of a confidential counsellor at the workplace, Third Action Programme for equal opportunities for women and men for the period 1991 to 1995, and the action programmes for equal opportunities for men and women adopted by the Council all emphasize the need for decisive action to combat sexual harassment (http://ec.europa.eu/justice/gender-equality/).

During this period there was a considerable difference in the legal definition of sexual harassment in the member states. For example Belgium, Ireland and the Netherlands, using EU soft law instruments, brought the most far-reaching legal reforms against sexual harassment, compared to Greece and Portugal, where the authorities ignore the sexual harassment issue. Despite some legal reforms in the early 1990s, implementation and enforcement mechanisms have thus far have been less effective than in the United States.

The definitions in Directive 2002/73/EC were adopted as a result of the activity of feminist organizations, such as from the French Association contre les Violences Faites au Travail (AVFT), British Woman against Sexual Harassment (WASH) and Danish Handen, and from scientific and social research workers, members of trade unions, lawyers and representatives from the state institutions, who created institutional changes in the European Union that open the door for legal change.

In the Code of Practice on the protection of the dignity of women and men at work, *sexual harassment* is defined as unwanted conduct of a sexual nature, or other conduct based on sex affecting the dignity of women and men at work, including the conduct of superiors and colleagues, which is unacceptable and may, in certain circumstances, be contrary to the principle of equal treatment; conduct of a sexual nature, or other conduct based on sex affecting the dignity of women and men at work, including conduct of superiors and colleagues, is unacceptable if:

a   such conduct is unwanted, unreasonable and offensive to the recipient;
b   a person's rejection of, or submission to, such conduct on the part of employers or workers (including superiors or colleagues) is used explicitly or implicitly as a basis for a decision which affects that person's access to vocational training, access to employment, continued employment, promotion, salary or any other employment decisions; and/or
c   such conduct creates an intimidating, hostile or humiliating work environment for the recipient (Commission code of practice on sexual harassment, Official Journal L49 of 24 February 1992).

EU Directive 2002/73/EC defines two forms of harassment: harassment related to sex and harassment of a sexual nature. Harassment (non-sexual) is defined as: 'where an unwanted conduct related to the sex of a person occurs with the purpose or effect of violating the dignity of a person, and of creating an intimidating, hostile, degrading, humiliating or offensive environment'. This definition of harassment related to sex is the same as the harassment definitions included in the earlier adopted Council Directive 2000/43/EC (European Commission [2000a], OJ L180/22) of 29 June 2000 implementing the principle of equal treatment between persons irrespective of racial or ethnic origin and the Council Directive 2000/78/EC (European Commission [2000b], OJ L303/16) of 27 November 2000 establishing a general framework for equal treatment in employment and occupation. Together, these three Directives prohibit harassment in the workplace that is related to sex, religion or belief, disability, age, sexual orientation, race and ethnic origin so long as the conduct is unwanted; its purpose or effect is to violate the dignity of a person and it creates an intimidating, hostile, degrading, humiliating or offensive environment.

Sexual harassment is defined as 'any form of unwanted verbal, non-verbal or physical conduct of a sexual nature occurs, with the purpose or effect of violating the dignity of a person, in particular when creating an intimidating, hostile, degrading, humiliating or offensive environment'. This definition reflects the definition of sexual harassment adopted by the EU Commission in 1991 in its recommended Code of Practice on sexual harassment. This concept of harassment is also similar to that under United States law, examples of which are unwanted sexual comments, touching and propositions.

It is important to note that the Directive prohibits both 'quid pro quo' and 'hostile work environment' harassment. Hostile work environment harassment related to sex and of a sexual nature is addressed in the definitions described above with the reference to the creation of 'an intimidating, hostile, degrading, humiliating or offensive environment'. In connection with the definitions of harassment and sexual harassment, the Directive clarifies that harassment or sexual harassment may not be used as a basis for a decision affecting that person (Magurová, 2008).

There are several important elements that arise from the definitions included in the Directive 2002/73/EC. Sexual harassment is defined as a form of sex discrimination. Member states are required to establish national bodies for the enforcement of equal opportunities. This is a wide definition of sexual harassment which means that in practice victims can subjectively define what sexual harassment in the workplace means based on their own country. This is very important because Directive 2002/73/EC defines sexual harassment from the victim's perspective as 'unwanted conduct'. The purpose of the harasser would not be valued for the case law.

Directive 2002/73/EC requires employees in member states, in accordance with their national law, collective agreements, and practice, to take measures for elimination of all forms of gender discrimination, particularly harassment and sexual harassment in the workplace. The Directive requires member states in national laws to provide legal procedures for victims of sexual harassment on the workplace, which should be available even after their contract agreement has ended. Directive 2002/73/EC forbids member states from capping compensation or reparation to victims of discrimination, including harassment or sexual harassment, except in 'cases where the employer can prove that the only damage suffered by an applicant as a result of discrimination within the meaning of the Directive is the refusal to take his/her job application into consideration.'

EU Directive 2006/54/EC (European Commission, 2006) on the implementation of the principle of equal opportunities and equal treatment of men and women in matters of employment and occupation (recast version) defines harassment and sexual harassment as follows:

- Harassment – where unwanted conduct related to the sex of a person occurs with the purpose or effect of violating the dignity of a person, and of creating an intimidating, hostile, degrading, humiliating or offensive environment (European Commission [2006], Article 2/1/c).
- Sexual harassment – where any form of unwanted verbal, non-verbal or physical conduct of a sexual nature occurs, with the purpose or effect of violating the dignity of a person, in particular when creating an intimidating, hostile, degrading, humiliating or offensive environment (European Commission [2006], Article 2/1/d).

Council Directive 97/80/EC of 15 December 1997 on the burden of proof in cases of discrimination based on sex regulates that member states shall take such measures to ensure that, when persons who consider themselves wronged because the principle of equal treatment has not been applied to them establish before a court or other competent authority, facts from which it may be presumed that there has been direct or indirect discrimination, it shall be for the respondent to prove that there has been no breach of the principle of equal treatment. The Directive switches the burden of proof onto the respondent, so in practical terms it is easier for the plaintiff to prove discrimination.

The Weaknesses of Directive 2002/73/EC for Equal Treatment

Directive 2002/73/EC marked important steps towards legally defining harassment and sexual harassment but also creates obstacles. The definition for sexual harassment does not specify if only harassment during work time is covered, or also includes outside work, during work parties, professional travelling or private parties. The Directive does not apply to health care services or households so additional legal Acts are necessary.

Member states must also encourage employers and those responsible for vocational training to institute preventive measures to protect against harassment and sexual harassment in the workplace. The fact that member states have a discretionary right to implement the preventive measures means that they will vary from country to country. This inconsistency in sexual harassment policy in the member states could prevent the victims from using legal procedures, especially the work agreement. The victims would fear the loss of their jobs and other repercussions when processing cases against sexual harassment. Usually they decide to use their rights after losing the job or finishing the contract agreement, and it is important that the internal laws of member states are strengthened to protect the position of victims of sexual harassment.

A few member states, in accordance with their legislative and institutional capacities, require employers to provide educational programmes for raising the awareness of workers' rights. The Directive allows for non-governmental organizations and trade unions to take part in the legal procedures either on behalf of or in support of discrimination complainants, with their approval, in any judicial and/or administrative procedure provided for the enforcement of obligations under the Directive.

The Practices and Recommendations for the EU Member States

All member states have brought in national laws against sexual harassment in the workplace. Most countries have included explicit definitions in employment legislation, while Estonia, Italy, Spain and the United Kingdom deal with it implicitly. Greece and Latvia were the last two countries to adopt laws against sexual harassment in the workplace. Codes of Practice dealing with sexual harassment/harassment based on sex are in place in 11 member states (Austria, Finland, Ireland, Italy, Malta, Lithuania, Luxembourg, Netherlands, Slovenia, Spain and the United Kingdom). In Ireland and the United Kingdom the Code of Practice can be taken into account by tribunals. Codes of Practice cover verbal, non-verbal and physical activities.

In the member states there is little consistency of practice in relation to bodies to which complaints of work-related sexual harassment can be brought and the associated support mechanisms and remedies.

According the *Report on Sexual Harassment in the Workplace in the EU Member States*, the best practices for financial compensation awarded by courts in respect of sexual harassment/ harassment based on sex are in Ireland and the United Kingdom. The highest award described was £1.37 million sterling (in the United Kingdom) and £30,000 in Ireland. It is important that in the future member states show how often sexual harassment at the workplace occurs and to what extent employees are able to report work-related sexual harassment (benchmarking indicators). There is an urgent need to collect statistical information about preventive policy and sanctions and conduct research to get more insight into variables influencing sexual harassment at work.

For example, in Slovakia the European anti-discrimination legislation was incorporated into the Labour Code, Employment Act and Services Act. The transposition finished with the adoption of the Anti-Discrimination Act in 2004. In the Czech Republic EU anti-discrimination legislation was incorporated into national law. The Czech Republic has ratified all the instruments for combating discrimination in the two main international human rights systems, the United Nations and the Council of Europe, including the UNESCO Convention against Discrimination in Education, International Labour Organization Convention No. 111 and the International Convention on the Elimination of All Forms of Racial Discrimination. The country is also a party to the European Convention for the Protection of Human Rights and Fundamental Freedoms, the International Covenant on Civil and Political Rights and the International Covenant on Economic, Social and Cultural Rights. The national legal system is framed by the Czech Constitution, which refers to the Charter of Fundamental Rights and Freedoms of the Czech Republic as a part of its constitutional provisions. Of the new member states, in Bulgaria the Protection against Discrimination Act 2004 is the main anti-discrimination legislation, which was enacted in order to incorporate EC equality Directives. It is a single equality law universally banning discrimination on a range of grounds, explicitly including race/ethnicity, sex, religion/belief, sexual orientation, disability and age, and providing uniform standards of protection and remedies.

The European Network of Legal Experts in the Non-discrimination Field was set up in order to provide the Commission with independent information and advice on the transposition of the Directives into national law, their practical implementation, the national initiatives in the field of anti-discrimination legislation and related policy developments, the impact of national court rulings that have the effect of establishing jurisprudence on the level of protection against discrimination provided by national law, the potential conformity of national developments with the requirements of Community law and the impact of judgments of the European Court of Justice and the European Court of Human Rights on national law (McGolgan, 2004).

Case Study: The Republic of Macedonia

The Constitution of the Republic of Macedonia (Constitution of Macedonia, 1991) is a written Constitution and the country's highest legal Act. It accepts international law as part of domestic law, making international law higher than domestic laws and bylaws. Article 118 of the Macedonian Constitution regulates that the international agreements ratified in compliance with the Constitution and the national laws are part of the internal legal order and thus could not be subject to amendment. The

Constitution provides for protection against discrimination. It upholds equality of the citizens before the Constitution and before law, stating that citizens of the Republic of Macedonia are equal in their freedoms and rights, regardless of gender, race, colour, national and social origin, political and religious conviction, property and social status. It foresees a protection mechanism for all who find their human rights and freedoms breached, in front of the Constitutional court. Upholding the monism principle on application of international law (Brindusa, 2007), the Constitution provides for the domestic use of these documents, thus also for those providing for protection against non-discrimination and upholding the principle of equality.

In April 2010, the Anti-Discrimination Law (Official Gazette No. 50/2010), the first comprehensive legislation on anti-discrimination, was adopted in the process of approximation of the domestic legislation with the EU *acquis*. This law does not comply with the Directives regarding minimum protected grounds, definitions and forms of discrimination, victimization, effective, proportionate and dissuasive sanctions, use of statistical data or dialogue with the NGO sector. The equality body established with the law cannot be seen as meeting the requirements of Directive 2000/43 (European Commission, 2000a). The Anti-Discrimination Law protects on the following grounds: colour, gender, belonging to a marginalized group, ethnic affiliation, language, citizenship, social origin, education, political affiliation, personal or social status, family or marital status, property ownership and health condition, or any other ground foreseen by law or a ratified international treaty.

The Anti-Discrimination Law is applicable in both the private and the public sector and applies to all fields. The law notes that specific attention should be paid to the fields of employment and working relations, membership of and involvement in trade unions, political parties, NGOs, foundations, and other membership organizations, social security, including social protection, pensions and disability insurance, health insurance and healthcare, education, access to goods and services and housing. Thus this law goes beyond the Directives. Other laws also include discrimination provisions, defining the material scope. In the field of employment, aside from the Anti-Discrimination Law, there is also the Labour Law which prohibits discrimination in all aspects listed in the Directives. These apply both to the public and private sector.

The Anti-Discrimination Law provided for the establishment of the first equality body in the country, a Commission on Protection against Discrimination. Its members were elected in December 2010, and it started functioning in 2011. The Commission works on cases of discrimination covered by the Anti-Discrimination Law. These grounds are sex, race, colour of skin, gender, belonging to a marginalized group, ethnicity, language, citizenship, social origin, religion or religious belief, other sorts of belief, education, political affiliation, personal or social status, mental or physical disability, age, family or marital status, property ownership, health condition, or any other ground stipulated in law or a ratified national treaty. The Commission received 77 cases in 2012 (compared to 60 cases in 2011). Most were on the grounds of ethnicity, health status, belonging to a marginalized group, personal or social status, mental or physical disability, education and social origin. The majority of the cases were in the areas of employment and labour relations, social security, access to goods and services, and judiciary and administration. The body does not provide statistics as to how many of these cases were processed and/or were closed in 2012 (Kotevska, 2012).

Macedonian Labour Law in general is harmonized with the EU Directives. Article 9 forbids harassment and gender harassment which is different from the terminology used in the Directive for equal treatment 2002/73/EC (sexual harassment; Official Gazette, No. 60/05);

Gender is not particularly emphasized in the harassment definition, which is not the case in the definition used in the EU Equal Treatment Directive. The same article provides that the employee is obliged that employers will not be victims of harassment and sexual harassment and that the employee would protect the personality and dignity of others such as the employers' privacy. However, it is not clear what measures and activities the employee should take for its implementation. The article appears to fulfil the necessity for legal definition in the national legislation for sexual harassment rather than to provide concrete measures for overcoming similar situations in everyday life.

Macedonian Labour Law is harmonized with the EU Directives in the area of employment but the sexual harassment is not properly addressed, which would result in bad practice. The Macedonian population is not well informed about workers' rights for protecting their dignity and there are no educational programmes for raising awareness in the public and private sphere.

In 2006 the Law for equal opportunities for men and women (Official Gazette No. 6/06) was adopted and is similar to the laws for equal opportunities in central and southeastern Europe. Because of stereotypes and prejudice some of these countries had difficulty recognizing sexual harassment as a new form of discrimination based on sexual behaviour in the workplace. The first step was recognizing the existence of sexual harassment de facto and then de jure, defining it in the national laws in the member states. The new laws for equal opportunities for men and women in the Czech Republic, Lithuania, Romania, Bulgaria, Estonia and Poland brought important legal changes without significant improvements in practical life. The relevance of the problem and the specific features of sexual harassment as a form of discrimination in the workplace are still not properly addressed (ILO, 2007). In the Republic of Macedonia no research has been undertaken by the Macedonian government, which shows that the problem is completely ignored by the relevant institutions. There is also no relevant case law on sexual harassment.

The existing Macedonian legislation on psychological and sexual harassment in the workplace was brief, incomplete and insufficient in terms of concrete and complete regulation and other issues relating to harassment in the workplace. In order to provide a more comprehensive legal framework that would specifically regulate issues concerning the rights, obligations and responsibilities of employers and employees about the prevention of harassment in the workplace, as well as measures and procedures to protect against harassment in the workplace, the new special law for protection against harassment in the workplace was adopted.

Through the establishment of preventive and other measures for protection against harassment in the workplace and creating special procedures for protection against harassment in the workplace, judicial workers will have a real opportunity to prove harassment. The law results from analysis conducted in several member states, such as the conditions and experiences of the past when procedures were initiated to protect against harassment in the workplace.

The greatest legal improvement was made with the adoption of the new Law for prevention of harassment in the workplace (Official Gazette No. 79, 31 May 2013).

Article 5 paragraph 2 defines sexual harassment as any verbal, non-verbal, or physical conduct of a sexual nature which has the purpose or a violation of the dignity of a candidate for employment, and that causes fear or creates discomfort, humiliation. The employer is obliged to provide the employee with work in a healthy workplace environment under conditions which ensure respect for the dignity, integrity, and health of the worker. The employer is also obligated to take concrete measures to prevent harassment in the workplace. The law regulates the procedure for protecting the worker from harassment in the workplace, and the procedure begins with the employer and is entirely regulated within the law. The worker has the right to bring a court procedure in a case when they are not satisfied with the procedure that begins with the employer. Unfortunately, there is no relevant case study for the efficiency of the law in practice since it was adopted during the 2012.

Conclusions

EU law and primary and secondary legislation such as the important case law of the European Court of Justice are the most relevant legal Acts concerning gender equality and non-discrimination. A major improvement was made with the Treaty of Amsterdam by including a new article, article 13, which prevents discrimination with new legal bases apart from gender.

The Council of Ministers has adopted an important secondary legislation for equal treatment of men and women. EU Directive 2002/73/EC defines two forms of harassment: harassment related to sex and harassment of sexual nature. Also, the EU Directive 2006/54/EC on the implementation of the principle of equal opportunities and equal treatment of men and women in matters of employment and occupation (recast version) defines harassment and sexual harassment. All member states have brought in national laws against sexual harassment in the workplace, and most countries have included definitions in their employment legislation. However, in member states there is little consistency of practice in relation to bodies to which complaints of work-related sexual harassment can be brought and the associated support mechanisms and remedies. The relevance of the problem and the specific features of sexual harassment as a form of discrimination in the workplace are still not properly addressed. The European Network of Legal Experts in the Non-discrimination Field was set up in order to provide the Commission with independent information and advice on the incorporation of the Directives into national law, their practical implementation, the national initiatives in the field of anti-discrimination legislation and related policy developments.

In our Republic of Macedonia case study in April 2010, the Anti-Discrimination Law as the first comprehensive legislation on anti-discrimination was adopted in the process of approximation of the domestic legislation with the EU *acquis*. Anti-Discrimination Law provided for the establishment of the first equality body in the country, a Commission on Protection against Discrimination. Macedonian Labour Law in general is harmonized with the EU Directives. Article 9 forbids harassment and gender harassment, which is different from the terminology used in the Directive for equal treatment 2002/73/EC (sexual harassment). The biggest legal improvement was effected with the adoption of the new Law for protection of harassment in the workplace. Article 5 paragraph 2 defines sexual harassment as any verbal, non-verbal, or physical conduct of a sexual nature which has the purpose or a violation of the dignity of a candidate for employment, and which causes fear or creates discomfort, humiliation.

Notes

1 Treaty of Amsterdam amending the Treaty on European Union, the treaties establishing the European Communities and certain related acts, Official Journal C350 from 10/11/1997.
2 Open Society Institute Network women's programme, *Equal Opportunities for Women and Men*, Monitoring law and practice in new member states and accession countries of the European Union, 2005.

References

Brindusa, M. (2007), The Dualist and Monist Theories. International Laws Comprehension of These Theories. *The Juridical Current Journal*, ISSN 1224 9173, Available at: http://revcur entjur.ro/arhiva/attachments_200712/recjurid071_22F.pdf/ (Retrieved 6 March 2014).

Constitution of Macedonia. (1991), Constitution of the Republic of Macedonia. *Assembly of the Republic of Macedonia.* Available at: http://sobranie.mk/en/default-en.asp?ItemID=9F7452B F44EE814B8DB897C1858B71FF/ (Retrieved 5 March 2014).

International Labour Office. (2007), Equality at Work: Tackling the Challenges Global Report Under the Follow-Up to the ILO Declaration on Fundamental Principles and Rights at Work, 96th Session 2007 Report I (B), Geneva, Available at: http://www.ilo.org/public/english/ standards/relm/ilc/ilc96/pdf/rep-i-b.pdf (Retrieved 6 March 2014).

Kotevska, B. (2012), *Executive Summary Country Report Macedonia (FYR) 2012 on Measures to Combat Discrimination.* Macedonia: European Network of Legal Experts in Non-discrimination.

Magurová, Z. (2008), Institute of State and Law Slovak Academy of Sciences, Bratislava, Exposure of Woman Workers to Violence and Sexual Harassment at Workplace (Slovak and Czech Experience). Seminar on Protection of Women Workers and Gender Equality, Ankara, 2–3 June 2008.

McGolgan, Aileen. (2004), Report on Sexual Harassment in the Workplace in EU Member States, June 2004. Available at: http://www.justice.ie/en/JELR/SexualHrrsmtRpt.pdf/ Files/SexualHrrsmtRpt.pdf (Retrieved 5 March 2014).

Legal Acts

European Commission. (1975), Council Directive 75/117 of 10 February 1975 on the Approximation of the Laws of the Member States Relating to the Application of the Principle of Equal Pay for Men and Woman, 1975 OJ L45/19.

———. (1976), Council Directive 76/207 of 9 February 1976 on the Implementation of the Principle of Equal Treatment for Men and Woman as Regards Access to Employment, Vocational Training and Promotion, and Working Conditions, 1976 OJ L39/40.

———. (2000a), Council Directive 2000/43/EC of 29 June 2000 Implementing the Principle of Equal Treatment Between Persons Irrespective of Racial or Ethnic Origin, [2000] OJ L180.

———. (2000b), Council Directive 2000/78/EC of 27 November 2000 Establishing a General Equal Treatment in Employment and Occupation, [2000] OJ L303.

———. (2002), Directive 2001/73/EC of the European Parliament and of the Council of 23 September 2002 amending Council Directive 76/207/EEC on the Implementation of the Principle of Equal Treatment for Men and Woman as Regards Access to Employment, Vocational Training and Promotion, and Working Condition, OJ L269 of 5 October 2002.

———. (2006), Directive of the European Parliament and of the Council on the Implementation of the Principle of Equal Treatment of Men and Women in Matters of Employment and Occupation (Recast Version), OJ L204/23 of 26 July 2006.

Part III

Corporate Sustainability and Women

Chapter 12

Strengthening Women Stakeholders with Social Responsibility

Does It Really Work?

Duygu Türker and Senem Yılmaz

Introduction

Sustainable development (WCED, 1987) is a key phenomenon of recent decades and has provided a viable framework for both practitioners and policy-makers to overcome increasing economic, environmental and social problems. Today, most business organizations have begun to accept its main philosophy and try to meet the challenges of the triple bottom line within their organizational system (Jamali, 2006). In doing so, they need to convert their system into a sustainable one (Figge et al., 2002) focusing on the core functions of business, such as the production (Robèrt et al., 2002) or procurement process (Altuntaş and Türker, 2012; Linton, Klassen and Jayaraman, 2007). In a wider sense, however, the business organizations should also confront the economic, social and environmental claims of their stakeholders and adopt corporate social responsibility (CSR) as a management approach (Steurer et al., 2005).

CSR, which can be defined as the economic, legal, ethical, and discretionary expectations of society at a given point in time (Carroll, 1979: 500), has become a significant component of policy recommendations to ensure the sustainability of enterprises at the national or international level. For instance, the European Union (EU) defines the concept as 'the responsibility of enterprises for their impacts on society' (CEC, 2011: 6) and promotes it as part of the Europe 2020 strategy for smart, sustainable and inclusive growth. On the other hand, in order to address the economic, social and environmental problems of globalization, the Organization for Economic Cooperation and Development (OECD) has also announced its guidelines for multinational enterprises (MNEs) as 'the only multilaterally agreed and comprehensive code of responsible business conduct that governments have committed to promoting' (OECD, 2011: 3). In line with the OECD's guideline, other international organizations have also promoted similar international frameworks (e.g. the United Nations Global Compact, the International Star [ISO] 26000 Guidance Standard, the International Labour Organization's Tripartite Declaration of Principles concerning Multinational Enterprises on Social Policy – the ILO MNE Declaration) and the composition of these instruments is recommended to business organizations by European Commission (EC) as a formal approach to CSR (EC, 2013).

While CSR is initiated by the organizations in developed countries, companies in a developing context have also been interested in CSR. Despite the lack of structural support at the national policy-making level, it seems that business communities in developing countries like the voluntarily nature of this framework in addressing the increasing expectations of society (Türker and Altuntaş, 2012). CSR captures the growing interest of practitioners in those countries who have recognized the positive impacts of CSR on various organizational outcomes, such as increasing the organizational commitment of current employees (Peterson, 2004; Türker, 2009), attracting prospective employees (Turban and Greening, 1997), increasing consumer trust (Pivato, Misani and Tencati, 2008), strengthening stakeholder relationships (Sen, Bhattacharya and Korschun, 2006) or improving corporate reputation (Lewis, 2003). CSR has become a popular tool for companies wanting to balance their relations with society. It is clear that this 'business case' approach towards CSR (Carroll and Shabana, 2010; Weber, 2008) might result in opportunism among managers (Nijhof and Jeurissen, 2010) in such countries and, because CSR can be understood in a very superficial way, it can manifest itself in spending more money on advertising than on social responsibility activities. However, even this stage of the adoption process can be seen as valuable in paving the way to developing a deeper understanding with which to combat the growing problems of developing countries.

This study focuses particularly on the problems of women in developing countries and attempts to analyse the socially responsible approaches of companies towards these women stakeholders. Considering the overall gender inequalities in this context, many women face diverse problems, such as poverty, discrimination or crime during their lifetime. These problems not only affect their health and well-being (Belle and Doucet, 2003), but also create a significant economic loss and cause many social problems in the long term. Besides the enforcement of related laws by public authorities, business organizations in this context should also be involved in the process of contributing to the solution of such problems, and CSR can be the best option for their involvement in the process. In this study we analyse how women stakeholders are integrated into the CSR concept in practice within the developing country context. After explaining the problems briefly, a theoretical framework was derived from the CSR and stakeholder management literature. Based on this framework, a qualitative study was conducted on a sample of 15 CSR projects in 12 companies towards women stakeholders in Turkey. The study both reveals the nature of such CSR involvement and discusses the extent to which the problems of women are recognized by the business community and how effective these CSR projects are for the solution of women's increasing problems in Turkey.

CSR towards Women Stakeholders in Developing Countries

The need for a paradigm shift in management theory towards sustainable development (Gladwin, Kennelly and Krause, 1995) that can provide a real equality among all stakeholders has been discussed for a long time. Although achieving a consensus on this paradigm, which Gladwin, Kennelly and Krause (1995) call 'sustaincentrism', is difficult, the increasing interest of business organizations in social and environmental problems can be viewed as the initial step of this transition process. As we said earlier, the concept of CSR has provided a useful framework for organizations when they work out and operationalize sustainable development at the micro level. Therefore,

CSR has been frequently practiced during the last decades and, after all these years of practice, has also proliferated and diversified in terms of its nature, structure and coverage.

Today, aware of the emphasis of sustainable development against the domination of men over women and nature (Warren, 1994), companies have begun to formulate and implement CSR activities towards their indirect stakeholders (Türker and Altuntaş, 2013) such as the natural environment or disadvantaged groups such as orphans, handicapped people, minorities, immigrants or women. Although they are usually neglected due to their attributed features in terms of power, legitimacy or urgency (Mitchell, Agle and Wood, 1997: 854), some companies do try to find innovative ways of balancing the interests of these stakeholders. This corporate attention is particularly meaningful for developing countries, in which the economic, social and environmental problems are much greater and harder to solve. For instance, the study of Jamali and Mirshak (2007) on a sample of eight companies in Lebanon indicated that despite the lack of measurement systems for the outcome, the scope and spectrum of CSR is extremely wide among companies, including donations for orphans and handicapped people or activities for supporting education, art, culture, sport or music, etc. Because governments in developing countries usually fail to recognize and/or provide adequate resources for these growing problems, the support of non-governmental organizations (NGOs) and business enterprises is vital for the solution to such problems. One of the major problems in developing countries, gender-related issues, should also be addressed through the collaborative efforts of various sectors.

Since 'women's empowerment and the promotion of gender equality are key to achieving sustainable development' (World Bank, 2013), the indicators of gender equality are closely monitored by national and international organizations. The results of such statistical reports and analysis show that gender inequalities are most obvious in developing and underdeveloped countries and that women have problems in many areas such as education, health, participation in the labour force, political mechanisms, etc. Table 12.1 presents some indicators of gender equality for the developing parts of the world. It can be seen that the rates for females are lower than the rates for males in almost all indicators in developing regions. Women are not only less educated and literate than men, they participate in economic life at a lower level than their male counterparts. Compared to OECD members as a representation of developed world, there is a need for more progress in all indicators of development.

Although it is an OECD member, Turkey is also a developing country and shares the common characteristics of other developing countries to a great extent. While the expected years of schooling for women is around 13.18, labour participation rate and literacy rate of adult females (the population aged 15+) are 28.10 and 85.34, respectively (World Bank, 2013). Compared with other OECD countries, Turkey has the lowest rate of female employment levels among all members (TurkStat, 2012). Table 12.2 shows that despite the decrease in the unemployment rate in both genders since 2005, the ratio of female unemployed is higher than male unemployed in all years. On the other hand, although female employees are better paid in total, it seems that the gender pay gap is not closed by education in Turkey and it is still around 16 per cent among people who have a higher education degree.

Table 12.1 Selected indicators of gender equality in the developing world (2011)

Indicator Name	OED	CFR	CAM	CAS	EAP	ESA	ESS	EER	ECA	LAC	MNA	MDE	PAC	SAM	SEA	SER	SSA
GDP per capita (current US$)	3,696	1,497	8,167	4,236	4,689	551	5,370	6,255	6,821	9,353	4,614	5,244	2,258	10,29	3,154	8,863	1,423
Expected years of schooling, female	16.16	8.06	13.25	12.43	12.17	9.31	12.22	14.99	13.36	14.08	11.61	10.88	–	14.59	12.21	13.11	8.58
Expected years of schooling, male	15.58	10.44	13.07	12.74	11.79	10.01	11.63	14.34	13.65	13.48	12.45	12.16	–	13.79	12.14	13.89	9.75
Labour participation rate, female*	50.88	67.35	44.97	54.58	65.20	68.40	67.75	50.17	45.58	53.73	19.82	16.96	65.11	57.63	58.82	34.74	63.11
Labour participation rate, male*	69.45	75.11	81.11	75.84	80.61	80.46	80.13	63.72	69.05	80.17	72.49	71.37	75.27	80.47	81.97	70.60	76.30
Literacy rate, adult female*	–	50.59	89.57	99.40	92.07	59.51	92.85	98.87	96.71	90.60	69.90	75.41	66.00	91.72	90.47	93.05	51.23
Literacy rate, adult male*	–	75.33	92.51	99.69	96.74	73.57	97.52	99.29	99.02	91.97	84.91	88.53	71.81	92.45	95.01	98.42	68.77
Total enrolment, primary, female (%)	98.20	72.44	98.91	94.43	96.91	83.90	98.02	92.22	95.27	95.73	91.52	87.65	–	95.71	96.13	97.07	75.26
Total enrolment, primary, male (%)	97.96	78.84	98.33	96.26	96.58	86.86	97.87	91.89	96.09	94.99	96.31	93.58	–	94.71	95.11	97.84	79.24

Source: World Bank (2013).

* Percentage of male/female population ages 15+.

Note: OED: OECD members; Developing only in the following regions: CFR: Central Africa; CAM: Central America; CAS: Central Asia; EAP: East Asia and Pacific; ESA: East and Southern Africa; ESS: Eastern Africa; EER: Eastern Europe; ECA: Europe and Central Asia; LAC: Latin America and Caribbean; MNA: Middle East and North Africa; MDE: Middle East; PAC: Pacific; SAM: South America; SEA: South-Eastern Asia; SER: Southern Europe; SSA: Sub-Saharan Africa.

Table 12.2 Selected indicators of gender equality in the developing world (2011)

Unemployment rate (%)			Gender pay gap 2010 (%)		Physical/sexual violence		
Years	Female*	Male*	Education level	Rate	Education level	Lifetime violence	Last 12 months
2005	11.2	10.5	Primary school and below	16.5	Uneducated	55.7	17.4
2006	11.1	9.9	Primary and secondary school	16.7	First level primary school	42.2	13.1
2007	11.0	10.0	High school	10.1	Second level primary school	38.5	15.4
2008	11.6	10.7	Vocational school	19.5	High school and above	27.2	10
2009	14.3	13.9	Higher education	16.1			
2010	13.0	11.4					
2011	11.3	9.2					
2012	10.8	8.5					

Source: TurkStat (2012).

* The population aged 15+.

The representation of women in managerial positions is still very low when compared with other developed countries. For instance, in terms of the proportion of female deputies, Turkey is 43rd in the list of 51 selected countries, with a ratio of 14.4 per cent, and the number of female professors, public prosecutors or judges is much lower than that of their male counterparts. In addition to these problems, women in Turkey have been increasingly exposed to physical/sexual violence during the last decade. Table 12.2 shows that education can play a functional role in reducing violence against women in Turkey – but it does not solve the problem as a whole.

Women in Turkey have suffered significantly from problems in the areas of education, employment and health for a long time (Kağıtçıbaşı, 1999). Additionally, violence against women, which has been embedded into the socio-cultural traditions of society, becomes a major problem that threatens the lives of women. According to Kağıtçıbaşı (1999), regional inequalities (between the developed western and less developed eastern part of the country) and educational problems can be seen as the main factors that directly affect the overall well-being of women in Turkey. Since the solution of such problems needs a long-term orientation that will focus on social, cultural, economic, political and legal dimensions of gender issues, a high degree of collaboration among governmental, non-governmental and business organizations is required to generate a sustainable future for developing countries. In doing so, each of these sectors can pool their diverse expertise on a given aspect and share their experiences with each other in solving these complicated problems. CSR can be a way of initiating or maintaining such cooperation in the solution to gender-related problems in developing countries. Therefore it is important to investigate whether CSR towards women stakeholders can contribute to the solutions of growing problems in a developing country context.

Methodology

Sample Selection, Data Collection and Analysis

In this study, the CSR projects that focus on women stakeholders were identified through a two-step Web search of researchers. After obtaining a list of CSR projects from national newspapers, CSR networks and company websites, the projects for women stakeholders were selected for further analysis. At the end of the process, a total of 15 projects from 12 companies were identified and the data on projects were collected through the official Web page of each project. These collected data were analysed through content analysis, which 'aims at a quantitative classification of a given body of content, in terms of a system of categories' (Kaplan, 1943: 1). In doing so, the coding categories were first identified to find out the underlying nature and structure of each project.

Table 12.3 shows each category and their subcategories. For instance, while target stakeholder/s of each project were analysed based on the demographics of these women, the stated problem in the projects was classified into 10 subcategories. Depending on the scale and content of projects, they might fall into two or more categories simultaneously. The main activity of each project was classified based on five subcategories and the sustainability theme was analysed based on the three core dimensions of sustainable development. Additionally, the degree of relatedness between the project theme and the sector of company was also analysed in the study to evaluate whether the companies use and transfer their expertise into their CSR projects. Based on Husted's 2003 study, the governance model of each project was classified into three subcategories as outsourcing CSR through charitable contributions, internalizing it through in-house projects or using a collaborative model. In order to understand the structure of a collaborative model, the partners of projects were also analysed based on four groups of organization. In the last category, the concrete results of projects were classified into four main groups in terms the scale of projects and their impact on stakeholders. In addition to this analysis, the study also provided the descriptive analysis of each project.

In order to increase the objectivity of the process of analysis, two researchers performed the analysis of data individually based on the predetermined rules and procedures (Holsti, 1969). During this process, the researchers aim to observe and reveal the existence of each category (Bailey, 1994) on the website of each project. Any dispute about the existence of a category or its content was resolved with the involvement of a third researcher (Weber, 1990: 17). The reliability of the analysis was thus ensured during the data collection process.

Findings

Table 12.4 shows both the descriptive and content analysis of 15 CSR projects of 12 companies, all of which are large-scale organizations in Turkey. The companies operate in various sectors, including telecommunication (two companies), electric/electronic (two companies as manufacturer and retailer), life insurance, personal products, non-food retailer, media, textiles and agriculture. Two projects are executed by the holding companies. While all of them are current projects, the oldest

Table 12.3 Descriptive and content analysis of CSR projects

Main category	Subcategories
Target stakeholder/s	Demographics of women stakeholders (age, education level, income, geography etc.)
Stated problem	Cultural, education, employment, entrepreneurship, environment, health, legal, social, political, technology
Main activity	Raising awareness, informing, networking, lobbying, providing something tangible (fund training, employment, etc.)
Sustainability theme	Economic, social, environmental
Task/project-relatedness	Yes/No
Governance model	Charitable contributions, in-house projects, collaborative model
Partner/s	NGO, GO, IGO, BO
Concrete result	Scale of project (small or large) and impact of project (minor or major): small-scale minor impact (SMi); small-scale major impact (SMa); large-scale minor impact (LMi); large-scale major impact (LMa)]

Source: Anadolu Hayat (2013a, b); Avon (2013); Borusan Holding (2013); Dogan Holding (2013a, b); Kale Grup (2013); Mudo/Boyner Holding (2013); Profilo (2013); Teknosa (2013); Toros Tarım (2013); Turkcell (2013a, b); Vodafone Vakfi (2013).

*NGO: Non-governmental Organization; GO: Governmental Organization; IGO: Intergovernmental Organization; BO: Business Organization.

project was started by Avon in 1998 and the most recent initiated by Borusan Holding in 2013. The average time coverage of projects is around six years. Among all projects, only those of Borusan Holding, Boyner and Kale Grup have specific time coverage and clear performance indicators for their successful completion. For instance, Borusan Holding's project aims to build new childcare centres in 10 organized industry zones by 2016. Although the specific time period is not stated, Turkcell's Women Empowerment in Economy project has set its performance indicator as achieving 100,000 women employees in the next four years.

Table 12.4 shows that the objectives of projects range from providing equal opportunities in education and social life to increasing the economic, social or political participation of women.

This variety of projects is in line with the various problems of women in Turkey; the analysis of stated problems shows that the majority of projects focus on the economic (employment/entrepreneurship) (eight projects) and social (five projects) problems of women. Considering the relatively higher unemployment rate among women, the projects aim to *help* women to be employed (Project no. 1), *provide* childcare services for working women (Project no. 4), *prevent* the poverty of women and *increase* their employment (Project no. 5), *provide* employment opportunities (Project nos 6, 8 and, 9), *support* women to participate in the economy (Project no. 14), and *increase* their entrepreneurial activities (Project no. 15). In three of these projects (Project nos 5, 6 and 9), the economic problems are closely linked with the social problems women face and the projects aim to strengthen women in social life by supporting their economic well-being. Since violence against women has become a major problem in Turkey, three of the projects (5, 6 and 7) mention this social problem and two of them (6 and 7) focus on raising public awareness of the issue. Additionally, while two projects mention educational (1 and 13) and environmental (10 and 12) problems, other problems are addressed by only a single firm (e.g. culture, Project no. 2;

Table 12.4 Descriptive and content analysis of CSR projects

No.	Company	Sector	Project Title	Period	Project Objective	Stakeholder/s	Stated Problem
1	Anadolu Hayat Emeklilik	Life Insurance	Geleceğin Sigortasi Kizlarimiz (Girls: the Insurance of Our Future)	2005–...	Support the students of insurance departments from high school to graduation and help their employment	Uneducated / low-income girls	Employment+ education
2	Anadolu Hayat Emeklilik	Life Insurance	Kadın Gözüyle Hayattan Kareler Fotograf Yarışması (Shots from Life as Seen by Women)	2007–...	Contribute to social and cultural development of women and provide a platform for their freedom of expression	Women	Social + cultural
3	Avon	Personal products	Meme Kanseri ile Mücadele (Fight Against Breast Cancer)	1998–...	Raise awareness, inform, educate, and support research on breast cancer	Women	Health
4	Borusan Holding	Holding (Conglomerate)	Annemin İşi Benim Geleceğim (My Mom's Job is My Future)	2013–2016	Provide childcare services to increase women's employment rate in industry and improve the mental and physical development of children	Women who have child/children	Employment
5	Boyner Holding	Non-Food Retail Group	Nar Taneleri (Pomegranate Arils – Strong Young Women, Happier Future)	2009–2015	Prevent the poverty of women; increase the employment of women; prevent violence against women; to struggle against social exclusion; increase joint activities among various sectors	Young women aged 18–24 years who grew up in orphanages	Employment + social
6	Hürriyet	Media	Haklı Kadın Platformu (Rightful Women Platform)	2011–...	Increase women's participation in parliament, protect from violence, provide employment opportunity, help enact laws to ensure gender equality	Women	Employment+ social + legal + political
7	Hürriyet	Media	Aile İçi Şiddete Son (Fight against Domestic Violence)	2004–...	Raise awareness of violence against women and provide information/consultancy services to women	Women who are exposed to violence	Social (Violence)

#	Company	Sector	Program	Year	Description	Target	Category
8	Kale Grup	Holding (Conglomerate)	Kadın Usta (Skilled Women)	2009–2015	Provide employment opportunity to women in men-dominant sectors of construction	Low-income and unemployed women	Employment
9	Mudo	Textile	Argande	2008–...	Provide employment and education to women in southwestern region in the garment industry	Low-income women in southwestern region	Employment + social
10	Profilo	Electric/Electronics (Manufacturer)	Türkiye Enerjisini Topluyor (Turkey is Collecting its Energy)	2010–...	Inform housewives on energy saving to protect natural resources	Housewives	Environment
11	Teknosa	Electric/Electronics (Retailer)	Kadın için Teknoloji (Technology for Women)	2007–...	Make technology an integral part of women's lives; contribute to their personal development, cultural and social lives	Women in regions where the facilities are limited	Technology
12	Toros Tarim	Agriculture	Kadın Çiftçilere Eğitim ve Destek Projesi (Project for Education and Support for Women Farmers)	2010–...	Educate women farmers, who make paramount contribution to agricultural labour in Turkey, on the correct and balanced use of chemical fertilizers, one of the most important inputs in agriculture	Women working in agriculture sector	Environment
13	Turkcell	Telecommunication	Kardelenler (Snowdrops)	2000–...	Provide equal opportunities in education for underprivileged girls mainly in rural areas of Turkey	Low-income girls in the rural areas	Education
14	Turkcell	Telecommunication	Ekonomiye Kadın Gücü (Women Empowerment in Economy)	2012–...	Support women to participate in the economy through this mobile for development campaign	Low-income women	Entrepreneurship
15	Vodafone	Telecommunication	Önce Kadın Programı (Woman First Programme)	2010–...	Identify the attitudes and needs of women to increase their access to mobile technology in entrepreneurial activities by providing products and projects for communication	Employed or unemployed women aged 15–65	Entrepreneurship

(Continued)

Table 12.4 (Continued)

No.	Main Activity	Sustainability Theme	Task/ Project Relatedness	Governance Model	Partners*	Performance Indicators	Concrete Results/Outcomes
1	Providing funds (scholarship)	Economic + social	Yes	Collaborative	1 NGO + 1 GO	N/A	SMa: start with 500 students – 100 new students in 2010–11
2	Raising awareness (organizing a photography contest)	Social (cultural)	No	In-house	N/A	N/A	LMi: 7,000 applicants with 32,000 photos since 2007 (In 2013 1,134 applicants with 5,143 photos); 44 photos were archived by the company and collectors
3	Executing multiple programmes (raising awareness, informing, training, free check-up, donating through the sale of project products)	Social (health)	No	Collaborative	1 NGO + various hospitals/ clinics	N/A	LMa: provided funds (2,200,000 TL); 10,000 check-ups in 23 cities; 17 meetings in 14 cities; donating equipment to 7 hospitals; organizing race walk/ fashion show; initiating a call centre
4	Providing childcare centres	Economic + social	No	Collaborative	2 GOs	Centres in 10 organized industry zones till 2016	SMa: architectural design contest was resulted to build centres
5	Providing training/ employment (gender equality)	Economic + social	No	Collaborative	1 NGO + 1 IGO + 3 GO + 1 BO	2013–2015 strategy – continue the project with new cooperation	SMa: educated 162 women for 15 days and mentored for 1 year (51% find job; 33% continue education; 16% seek job)
6	Raising awareness, networking, lobbying (gender equality)	Social	Yes	Collaborative	41 NGOs + individual members	N/A	LMi: expanded the network
7	Raising awareness, informing, providing training (violence)	Social	Yes	Collaborative	NGOs + GOs + BOs	N/A	LMi: 35,775 calls from all cities of Turkey/14 countries to the emergency call centre of project; educated 45,000 people; organized conferences

#	Activity	Category		Type	Partners	Target	Outcomes
8	Providing training (construction)	Economic	Yes	Collaborative	1 NGO + 1 GO	Provide education to 1,250 unemployed women till 2015	SMa: educated 75 women; employed 254 persons in 12 cities; replaced 22 school toilets
9	Providing training/ employment	Economic	Yes	Collaborative	2 IGO + 2 GO	N/A	SMa: provided employment for 200 women in the manufacturing firms of ARGENDE in Batman ve Mardin
10	Raising awareness, informing (energy saving)	Environmental	Yes	In-house	N/A	N/A	SMi: informing 1,000 households/12,000 housewives
11	Providing training (computer literacy)	Economic	Yes	In-house	N/A	N/A	LMi: educated 12,000; awarded the CSR practices of NGO
12	Providing training	Environmental	Yes	In-house	N/A	N/A	SMi: organized education sessions in Izmir and Antalya
13	Providing funds (scholarship)	Economic + social	No	Collaborative	1 NGO	Number of students	LMa: 29,000 students are funded, 17,000 students graduated from high school, 1,800 students graduated from universities
14	Providing a Web-based communication platform between the fundraiser and women	Economic + social	Yes	Collaborative	2 NGOs	100,000 women in 4 years	N/A
15	Executing multiple programmes (conducting research; providing communication products/projects, training, providing funds [credit])	Economic (technological)	Yes	Collaborative	4 NGOs + 1 GO + 1 BO	N/A	LMi: conducted research on a sample of housewives and working women (1,607) aged 15 and 65 in 16 cities for a period four months starting in August 2011; educated 1,300 women on technological issues; provide funds to 3 entrepreneur women; started online retailing services

Source: Anadolu Hayat (2013a, 2013b); Avon (2013); Borusan Holding (2013); Dogan Holding (2013a, 2013b); Kale Grup (2013); Mudo (2013); Profilo (2013); Teknosa (2013); Toros Tarim (2013); Turkcell (2013a, 2013b); Vodafone Vakfi (2013).

* NGO: Non-governmental Organization; GO: Governmental Organization; IGO: Intergovernmental Organization; BO: Business Organization.

health, Project no. 3; legal and political; Project no. 6; and technological problems, Project no. 11).

Depending on the perceived problems addressed by the projects, we note that target stakeholders in most of these projects are disadvantaged women, who are defined in terms of education, income and region. While five projects aim to reach all women stakeholders without segmenting them (Project nos 2, 3, 6, 10 and 15), the rest of them specifically focus on women who are in a low-income group (Project no. 14), are uneducated/in a low-income group (Project no. 1), are unemployed/in a low-income group (Project no. 8), are in a low-income group in the south-eastern region (Project no. 9), are living in regions where the facilities are limited (Project no. 11), are in a low-income group in the rural areas (Project no. 13), have a child or children (Project no. 4), grew up in orphanages (Project no. 5), are exposed to violence (Project no. 7) and are working in the agriculture sector (Project no. 12).

The analysis of the main activity in projects shows that almost all of them provide something tangible to their target stakeholder, such as funds (1 and 13), childcare services (4), training (5, 7, 8, 9, 11 and 12), employment (5 and 9) or a Web-based communication platform (14). While two projects, 3 and 15, execute several subprogrammes simultaneously, four of them, 2, 6, 7 and 10, are involved in raising awareness, informing, networking and lobbying activities. On the other hand, four projects, 8, 9, 11 and 15, focus on economic issues; four of them emphasize social needs, 2, 3, 6 and 7; and five projects engage in both the economic and social dimensions of a sustainability theme, 1, 4, 5, 13 and 14. Only two of these projects are related to the environmental theme of sustainability, 10 and 12. Women become the target stakeholders in both of these projects as the consumers of products provided by the companies.

The analysis of task/project-relatedness indicates that the themes of 10 projects closely overlap the sector of project-owner companies (Project nos 1, 6, 7, 8, 9, 10, 11, 12, 14 and 15). This indicates that companies usually prefer to transfer their field of expertise into their projects. For instance, while an insurance company (Project no. 1) is mainly interested in the educational and employment problems of women in insurance departments of universities, the company in the agriculture sector focuses on how women farmers use chemical fertilizers correctly (Project no. 12), or a company in the media sector (Project nos 6 and 7) tries to increase the level of communication and networking among women, and so on. On the other hand, five of these companies are involved in projects that are completely different from their major task or sector. For instance, the same insurance company (Project no. 2) is organizing a photography contest for women or is the producer of personal products for the health problems of women (Project no. 3).

However, the analysis of the governance model reveals that the companies mainly prefer to collaborate with other organizations when involved in CSR projects. We can see in Table 12.4 that the governance structures of 11 projects are collaborative and only four of them are the examples of in-house projects. Companies might close the gap between their areas of expertise and the expertise that is necessary for conducting a CSR project by joining forces with other organizations. The analysis of these partner organizations shows that companies mostly collaborate with NGOs (Project nos 1, 3, 5, 6, 7, 8, 13, 14 and 15) and GOs (Project nos 1, 4, 5, 7, 8, 9 and 15). While three companies are also collaborating with BOs (Project nos 5, 7 and 15), four of them are not working with any organization.

Finally, the outcomes of each project were also analysed to reveal whether these projects create any concrete change in the lives of women stakeholders. As explained previously, the projects can be classified into four groups:

1   Small-scale/minor impact: the projects in this group (nos 10 and 12) are both small-scale and create a minor impact on the target stakeholders. For instance, Profilo's Turkey Collecting Its Energy project aims to inform a limited number of women consumers on energy savings to protect the environment. On the other hand, Toros Tarım's CSR project provides education sessions for women farmers on the use of fertilizers.

2   Small-scale/major impact: the second group consists of five projects (nos 1, 4, 5, 8 and 9) which focus on a specific problem in order to provide a comprehensive solution. For instance, while 162 women were educated and 51 per cent of them were employed in the project of Boyner Holding, 75 women were educated and 254 women were employed in the project of Kale Grup. On the other hand, Boyner Holding provides employment opportunities for 200 women in their own manufacturing firm of Argande and sells their products all around the country. Although its governance model is classified as collaborative, this project can be viewed as a unique example for the intersection between the concepts of social responsibility and social entrepreneurship.

3   Large-scale/minor impact: this group contains five projects (nos 2, 6, 7, 11 and 15) and their overall aims are to raise awareness, inform or educate women stakeholders in the selected domain of the project. Although Vodafone is executing multiple programmes under its CSR project, the high degree of task/project-relatedness limits the real impact of this project. For instance, one of the programmes for this project provides some communication products/projects for women (consumers) within its product line and it seems that the company successfully combines its CSR with its marketing strategy. Although the governance model of this project is stated as collaborative, it might be seen as an example how a company can integrate its social responsibility into its core business.

4   Large-scale/major impact: this last group includes two projects, nos 3 and 13. Considering their time coverage (Avon's project in 1998/Turkcell's project in 2000), these are the oldest among the analysed projects. Partly due to the greater experience of these projects, their impact on the women stakeholders are more comprehensive and meaningful. For instance, depending on the company's effort to promote their project, Turkcell's Snowdrops has become one of the well-known projects in Turkey and its success motivates others in involving CSR activities also.

Note that only one project is not classified due to lack of information about its results on the company Web page. This is partly because the project was started in 2012 and has yet to obtain any concrete results.

Conclusion

CSR has been widely recognized as a useful framework that balances the relationship between society and business. According to the proponents of CSR, it can provide a significant mechanism that will contribute to the well-being of stakeholders and ultimately help to achieve the principles of sustainable development. It is clear that this attributed role of CSR is particularly important for developing countries when dealing with economic, social and environmental problems. This study focuses on the nature and effectiveness of CSR projects towards women stakeholders in a developing country. Based on the result of our analysis, we can say that companies in Turkey have begun to recognize the problems of women, and CSR is viewed as the main tool for providing a solution. However, the data collection process shows that the projects aimed directly at women stakeholders still constitute a small portion of growing CSR interests in Turkey. Considering the increasing problems of women stakeholders in economic, social, cultural, political, legal and environmental areas, companies should develop and implement more CSR projects in the future. Moreover, the analysis of the results reveals that the problems of poor, uneducated and low-income women are perceived as more urgent by the companies. The companies mostly focus on a stakeholder by emphasizing the economic and social theme of sustainability. However, recalling the gender pay gap and physical/sexual violence (by education level) in Turkey (Table 12.2), women who are well-educated and actively working also have many problems such as the glass ceiling, inequalities in payment and promotion, sexual harassment, etc. Therefore, companies would do well to develop more in-house projects for their own women employees to improve their well-being.

The results of the study also show that raising awareness or providing training is usually seen as the major solution to overcoming barriers for women. However, the growing problems of women stakeholders require more concrete responses from companies. The most effective way of involving CSR – under these circumstances – is to generate a *major impact* with either small- or large-scale projects. Despite the increasing interest in the former (small-scale/major impact projects), there is a need to develop the latter type of project more frequently. Considering the tendency to collaborate with other organizations, companies can easily overcome the lack of expertise in involving such specific problems of women stakeholders and develop large-scale projects. Additionally, as an implication for scholars, the analysis of the projects also reveals that companies find innovative ways of doing CSR activities. Besides Husted's (2003) classification on CSR governance models, these new forms can show companies how to combine *traditional* collaborative models with social entrepreneurship (Boyner Holding's Argande) or the company's core business activity (Vodafone's Woman First Programme).

References

Altuntaş, C. and Türker, D. (2012), Sustainable Supply Chains: A Content Analysis of Sustainability Reports. *Dokuz Eylül Üniversitesi Sosyal Bilimler Enstitüsü Dergisi* 14(3): 39–64.

Anadolu Hayat. (2013a), *Sosyal Sorumluluk.* Available at: http://www.anadoluhayat.com.tr/hakkimizda_genel/sosyal_sorumluluk.aspx (Retrieved 20 October 2013).

———. (2013b), *Kadın Gözüyle Hayattan Kareler.* Available at: http://www.anadoluhayat.com.tr/hakkimizda_genel/sosyal_sorumluluk/kadinGozuyleHayattanKareler.aspx (Retrieved 20 October 2013).

Avon. (2013), *Meme Kanseri.* Available at: http://www.avon.com.tr/PRSuite/static/microsites/avon-meme-kanseri/index.html (Retrieved 20 October 2013).

Bailey, K.D. (1994), *Methods of Social Research,* 4th edn. New York: The Free Press.

Belle, D. and Doucet, J. (2003), Poverty, Inequality, and Discrimination as Sources of Depression Among US Women. *Psychology of Women Quarterly* 27(2): 101–13.

Borusan Holding. (2013), Available at: http://www.borusan.com.tr/en/CommunityContribu
tion/MyMomsJobisMyFuture.aspx (Retrieved 20 October 2013).

Carroll, A.B. (1979), A Three-dimensional Conceptual Model of Corporate Social Performance. *Academy of Management Review* 4(4): 497–505.

———— and Shabana, K.M. (2010), The Business Case for Corporate Social Responsibility:
A Review of Concepts, Research and Practice. *International Journal of Management Reviews*
12(1): 85–105.

CEC (Commission of the European Communities). (2011), Communication from the Commission to the European Parliament, the Council, the European Economic and Social Committee and the Committee of the Regions – A Renewed EU Strategy 2011–14 for Corporate
Social Responsibility. Available at: http://ec.europa.eu/enterprise/policies/sustainable-
business/files/csr/new-csr/act_en.pdf (Retrieved 10 October 2013).

Dogan Holding. (2013a), *Haklı Kadın Platformu.* Available at: http://www.doganholding.com.
tr/kurumsal-sorumluluk/hakli-kadin-platformu.aspx (Retrieved 20 October 2013).

————. (2013b). *Aile İçi Şiddete Son.* Available at: http://www.doganholding.com.tr/kurumsal-
sosyal-sorumluk/aile-ici-siddete-son.aspx (Retrieved on 20 October 2013).

EC (European Commission). (2013), *CSR Guidelines and Principles.* Available at: http://
ec.europa.eu/enterprise/policies/sustainable-business/corporate-social-responsibility/
guidelines-principles/index_en.htm (Retrieved 10 October 2013).

Figge, F., Hahn, T., Schaltegger, S. and Wagner, M. (2002), The Sustainability Balanced Score-
card – Linking Sustainability Management to Business Strategy. *Business Strategy and the Environment* 11(5): 269–84.

Gladwin, T.N., Kennelly, J.J. and Krause, T.S. (1995), Shifting Paradigms for Sustainable Development: Implications for Management Theory and Research. *Academy of Management Review*
20(4): 874–907.

Holsti, O.R. (1969), *Content Analysis for the Social Science and Humanities.* Don Mills, ON:
Addison-Wesley Publishing Company.

Husted, B.W. (2003), Governance Choices for Corporate Social Responsibility: To Contribute,
Collaborate or Internalize? *Long Range Planning* 36(5): 481–98.

Jamali, D. (2006), Insights into Triple Bottom Line Integration from a Learning Organization
Perspective. *Business Process Management Journal* 12(6): 809–21.

———— and Mirshak, R. (2007), Corporate Social Responsibility (CSR): Theory and Practice in
a Developing Country Context. *Journal of Business Ethics* 72(3): 243–62.

Kağıtçıbaşı, Ç. (1999), *Türkiye'de kadının konumu: İnsanca gelisim düzeyi, eğitim, istihdam, sağlik
ve doğurganlik.* Paper presented at the International Conference on History of the Turkish Republic: A Reassessment, 10–12 December 1998, vol. 2, İstanbul: Tarih Vakfı Yayınları,
pp. 255–66.

Kale Grup. (2013), Sosyal Sorumluluk. Available at: http://www.kalegrubu.com.tr//tr-tr/kale-
grubu/basin-odasi/kaleden-haberler?recid=1769 (Retrieved 20 October 2013).

Kaplan, A. (1943), Content Analysis and the Theory of Signs. *Philosophy of Science* 10(4): 230–47.

Lewis, S. (2003), Reputation and Corporate Responsibility. *Journal of Communication Management* 7(4): 356–66.

Linton, J.D., Klassen, R. and Jayaraman, V. (2007), Sustainable Supply Chains: An Introduction. *Journal of Operations Management* 25(6): 1075–82.

Mitchell, R.K., Agle, B.R. and Wood, D.J. (1997), Toward a Theory of Stakeholder Identification and Salience: Defining the Principle of Who and What Really Counts. *The Academy of
Management Review* 22(4): 853–86.

Mudo. (2013), *Sosyal Sorumluluk.* Available at: http://www.mudo.com.tr/Kurumsal/sosyal-
sorumluluk-6 (Retrieved 20 October 2013).

Nijhof, A.H.J. and Jeurissen, R.J.M. (2010), The Glass Ceiling of Corporate Social Responsibility: Consequences of a Business Case Approach Towards CSR. *International Journal of Sociology
and Social Policy* 30(11/12): 618–31.

OECD (Organisation for Economic Cooperation and Development). (2011), *Guidelines for Multinational Enterprises*. Available at: http://www.oecd.org/daf/inv/mne/48004323.pdf (Retrieved 10 October 2013).

Peterson, D.K. (2004), The Relationship Between Perceptions of Corporate Citizenship and Organizational Commitment. *Business & Society* 43(3): 296–319.

Pivato, S., Misani, N. and Tencati, A. (2008), The Impact of Corporate Social Responsibility on Consumer Trust: The Case of Organic Food. *Business Ethics: A European Review* 17(1): 3–12.

Profilo. (2013), *Kurumsal Sosyal Sorumluluk Projeleri*. Available at: http://www.profilo.com.tr/profilo-d%C3%BCnyas%C4%B1/kurumsal-sosyal-sorumluluk-projeleri.html (Retrieved 20 October 2013).

Robèrt, K.-H., Schmidt-Bleek, B., Aloisi de Larderel, J., Basile, G., Jansen, J.L., Kuehr, R., Thomas, P.P., Suzuki, M., Hawken, P. and Wackernagel, M. (2002), Strategic Sustainable Development – Selection, Design and Synergies of Applied Tools. *Journal of Cleaner Production* 10(3): 197–214.

Sen, S., Bhattacharya, C.B. and Korschun, D. (2006), The Role of Corporate Social Responsibility in Strengthening Multiple Stakeholder Relationships: A Field Experiment. *Journal of the Academy of Marketing Science* 34(2): 158–66.

Steurer, R., Langer, M.E., Konrad, A. and Martinuzzi, A. (2005), Corporations, Stakeholders and Sustainable Development I: A Theoretical Exploration of Business–Society Relations. *Journal of Business Ethics* 61(3): 63–281.

Teknosa. (2013), *Kadın İçin Teknoloji*. Available at: http://www.teknosa.com/KurumsalSayfalar/Turkce/KadinIcinTeknoloji.aspx (Retrieved 20 October 2013).

Toros Tarım. (2013), *Kadın Çiftçiler Eğitim ve Destek Projesi*. Available at: http://www.toros.com.tr/sosyal-sorumluluk-grup-detay.asp?kategoriNo=1&grupNo=2&grupAdi=Kadın Çiftçiler Eğitim ve Destek Projesi (Retrieved 20 October 2013).

Turban, D.B. and Greening, D.W. (1997), Corporate Social Performance and Organizational Attractiveness to Prospective Employees. *Academy of Management Journal* 40(3): 658–72.

Turkcell. (2013a), *Kardelenler*. Available at: http://www.turkcell.com.tr/site/tr/turkcellhakkinda/Sayfalar/sosyal-sorumluluk/egitim/kardelenler/kardelenler.aspx.

———. (2013b), *Ekonomiye Kadın Gücü*. Available at: http://www.turkcell.com.tr/site/tr/turkcellhakkinda/Sayfalar/sosyal-sorumluluk/girisimcilik/Ekonomiye-Kadin-Gucu.aspx.

Türker, D. (2009), How Corporate Social Responsibility Influences Organizational Commitment. *Journal of Business Ethics* 89(2): 189–204.

——— and Altuntaş, C. (2012), Corporate Social Responsibility: A Framework for the Sustainable Future of Enlarged Europe. *Mustafa Kemal Üniversitesi Sosyal Bilimler Enstitüsü Dergisi* 9(18): 459–77.

——— and Altuntaş, C. (2013), Ethics of Social Responsibility to Indirect Stakeholders: A Strategic Perspective. *International Journal of Business Governance and Ethics* 8(2): 137–54.

TurkStat. (2012), *Women in Statistics*. Available at: http://www.tuik.gov.tr/Kitap.do?metod=KitapDetay&KT_ID=11&KITAP_ID=238 (Retrieved 15 October 2013).

Vodafone Vakfı. (2013), *Women Movement in Technology*. Available at: http://www.turkiyevodafonevakfi.org.tr/Women-Movement-in-Technology.php (Retrieved 20 October 2013).

Warren, K.J. (ed.) (1994), *Ecological Feminism: Environmental Philosophies*. London: Routledge.

Weber, M. (2008), The Business Case for Corporate Social Responsibility: A Company-level Measurement Approach for CSR. *European Management Journal* 26: 247–61.

Weber, R.P. (1990), *Basic Content Analysis*. Thousand Oaks, CA: Sage Publications.

WCED (World Commission on Environment and Development). (1987), *Our Common Future*. Oxford: Oxford University Press.

World Bank. (2013), *World Databank*. Available at: http://databank.worldbank.org/data/home.aspx (Retrieved 15 October 2013).

Chapter 13

Women and Social Sustainability

The Case of Canadian Agriculture

Amber J. Fletcher

Introduction

Social sustainability is the least discussed, and least clearly articulated, of the three 'pillars' of sustainable development: economic sustainability, environmental sustainability and social sustainability (United Nations, 2012). Various definitions of the concept exist. In one commonly cited definition, the Western Australian Council of Social Services (WACOSS) describes social sustainability as a situation where 'formal and informal processes, systems, structures and relationships actively support the capacity of current and future generations to create healthy and liveable communities' (as cited in van London and Ruijter, 2010: 18). There are several models and sets of indicators to measure and evaluate social sustainability (for example McKenzie, 2004; Western Australian Council of Social Service, n.d.); in general, these models emphasize principles of equity, diversity, democracy and strong social capital or interconnectedness. Social capital, similarly, has been variously defined. In their review of the concept, Adler and Kwon (2002) defined social capital as 'the goodwill that is engendered by the fabric of social relations and that can be mobilized to facilitate action' (17).

Like the two other 'pillars' of sustainability, social sustainability involves the continuity of communities and the well-being of future generations. It is this crucial component that links social sustainability and environmental sustainability. Future societies are dependent upon the long-term sustainability of natural ecosystems. Without this connection to environment, definitions of social sustainability simply – and uncritically – promote the preservation of social structures or communities, whether or not these structures or communities are environmentally responsible. One example of this disconnection is the definition of social sustainability provided in the Government of Canada's framework on corporate social responsibility. The framework defines social sustainability simply as 'improving local and global social conditions of workers, their families, communities and society at large' (Industry Canada, 2012). No reference is made to the social-environmental linkage.

In their 2011 article, Vallance, Perkins and Dixon broach the issue of whether some social structures should in fact be sustained. They suggest a threefold definition of social sustainability and connect each of the three components to environmental sustainability. They identify 'development sustainability', which means building social structures that address basic human needs; 'bridge sustainability' involves fostering behavioural changes that promote environmentally responsible attitudes in a society;

finally, 'maintenance sustainability' identifies which existing social practices can be maintained – and which must change – in order to be environmentally sustainable. In this chapter, I apply the concept of social sustainability to the current state of Canadian agriculture, focusing on its gendered and environmental dimensions. I suggest that cooperative forms of social capital, which were prevalent in the early decades of prairie agriculture, have now been overshadowed by a competitive, productivist paradigm. As family farmers are pressured to produce ever more, environmental practices are deemphasized. I argue the importance of preserving social structures and modes of production that reinforce and reward environmental awareness over unmitigated production levels.

Since the early days of European settlement in Canada, family farms[1] have dominated the agricultural landscape. In the latter half of the 1800s, the newly established Canadian government set out to populate the prairie region with family farms. This goal was motivated, in part, by the need to create a domestic market for agricultural implements being produced in central Canada (Fowke, 1957). The simultaneous rise of a world market for wheat meant that the Canadian west soon became a system of simple commodity producers, that is, a system of household-based farms producing a specialized commodity – wheat – for export (Buller, 1919; Friedmann, 1978). Therefore, the tariff-protected implement industry soon existed alongside an export-oriented agricultural market (Fowke, 1957; Friedmann, 1978). Early Western farmers found themselves as price-takers in a situation known as the 'cost-price squeeze' – they were 'squeezed' between high input costs in the domestic market and lowered prices for their grain exports on competitive world markets.

The early 1900s brought several decades of agrarian protest as farmers fought for economic control. Initially sparked by the unfair practices of railways and elevator handling companies, these movements lasted into the 1930s and resulted in the creation of several farmer-owned grain companies and farmer unions (McCrorie, 1964). Although political and social differences caused some discord between farmers (Stirling and Conway, 1988), sufficient class cohesion and social capital existed to facilitate a strong agrarian movement directed against large agribusiness interests and financial speculators.

The dominant history of prairie agriculture is a story of the 'heroic male leaders' who led this agrarian movement (Taylor, 2007: 33) and other adventurous, industrious men who took up farming in the region. Farm women also played important roles in establishing prairie agriculture, although their contributions have been submerged in the historical narrative. In the late 1800s and early 1900s, prairie women's lives were structured by a patriarchal gender ideology. Marriage and motherhood were seen as essential roles for women, while farming was constructed as a masculine pursuit (Binnie-Clark and Carter, 2007). Rarely have the contributions of farm women been seen as contributions to agriculture itself.

This gender ideology was (re)produced through settlement-era policy. Homesteading legislation limited the possibility of an independent livelihood for women. The *Dominion Lands Act* of 1872, for example, dictated that only 'heads of households' or men over 21 could apply for land on which to establish a farm. Due to the difficulty of arguing that a woman could indeed be a 'head of household', single female homesteaders were often forced to purchase or rent their land instead of receiving land from the government (Rollings-Magnusson, 1999). Property laws also discouraged women from leaving marriages and simultaneously reinforced men's control over resources (Rollings-Magnusson, 1999). These laws began to shift around 1918, when some property rights for women began to develop. However, women in most Canadian provinces did not receive full equal rights to matrimonial property, including farm and ranch businesses, until the late 1970s or early '80s.

The notion of farming as 'men's work' continues today. Women's farm contributions are often still viewed as peripheral or invisible (Alston, 1998; Kubik, 2005), and women are underrepresented as farm operators. In 2011, only 9 per cent of sole farm operators were women, and women comprised only 27 per cent of all farmers on sole or multiple-operator farms (Statistics Canada, 2011a). Nonetheless, women's contributions to the farm business are increasing. Although farm men continue to perform more field work than women, a 2006 comparative study found that Canadian farm women are more active in all farm tasks than they were in 1982 (Martz, 2006). Between 1982 and 2006, the percentage of farm women involved in grain hauling grew from 28 per cent to 54 per cent, and the percentage driving heavy harvesting machinery (known as 'combines') grew from 21 per cent to 36 per cent (Martz 2006). On many farm operations, farm women are also responsible for the majority of financial management and record-keeping.

In addition to farming work, farm women's labour is central to the farm household. Farm women continue to do the majority of household labour, such as cooking, cleaning and laundry. However, due to the interconnection of farm and household, domestic work on the farm often blurs the lines between 'productive' and 'reproductive', between 'farm' and 'domestic' labour (Kubik, 2005; Whatmore, 1991). In the early days of prairie agriculture, farm women's roles ranged from removing trees to clear farmland to raising livestock for the household's own consumption. Today, such subsistence practices have given way to highly industrialized farming. For contemporary farm women, 'household' work now includes such tasks as cleaning laundry sprayed with agricultural chemicals and cooking meals for 10 hired farm workers. Throughout history, farm women's work has been central to sustaining and reproducing the family farm as a productive unit.

Scholars have questioned why the family farm continues to exist in Canadian agriculture. Unlike many other household-based and simple commodity production systems that have disappeared under advanced capitalism, the family farm remains the primary mode of agricultural production in Canada. Despite much popular discourse about the demise of the family farm, only 4 per cent of farms in Canada are classified as 'non-family corporations' (Statistics Canada, 2011a). The family farm's endurance has been attributed to a variety of factors, including the adaptability or flexibility of the farm family's labour (for example Brookfield, 2008; Friedmann, 1978) or the fact that family farming is often motivated by the goals of personal consumption and farm reproduction rather than by a profit imperative (Friedmann, 1978).

Despite its continued existence, the family farm is changing dramatically. Contemporary farming on the Canadian prairies is now guided by economies of scale. Historical forms of cooperative farming have been overshadowed by a new ideology of 'farming as a business'. Large multinational agribusiness corporations have increased their presence at multiple links in the food chain, from seed inputs to marketing and export (Kuyek, 2007). Farm machinery has grown extremely large, complex and expensive. With such changes, prairie farming has become more competitive and industrialized. In order to keep apace with the rising price of inputs and to make a profit on expanding international markets, farmers have dramatically increased the size of their farms. Small- and medium-sized family farms are often unable to compete and many have been forced to leave the industry. In just four years between 2006 and 2011, the number of farms in the province of Saskatchewan dropped by nearly 17 per cent (Statistics Canada, 2011a). In the same time frame, average farm size increased by 10 per cent in the province of Alberta, by 13 per cent in Manitoba, and by 15 per cent – the highest increase in the country – in the province of Saskatchewan (Statistics Canada, 2011b).

Very little research has examined the implications of these changes for social and environmental sustainability in Canadian agriculture. Further, aside from some notable exceptions (Kubik, 2004; Martz, 2006), very little recent research has considered the gendered dimensions of the changing family farm in Canada. In this chapter, I draw on my research with farm women in the Canadian prairie province of Saskatchewan. I discuss farm women's roles and contributions toward social and environmental sustainability in contemporary family farming.

Methodology

The research discussed in this chapter was conducted between August 2011 and January 2012. I conducted in-depth, in-person interviews with 30 farm women from 27 communities across the Canadian prairie province of Saskatchewan, as well as key informant interviews with three leaders of major agricultural organizations. Participants were recruited using purposive and snowball sampling techniques. The interviews were a combination of open-ended, semi-structured questions and closed, quantitative questions that focused on women's understandings of recent changes in rural communities, agriculture and the environment. The results were coded using a mixed deductive and inductive technique assisted by NVivo 9 qualitative data processing software.

The average age of the study participants was 54 years (min = 31; max = 72), which reflects the statistical average for Saskatchewan farmers overall (Statistics Canada, 2011a). The participants' farms ranged in size from 800 to 12,000 acres, with an average size of 3,657 acres; this is slightly larger than the provincial average of 1,668 acres (Statistics Canada, 2011a). Farm types were also generally reflective of agriculture in the province: 16 participants produced both crops and livestock, 12 produced only crops, and two produced only livestock. Participants had spent an average length of 30.8 years in farming (min = 11; max = 52).

Findings

The Productivist Paradigm

In discussions about the current state of agriculture in Saskatchewan, two interconnected trends emerged most strongly. First, participants spoke about the growing power of large multinational corporations in agriculture. They expressed concern about the rising cost of farm inputs such as seed, agro-chemicals, and equipment. Some attributed rising input costs to a lack of competition in the inputs sector, which in many cases is dominated by only a few large companies.

Other participants noted the growing role of multinational corporations in producing new seed and chemical inputs. From the late 1800s to the mid-1980s, the creation of new seed varieties had been primarily a public endeavour that occurred in government or university-based plant breeding facilities, often in cooperation with farmers (Kuyek, 2007). This plant breeding consisted primarily of crossbreeding techniques. As Kuyek (2007) has argued, by the 1980s seed production paradigms began to shift toward an increasingly profit-focused system marked by a strong corporate presence. With this new system came the introduction of seeds genetically modified to tolerate specific conditions or agro-chemicals. Indeed, Canada is now amongst the top five countries in the world producing genetically modified (GM) crops (Beckie et al., 2011). GM seeds, which are designed for use with patented agro-chemicals and fertilizers, now represent approximately 95 per cent of the canola produced in Canada (Beckie et al., 2011). Most are accompanied by usage contracts that prevent farmers from reusing the seed; they must purchase new GM seed each year.

Farmers are drawn to GM technologies by the promise of higher productivity. Although the farm women perceived some benefits, such as higher crop yields, from these seed inputs, many also expressed a loss of control over their conditions of production. For example, one farm woman stated, 'I am concerned that it is corporations and not farmers driving the future as to which characteristics they want in the plants'. Participants were also critical of the growing rate of profit for corporations in the input sector. One farm woman attributed this to lack of competition:

> [Companies] can pretty much charge whatever they want . . . [we] used to have all these little grain companies or you could buy it privately from a farmer, and you had many more options. Now, especially with canola, you don't have any options. There are a couple of places to get it, and this is the price, and if you don't like it, well, then you don't get any. Simple.

A second, related theme was the growing size and industrialization of family farms in Canada. As the cost of production has risen, Canadian farmers have expanded the size of their farm operations – and nowhere is this trend more evident than in the prairie region. A strong majority (85 per cent) of participants in the study had either expanded or intensified their farm operation within the past 15 years. The main motivation for expanding was to ensure the profitability of the farm, especially for future generations. One farm woman summarized the financial motivation for farm size growth: 'Our farm has gotten bigger. The input costs have gotten huge and the return has stayed pretty much the same. You're just playing with bigger numbers and the profit at the end has pretty much stayed the same'.

These two interconnected themes illustrate the shift toward a more industrialized, productivist paradigm in Canadian agriculture. Faced with rising costs, fluctuating market prices, and the elimination of farm support programmes, farmers engage economies of scale as a form of adaptation to market conditions. As farms grow ever larger, farm women experience higher demand on their farm labour. Women reported driving great distances – sometimes as long as 40 minutes – to haul grain or deliver meals to farm workers. Typically, when hired labour is attainable, gender roles are reinforced and women are positioned as responsible for preparing meals for farm workers. However, in many regions hired labour is unattainable due to the draw of lucrative jobs in other industries, such as oil extraction and mining; even when labour is available, many farmers simply cannot afford to hire farm workers. Without hired workers, women become (in the words of many participants) 'hired men'. Indeed, although the most common job title used by participants was 'farmer' (n = 14), the majority also labelled themselves as 'employees' of the farm, or they described their farm work as 'helping' or 'assisting'. Men, in contrast, tended to be seen as the 'main' or 'primary' farmers and were attributed the locus of control over daily production decisions. Despite a heightened demand for women's labour in the fields, in the barns and in the household, farm women's contributions to agriculture remain under-recognized – sometimes even by the women themselves.

Rural Society in the Productivist Era

The new productivist paradigm has brought dramatic changes in the social fabric of rural Saskatchewan. The loss of many small- and medium-sized family farms has led to a decline in rural populations. Young people are leaving rural life for opportunities in urban areas; meanwhile, the growing competition and high cost of farming makes it an undesirable or unattainable career for many young people. With depopulation, many communities have lost businesses, schools and hospitals, which further fuels the trend. As farms grow larger and further apart, neighbourly relationships are lost.

Depopulation combines with ideological factors to deplete rural social capital. Rising competition for land and a more competitive business ideology have diminished cooperative relationships between farmers. Although farmers support each other during crises such as an illness or death, everyday cooperation has declined. The farmer-owned grain cooperatives established during the early 1900s have ceased to exist and their assets have been sold to large multinational grain corporations. Many farm women spoke of the loss of social capital in their communities:

> Coming out to the 'whoop-whoops' [social events] and getting people together to talk about things – there used to be a lot of that when I first started in farming in the early [19]80s. It was a lot more – what would you call it? – grassroots. But it doesn't seem to be the same anymore . . . people get . . . they're getting too tied up in farming as the business and not as the way of life.

Indeed, the cooperation of the early settlement era has given way to an individualistic ideology of 'farming as a business'. Some participants viewed this ideology as the source of rifts in the farming population. One participant noted that

> The most defined lines out here in terms of conflict right now are the individualistic versus the interdependent: the [farmers] that have been brainwashed into believing that they can survive on their own, and that they are completely on their own, versus the ones who recognize their interdependence.

Despite the powerful ideology of competitive individualism that accompanies the new productivist paradigm, many of the participants valued their communities and the historical social ties within them. Participants actively worked to maintain social capital in their communities. Almost all of the participants performed community volunteer work, although many expressed concern that the shrinking population had increased the amount of community work required to maintain social events and relationships. Many of the women also expressed their love of farming and their desire to maintain a farm lifestyle. One farm woman expressed this common sentiment by saying,

> In the end, I wouldn't trade the family life on the farm for anything. Nobody, in my 34 years of living here, has ever told me when to start or end my day. I feel fortunate that I was able to raise our three daughters on [the] family farm, which will be 100 years [old] next year.

Implications for Environmental Sustainability

Throughout the history of agriculture on the Canadian prairies, farmers have engaged in environmentally beneficial practices, such as the use of livestock manure as fertilizer. However, family farming should not be portrayed as always-already environmentally sustainable; to do so would be to forget history and to ignore the effect of broader economic conditions in shaping micro-level practices. After a catastrophic agricultural drought swept the plains of North America in the 1930s, there was a recognition that unsustainable farming practices had contributed, at least in part, to the extreme soil erosion that occurred. In an effort to establish a sustainable level of productivity, farmers had 'mined' the soil of its nutrients. As previously discussed, social capital was strong in the agricultural prairie region during the early 1900s, but this social capital was not accompanied by environmental sustainability. Environmental knowledge and practices were overshadowed by a survival imperative. Nonetheless, lessons from the 'Dirty Thirties' drought spurred the creation of institutional infrastructure, such as the federal government's Prairie Farm Rehabilitation Administration (PFRA), which encouraged environmentally sustainable farming practices such as the planting of tree shelterbelts for erosion prevention and the preservation of natural grasslands through a system of protected community pastures. Farmers learned from the experience of the 1930s, and knowledge of sustainable practices was passed through subsequent generations.

Today's productivist paradigm has caused another shift in farm practice. The prioritization of economic concerns over environmental sustainability can be seen in both policy and farming practice. In 2012, the federal government eliminated the shelterbelt programme originally operated by the PFRA and divested itself of the community pastures programme. Meanwhile, farmers have also engaged in productivist strategies for both adaptation and profit. While some family farmers today strive simply to maintain household consumption levels and reproduce the farm, others are driven by a profit motive. Many farmers have embraced the use of agro-chemicals and large-scale equipment to increase production levels. Some very large family farms, which often encompass more than 20,000 acres, use small aircraft to spread chemicals onto land and crops. Participants reported that farmers have removed tree shelterbelts to accommodate very large farm equipment. Many farmers lack storage capacity for the vast quantities of grain now being produced; as such, a new trend on prairie farms is the use of plastic 'grain bags', which act as temporary storage containers to hold tonnes of grain. Although recycling facilities for grain bags have begun to be established, participants reported that, due to inconvenience and lack of time, some farmers simply burn these containers after use.

Despite these environmentally unsustainable practices, most participants agreed that many farmers possess an environmental awareness and a desire to preserve the land for future generations. However, at the end of the day, farmers focused on financial sustainability and farm survival, which often took precedence over environmental practices. One participant expressed this view, saying, 'I think most [farmers] are very [environmentally] concerned but they can't afford to be'. A leader of one farm organization discussed the push for productivity through GM products, stating that '[farmers] have readily adopted these GM technologies, and a driving force in that is the cost-price squeeze. They're looking for the increased value in order to solve their profitability problem'.

While it is inaccurate to suggest that small farmers are uniformly more environmentally aware than large farmers, or vice versa, it is valid to compare the environmental implications of different farming paradigms. The productivity paradigm is associated with an asymmetrical valuation of economics over environment, ideologically and in practice. However, it should be noted that some productivity-focused farm practices may bring mixed environmental benefits: a new practice, known as 'minimum till' or 'zero till', has been embraced almost uniformly by farmers in the province of Saskatchewan. The practice replaces the traditional practice of soil tillage – a major contributor of soil erosion – with chemical methods of preparing the land for seeding. Although often described as an environmentally friendly practice, several farm women questioned whether the practice is truly more environmental due to the large amounts of chemicals used. As one woman pointed out, the practice also reinforces dependence on inputs purchased from large corporations:

> [Zero-till] really improves the quality of your land quite a bit . . . you don't lose topsoil and you have a lot more organic matter going back into the ground . . . but on the other hand, farmers have become slaves to the chemical company.

Participants were asked if they perceived a gender difference between men and women in terms of environmental awareness. Their answers were almost evenly divided, with 13 participants stating that farm women are more environmentally aware than farm men and 14 participants stating that environmental awareness tends to vary by family, not by individual. One participant was uncertain. However, it is notable that none of the participants felt that farm men were more environmentally aware than farm women.

Of the participants who felt that farm women were more environmentally aware, reasons varied dramatically. Some held essentialist views of women as more intuitive, caring and conscientious. Two participants felt that women might be more cautious about chemical use due to the prevalence of breast cancer. Many linked women's increased awareness to their roles in social reproduction, arguing that women may be more concerned about healthy food, about their children's future or might have learned about environmental issues from their children. This point is supported by recent research from Australia, in which participants linked rural women's increased environmental awareness to their household roles (Boetto and McKinnon, 2013). Relatedly, four participants explained that, because farm men often play the role of 'main farmer', they may be more attuned to issues of farm productivity and finances. This makes farm men more likely to emphasize productivity over the environment.

Discussion

In agriculture, social sustainability involves sustaining and preserving social structures that are linked to environmentally sustainable farming practice. With their concept of 'maintenance social sustainability', Vallance, Perkins and Dixon (2011) address how people's preferences and desired lifestyles may either advance or conflict with the goal of environmental sustainability, suggesting a potential trade-off between maintaining the environment or maintaining one's preferred lifestyle. Environmental initiatives need social appeal, and vice versa.

Family farmers in the Canadian prairies seek to maintain a preferred lifestyle that is, in many ways, very environmentally sustainable due to its emphasis on intergenerational farming. However, in the current situation, environmentally sustainable practices are at odds with economic profitability. Many farm women expressed their love of the land and their country lifestyle, and all but one participant expressed some concern about the current productivist paradigm of rapidly expanding farms and diminishing rural populations. The rewards for farming sustainably – such as the long-term health of the land for future generations – are currently being outweighed by short-term financial survival in a highly competitive and corporatized agricultural context. Further, as rural depopulation proceeds and children move to urban areas to advance their education or careers, the possibility of intergenerational transfer disappears and the long-term sustainability of the land is no longer a personal interest for some farmers.

Indeed, the productivist paradigm has led to a loss of social capital in rural areas. Social capital includes micro-level relationships between individuals as well as the broader social structures or systems in which those relationships are embedded (Adler and Kwon, 2002). In the history of prairie agriculture, these social structures included cooperative relations between farmers. In the early decades of the 1900s, rural social capital resulted in a strong agrarian protest movement as farmers pushed back against the economic power of large capital. Such resistance is not seen on the prairie today. Instead, farmers have adapted to the growing role of large capital in both the input and marketing sectors; they have done this primarily by expanding farm size and depending on high-cost chemical or GM inputs to increase productivity. Adaptation is more individualized than in the past.

Family farming as a mode of production possesses internally necessary characteristics that are conducive to both environmental and social sustainability. For example, past research on family farmers has shown the desire to preserve the land for children and grandchildren (Lind, 1995). However, depopulation and contemporary economic challenges have led some farm women to advise their children against a farming career (Roppel, Desmarais and Martz, 2006). Although family farming remains the dominant mode of agricultural production in Canada, broader economic conditions have reshaped the social relations of family farming and, with this, farmers' practices vis-à-vis the environment have also changed. Furthermore, some very large family farms have grown to the extent that they are now operated as capitalist ventures, wherein farm families become owners but not operators (Magnan, 2012). Many participants questioned the environmental sustainability of such operations; unlike family farmers, employees on large capitalist operations may not have an inherent interest in preserving the quality of the land for future generations. Further research on the environmental practices of specifically capitalist farming ventures is strongly needed.

In this chapter, I have drawn on my research with Saskatchewan family farmers to posit that most family farmers possess an environmental awareness. This awareness is grounded in their desire for long-term sustainability of the land, which in turn is usually motivated by the desire for intergenerational transfer of the farm. However, the productivist paradigm has forced many farmers into a system wherein economic profit and environmental sustainability are in conflict, forcing many to engage in environmentally unsustainable practices for short-term economic survival or gain, or somewhat paradoxically, to make the farm economically feasible for future generations.

The long-term survival of the family farm is, in part, attributable to the flexibility of family members' labour; in other words, family members are able to exploit their own labour to ensure the survival of the farm (Friedmann, 1978). Farm women are important, yet often under-recognized, contributors to farm survival. Farm women often view themselves as 'helpers' or 'employees' on the farm, which speaks to their relative disconnection from farm control vis-à-vis men, who are viewed as the 'main' or 'primary' farmer. While these 'main' farmers become encompassed within a productivist ideology of competition and profit, the farm women I interviewed often questioned the social and environmental implications of the current paradigm. Indeed, almost half of the women interviewed felt that women had a higher level of environmental awareness than men did; there were none who perceived farm men as more environmentally aware than farm women. It is women's relative distance from the productivist pressures that affords them a critical perspective; unfortunately, this distance also reinforces the historical invisibility of farm women's contributions – a fact which continues as farms grow larger and women experience growing demands on their farm and household labour.

Conclusion

Farm women make crucial contributions to the existence of the family farm as a mode of agricultural production on the Canadian prairies; without their labour, the long-term sustainability of the family farm model is uncertain. In this chapter, I have argued that the internal structure of family farming – its family based nature, the relationship of farmers to the land they live on and the desire for intergenerational inheritance – has facilitated environmental practices. If, as I have argued, the concept of social sustainability must also attend to environmental sustainability, then family farming is a social structure that should be maintained.

Today, however, family farmers face external pressure to produce ever more by any means necessary. This paradigm, which I have called the 'productivist paradigm', emerges from the broader trend of growing corporatization throughout the agricultural system. This trend has exacerbated the well-known 'cost-price squeeze': it has increased the cost of inputs and exposed farmers to competition on international markets. Farmers adapt by engaging large-scale and highly industrialized production techniques, including large amounts of agro-chemicals, the removal of trees to accommodate large farm equipment and use of patented GM seeds to increase productivity. Further, some family owned farms have extended toward a new, capitalist mode of production in which hired workers provide the majority of farm labour. Participants in this study expressed concern about the environmental implications of the productivist paradigm and its future directions.

The productivist paradigm of farming is associated with social relations of competition and an ideology of individualism, which have overshadowed historical forms of social capital and cooperation. In the early decades of the 1900s, family farmers overcame their political and demographic differences to form an agrarian movement against the extractive power of large capital and financial interests. Yet, this social capital was not accompanied by environmentally sustainable practices as farmers 'mined' the soil to establish their farm homesteads, resulting in high levels of soil erosion during the drought of the 1930s. Environmental sustainability, then, must be a key component of socially sustainable communities. Contemporary farming, in contrast, is marked by *both* competitive social relations (low social capital) *and* environmentally problematic farming strategies. Therefore, in this chapter I have argued the need to sustain a more cooperative form of agricultural society that emphasizes less competitive, less industrialized and more environmentally responsible forms of food production. From the perspective of many farm women interviewed in this study – women whose position as 'peripheral' farmers afforded them a more critical view of the productivist paradigm – the link between social and environmental sustainability is crucial to ensure sustainable agriculture practices for future generations.

Note

1 The 'family farm' has been variously defined. Roberts (1996) defined it as an enterprise in which the family or household retains 'ownership of business capital and land, exercises full management control, and supplies a significant proportion of the labour, although the farm may be integrated into circuits of capital through technological dependence, marketing linkages, and credit relations' (404). Brookfield (2008) suggested a similar definition but focused on land management instead of land ownership, since many family farms rent a portion of their land; he states, 'family management, coupled with substantial [family] work input, seems to adequately define family farms' (110). Others (for example Hill, 1993) have defined family farms by the proportion of labour contributed by family versus hired sources. In this chapter, I employ the definitions provided by Roberts and Brookfield; all participants represented farms wherein family members are owners, managers and central farm workers for the operation.

References

Adler, P.S. and Kwon, S.-W. (2002), Social Capital: Prospects for a New Concept. *Academy of Management Review* 27(1): 17–40.

Alston, M. (1998), Farm Women and Their Work: Why is it not Recognised? *Journal of Sociology* 34(1): 23–34.

Beckie, H.J., Harker, K.N., Legere, A., Morrison, M.J., Seguin-Swartz, G. and Falk, K.C. (2011), GM Canola: The Canadian Experience. *Farm Policy Journal* 8(1): 43–9.

Binnie-Clark, G. and Carter, S. (2007), *Wheat and Woman*. Toronto, ON: University of Toronto Press.

Boetto, H. and McKinnon, J. (2013), Rural Women and Climate Change: A Gender-inclusive Perspective. *Australian Social Work* 66(2): 234–47.

Brookfield, H. (2008), Family Farms Are Still Around: Time to Invert the Old Agrarian Question. *Geography Compass* 2(1): 108–26.

Buller, A.H.R. (1919), *Essays on Wheat*. New York: Macmillan.

Fowke, V.C. (1957), *The National Policy and the Wheat Economy*. Toronto, ON: University of Toronto Press.

Friedmann, H. (1978), World Market, State, and Family Farm: Social Bases of Household Production in the Era of Wage Labor. *Comparative Studies in Society and History* 20(4): 545–86.

Hill, B. (1993), The 'Myth' of the Family Farm: Defining the Family Farm and Assessing its Importance in the European Community. *Journal of Rural Studies* 9(4): 359–70.

Industry Canada. (2012), *Social Sustainability*. Available at: http://www.ic.gc.ca/eic/site/csr-rse.nsf/eng/rs00590.html/ (Retrieved 10 October 2013).

Kubik, W. (2004), The Changing Roles of Farm Women and the Consequences for their Health, Well-being, and Quality of Life. Unpublished doctoral dissertation, University of Regina, Regina, Saskatchewan.

———. (2005), Farm Women: The Hidden Subsidy in our Food. *Canadian Woman Studies* 24(4): 85–90.

Kuyek, D. (2007), Sowing the Seeds of Corporate Agriculture: The Rise of Canada's Third Seed Regime. *Studies in Political Economy* 80: 31–54.

Lind, C. (1995), *Something's Wrong Somewhere: Globalization, Community and the Moral Economy of the Farm Crisis*. Halifax, NS: Fernwood Books.

Londen, S. van and de Ruijter, A. (2010), 'Sustainable diversity', in M. Janssens, M. Bechtoldt, A. de Ruijter, D. Pinelli, G. Prarolo and V.M.K. Stenius (eds), *The Sustainability of Cultural Diversity: Nations, Cities, and Organizations*. Cheltenham: Edward Elgar, pp. 3–31.

Magnan, A. (2012), New Avenues of Farm Corporatization in the Prairie Grains Sector: Farm Family Entrepreneurs and the Case of One Earth Farms. *Agriculture and Human Values* 29(2): 161–75.

Martz, D.J.F. (2006), Canadian Farm Women and Their Families: Restructuring, Work and Decision-making. Unpublished doctoral dissertation, University of Saskatchewan, Saskatoon, Saskatchewan.

McCrorie, J.N. (1964), *In Union is Strength*. Saskatoon, SK: Centre for Community Studies, University of Saskatchewan.

McKenzie, S. (2004), *Social Sustainability: Towards Some Definitions*. Hawke Research Institute, University of South Australia. Available at: http://w3.unisa.edu.au/hawkeinstitute/publications/downloads/wp27.pdf (Retrieved 13 June 2016).

Roberts, R. (1996), Recasting the 'Agrarian Question': The Reproduction of Family Farming in the Southern High Plains. *Economic Geography* 72(4): 398–415.

Rollings-Magnusson, S. (1999), Hidden Homesteaders: Women, the State and Patriarchy in the Saskatchewan Wheat Economy, 1870–1930. *Prairie Forum* 24(2): 171–83.

Roppel, C., Desmarais, A.A. and Martz, D. (2006), *Farm Women and Canadian Agricultural Policy*. Ottawa, ON: Status of Women Canada. Available at: http://www.aic.ca/gender/pdf/Farm_Women.pdf/ (Retrieved 13 June 2016).

Statistics Canada. (2011a), *2011 Census of Agriculture*. Ottawa, ON: Government of Canada. Available at: http://www.statcan.gc.ca/dailyquotidien/120510/dq120510a-eng.htm/ (Retrieved 13 June 2016).

———. (2011b), *Snapshot of Canadian Agriculture: Farm and Farm Operator Data* (No. 95–640-XWE). Available at: http://www.statcan.gc.ca/pub/95–640-x/2012002/01-eng.htm/ (Retrieved 13 June 2016).

Stirling, R. and Conway, J. (1988), 'Fractions among Prairie farmers', in G.S. Basran and D.A. Hay (eds), *The Political Economy of Agriculture in Western Canada*. Toronto, ON: Garamond Press, pp. 73–86.

Taylor, G.M. (2007), '"What can we, the plain common people, do?": Violet McNaughton and the Hillview Local of the Saskatchewan Grain Growers Association', in M. Knuttila and R. Stirling (eds), *The Prairie Agrarian Movement Revisited*. Regina, SK: Canadian Plains Research Center Press, pp. 31–60.

United Nations. (2012), *Report of the United Nations Conference on Sustainable Development, Rio de Janeiro, 20–22 June 2012*. New York: United Nations.

Vallance, S., Perkins, H.C. and Dixon, J.E. (2011), What is Social Sustainability? A Clarification of Concepts. *Geoforum* 42(3): 342–8.

Western Australian Council of Social Service. (n.d.), *WACOSS Model of Social Sustainability*. Available at: http://www.wacoss.org.au/Libraries/State_Election_2013_Documents/WACOSS_Model_of_Social_Sustainability.sflb.ashx/ (Retrieved 13 June 2016).

Whatmore, S. (1991), *Farming Women: Gender, Work, and Family Enterprise*. London: Macmillan.

Chapter 14

Women Absent in Environmental Politics

Gender Mainstreaming in Environmental Policies

Arzu İrge Özyol and Nesrin Çobanoğlu

Introduction: Conceptual Background

In many international human rights instruments, including the 'Convention on the Elimination of All Forms of Discrimination against Women'[1], gender equality is accepted as an inalienable and integral part of human rights and fundamental freedoms, and it is essential for sustainable development, peace and security as well. It is also important to emphasize that the concept of gender does not only relate to women. Gender refers to both women and men and relations between them. Since the Beijing Conference in 1995, gender equity has been used as a term to provide balance between women and men. Gender equity denotes an element of interpretation of social justice, usually based on tradition, custom, religion or culture. However, it couldn't be possible to explain the advancement of women by the term gender equity. During the Beijing Conference, it was agreed that the term equality would be used. Gender equality means that the rights, responsibilities and opportunities of individuals will not depend on whether they are born male or female. Equality does not mean 'the same as'. In other words, promotion of gender equality does not mean that women and men will become the same. Equality involves ensuring that the perceptions, interests, needs, roles, responsibilities and priorities of women and men will be given equal weight in planning and decision making.

There is a dual rationale for promoting gender equality. First, equality between women and men – equal rights, opportunities and responsibilities – is a manner of human rights and social justice. And second, equality between women and men is also a precondition for sustainable development. The perceptions, interests, needs and priorities of both women and men must be taken into consideration not only as a matter of social justice: they are necessary to enrich development processes (http://www.un.org/womenwatch/osagi/pdf/factsheet1.pdf).

Some results obtained from field studies also show that gender equality is the fundamental issue regarding economic efficiency. For instance, the same opportunities regarding agricultural raw materials and vehicles are given to the women farmers in Kenya as men farmers; the amount of agricultural produce could potentially increase by more than 20 per cent. Another dramatic example is from Tanzania. If women coffee and banana growers spent less time on household chores, it will be possible to increase household cash incomes by 10 per cent, labour productivity by 15 per cent and capital productivity by 44 per cent.

Importance of Gender Mainstreaming in Environmental Policy-making

Women use and manage natural resources in order to perpetuate their families and communities. Women manage and rehabilitate natural resources and so they play a key role in providing sustainable development. Although they create direct effects on the quality and sustainability of the life for today's and future generations, women are not available in political and decision-making processes. However, if exploitation of nature and women is not ended, it is not possible to provide sustainable development.

This conceptual change in gender equality brings back gender mainstreaming strategies. Gender mainstreaming does not entail developing different development projects for women. Gender mainstreaming entails putting women's components within existing projects, programmes and policies. In order to reflect gender perspective on policies, the following questions should be answered. What are the impacts of the decisions on women and men? What is the resource allocation for women and men? What are the roles of women and men regarding policy development, implementation and monitoring? How are the norms and standards determined?

Methodology and Future Research Comments

For this study, a secondary research technique is used. Sets of documents were reviewed specifically in terms of gender rationale and environmental policy approaches:

1   Selected literature reviews of gender and environmental theory and practice.
2   Gender and environmental policy documents and official records from various bilateral and multilateral institutions.

The review adopts familiar working definitions of a number of basic gender and environmental concepts at a global level, although use of the gender mainstreaming strategy varies across countries and policy sectors. However, by the following steps, the implementation of gender mainstreaming strategy in environmental policies will be examined for different countries and a comparative analysis will be made within supranational organizations. Special focus is placed not only on the analysis of policy formulation and decision making, but also the implementation and evaluation of these decisions and the subsequent evaluation of their outcomes.

Gender Mainstreaming

Definition of Gender Mainstreaming in Its Broadest Sense

A gender perspective raises some questions. The first question is about whether or not women and men have access to natural resources at the same level. In order to answer this question it is important to collect sex-disaggregated data on the use of access to resources, and so on. It is also critical to ensure a consultation process to identify priorities for women as well as for men. The second question is about whether or not various policy options will affect women and men differently. The third question is about the impacts of fiscal policy, structure of taxation and budget allocations on women and men respectively.

The strategy of mainstreaming is defined in the ECOSOC Agreed Conclusions, 1997/2 (United Nations, 1997) as:

> The process of assessing the implications for women and men of any planned action, including legislation, policies or programs, in all areas and at all levels. It is a strategy for making women's as well as men's concerns and experiences an integral dimension of the design, implementation, monitoring and evaluation of policies and programs in all political, economic and social spheres so that women and men benefit equally and inequality is not perpetuated. The ultimate goal is to achieve gender equality.

Before implementing gender mainstreaming strategy, the following elements could be taken as starting points to explore how and why gender differences and inequalities are occurring in many specific situations: inequalities in political power (access to decision making, representation), inequalities within households, inequalities in labour markets, inequalities in strategies for HIV/AIDS prevention, inequalities in strategies to eliminate violence against women, differences in legal status and entitlements, inequalities in the domestic/unpaid sector.

It should be borne in mind that gender mainstreaming is a key strategy for achieving gender equality and the empowerment of women. The main elements that should be taken into consideration are as follows:

- Capacity building and institutional development is a fundamental issue to apply gender mainstreaming strategy for both private and public bodies. First, equality should be provided regarding the number of women and men, from senior decision-making levels to workers. Second, mandatory structures and mechanisms should be ensured to reflect the concerns of both women and men in planning and decision making.
- Accountability processes and mechanisms will be strengthened in order to make possible the implementation of gender mainstreaming on different policy areas at all levels.
- Participatory mechanisms should be supported to accelerate the processes. Working groups with the responsibility to advocate for gender equality issues might be formed. The members of these groups act as a catalyst rather than holding the overall responsibility for implementation of gender mainstreaming.
- In order to provide timely information to senior managers to enable them to make strategic decisions, indicators could be determined, measurement protocols could be developed and results-based management could be realized.

- In the context of monitoring, evaluation, audit and reporting, common indicators and benchmarks are determined to measure progress. This approach will help to close the gap in the collection and analysis of sex-disaggregated data. Lack of sex-disaggregated data is one of the major barriers to realizing accurate assessment on policies and programmes which are related to promoting gender equality and empowering women.
- To achieve desired outcomes during the implementation of gender mainstreaming, accurate allocation of human and financial resources is provided. However, developing and strengthening the staff with a capacity and competency in gender analysis is essential to implement gender mainstreaming into policies and programmes successfully.
- Collecting sex-disaggregated data is the major tool for accurate allocation of existing resources such as water, land and forest among men and women.
- Coherence and coordination of the efforts among different stakeholders in the implementation of the gender mainstreaming strategy is a vital element to reach gender equality goals.

Gender Mainstreaming in Policy Development

Gender mainstreaming in policy analysis and development is implemented to determine the impacts of policies on women and men; how this impacts could vary regarding gender differences and inequalities. It should also enable decision makers to reduce the gender gap. In the first step, gender perspectives should be reflected to the formulation of the policy. The accurate formulation is important in the means of fixing the proper scope of the constructive process. Second, gender-disaggregated data is obtained to analyse the gender differences and inequalities in the framework of the scope. The third important point is the assessment of the implications of different options that could have different costs, benefits and consequences for women and men. Fourth, gender perspectives should also be taken into account in the determination of relevant stakeholders and different options to define different needs, expectations and information. In addition, the involvement of civil society and public bodies is extremely important to seek meaningful inputs from both women and men.

Historical Overview on Gender Mainstreaming

Professor Gita Sen (Kabeer, 2003) of Stanford University emphasized the importance of gender issues for development policy:

> A gender perspective means that women stand at the crossroads between production and reproduction, between economic activity and the care of human beings, and therefore between economic growth and human development. They are workers in both spheres — those most responsible and therefore with most at stake, those who suffer most when two spheres meet at cross-purposes, and those most sensitive to the need for better integration between the two.

When we look over poverty reduction policies, we have determined that a serious transition was observed from 1960 to the present. In the early post-war years, development policy emphasized economic growth. In fact, development was equated by industrialization with import substitution. However, by the end of the 1960s, it was obvious that such strategies had failed to bring about the expected reductions in poverty and inequality (Kabeer, 2003: 4). In the 1970s, there was great concern about the productivity of small farmers. The 1970s were the years when the link between women and poverty was established. Attention was drawn to the disproportionate number of female-headed households who were largely responsible for meeting family 'basic needs'. This led to the spread of income-generating projects for women. But these projects had limited impact on the marginalized status of women in the development process (Kabeer, 2003: 13).

Poverty reduction strategies became more important than the problems of unsustainable budget deficits and the balance of payments in the 1980s (Kabeer, 2003: 4). In the 1990s, the poverty agenda of World Development Report (WDR) underlined the importance of broad-based and labour-intensive strategies. Generating income-earning opportunities and developing basic health and education services upheld the improvement in the productivity of the labour force (Kabeer, 2003: 5). WDR is important for feminist history because in its analysis there is a part regarding the gender dimension of poverty: the data on health, nutrition, education and labour-force participation showed that women were often disadvantaged compared to men (Kabeer, 2003: 14). The first Human Development Report (HDR) also touched on gender issues in 1990s. It noted that the increasing number of female-headed households has led to a 'feminization of poverty'. The 1995 report focused on gender inequality in parallel with the outcomes of the UN Fourth Conference on Women in Beijing. It stated that the purpose of development is to increase overall quality of life, not just income. It also figured out that there are 1.3 million people in poverty and 70 per cent are women (Kabeer, 2003: 15).

The 2000 World Development Report was more comprehensive than 1990 WDR regarding gender equality. Gender issues were discussed in different dimensions such as opportunity, empowerment, security, and so on. Although some changes in development policies were observed from the 1970s to the 2000s, it is easily said that Millennium Developments Goals (MDGs) are the milestones in the means of gender needs being clearly understood as a cross-cutting socio-cultural variable. The Millennium Declaration laid out a number of key development goals framed to reflect its fundamental values. Along with the reduction of poverty and hunger, these commitments included the promotion of human development and environmental sustainability. In addition, they included an explicit commitment to gender equality as that no individual and no nation must be denied the opportunity to benefit from development. The equality of rights and opportunities of men and women must be assured (Kabeer, 2003). Director General of International Union for Conservation of Nature (United Nations, 2013) Julia Marton-Lefevre said that 'the third MDG is dedicated to promoting gender equality and the empowerment of women. When we look at the other seven goals, it is clear that none of them are possible without the inclusion of gender considerations'.[2] In Table 14.1, there are some examples of the key links between gender and MDGs.

Table 14.1 Key links between gender and MDGs

Millennium development goals	Examples of gender, environment and energy linkages
Eradicate extreme poverty and hunger	Women represent the majority of those in extreme poverty and their livelihood strategies, and food, water and fuel supplies, often depend directly on healthy ecosystems.
Achieve universal primary education	Time spent collecting water and fuel wood by children, especially girls, reduces school attendance.
Promote gender equality and empower women	Women's time constraints and burdens related to collecting water and fuel wood, and unequal access to land and other natural resources, limit their ability to be active in social and political organizations.
Reduce child mortality	Women's inability to provide clean water for their families results in deaths from diseases such as diarrhoea and cholera, especially among children under the age of five.
Improve maternal health	Indoor air pollution from burning biomass fuels and injuries from carrying heavy loads of water and fuel wood adversely affect women's health and add to risks of complications during pregnancy.
Combat major diseases	Environmental risk factors such as water contamination and lack of sanitation, may have differing impacts on men and women, boys and girls.
Ensure environmental sustainability	Men and women both have important roles to play in environmental conservation efforts.

Source: *Gender mainstreaming: a key driver of development in environment and energy* (United Nations, 2007).

The Importance of Women in Ecosystems

Women and the Environment

The primary concerns about gender differences in some practical areas are related to the fact that adverse environmental conditions and a lack of energy services tend to have a more negative effect on women than on men. This is largely due to women's traditional roles and responsibilities. Inequalities coming from sociological gender roles limit women's control over and access to environmental and energy resources as compared to men. In many developing countries, women, as farmers and pastoralists, with primary responsibility for household food production, are the principal users of the land and natural resources. However, women generally do not own the land or control the allocation of natural resources.

Another major difference between men and women is related to access to water resources. In areas where there is no pumped water, and supplies are scarce due to seasonal dry periods or drought conditions, women can spend many hours per week trying to get enough water. Improved water and sanitation facilities can give time to women for productive activities, and girls more time for school, besides safeguarding their safety, dignity and physical well-being. In addition to getting water, women in developing countries also spend a great deal of time collecting traditional biomass fuels such as wood, dung and agricultural wastes for household needs. Over 1.6 billion people rely on these fuels, and the collection and management of these fuels is primarily done by women. When environmental degradation makes fuel supplies more difficult to find, women have to spend more time and effort searching for fuels long distances from home with consequently less time for other responsibilities. They are also at greater risk of rape, animal attacks and other threats as they travel farther away from home (UNDP training manual: 11–13). Women have no chance to use appropriate fuel with affordable prices, and have to spend more time and energy reaching traditional sources such as coal, wood and dried cow dung in order to prepare food and heat. Rural women have to cultivate without modern agricultural vehicles in order to provide their food. They spend additional time providing water from fountains, wells and rivers if they have no infrastructure or water pumps in their homes. In downscale areas, women are being exposed to open fires to prepare food and heat for long hours. Physiological differences between men and women also affect their relative susceptibility to adverse health impacts from exposure to toxic chemicals. However, due to direct interaction with gaseous particulates, carbon monoxide, benzene and some poisonous chemical compounds, 1.6 million people die every year. Air pollution also causes cataracts and low birth weight (Mies and Vandana, 1993). In many areas, rural women and men have different types of knowledge, and value different things, about natural resources and biodiversity conservation. Women may place more value on forests for the collection of fruits, nuts and medical plants. However, deforestation not only leads to loss of valuable health and food resources but also affects the amount of time and distance women must travel to secure fuel and water.

Main Approaches used to Interpret the Gender–Environment Relationship

Aguilar (2002) argues that sustainable development is not possible without equity. This implies that gender equality and equity are not only a question of fundamental human rights and social justice but are also precondition for environmental conservation, sustainable development and human security. Table 14.2 shows the constructive notices of main models that are used to interpret the gender–environment relationship.

Eco-feminist approach

According to an eco-feminist approach, women are considered as unique without considering differences such as ethnic background, social class, age and other factors. Paternal and capitalist systems have been established to dominate, exploit and domesticate both women and nature. Eco-feminists have based their system on hierarchical dilemmas dualisms of the Western world such as culture/nature, women/men, mind/body, intelligence/emotions and materialism/morale. However, women are surrounded by nature, body, emotion and morale in a negative way whereas men are accepted as the representatives of the one-dimensional public sphere that has been materialized by culture, mind, intelligence and materialism. Patriarchal communities bear themselves with the destructive attitudes such as aggression, competitiveness and preconception. Under these circumstances, in the public areas where women are excluded, environmental problems are growing exponentially.

Table 14.2 Main modules used to interpret the 'gender–environment' relationship

Eco-feminist approach	Women in development approach (WID)	Gender and development approach (GAD)
Conceptualizes the relationship of women with nature, maintaining that there is a strong link between the two. Maintains that women's experiences (biological or cultural) give them a different natural mindset, a special knowledge that will enable them to save the planet and a tendency to protect the environment.	Assumes that women are the main volunteers in the fight against environmental degradation. Stresses the potential of women's role as day-to-day administrators of natural resources. Much is made of women's vulnerability to environmental change due to their dependence on these resources. Development projects and programmes centre on women and their needs as individuals and groups.	Maintains that participation rate of women in labour markets and decision making levels are equal with the participation rates of men. Maintains that there is no difference regarding access to information and knowledge are same for women and men. Accounts for social relationships of production and power. Identifies and seeks to evaluate the differences that exist between women and men by emphasizing the social, historical and cultural nature of the processes of subordination and negotiation in which they are involved.

Source: *Cornell Journal of Law and Public Policy*, 22: 670.

Eco-feminism is a biology-centred environmental movement along with its cultural and social connections. It is a melting pot of ecology and feminism. It emerged as a reaction to men's treatment of nature as they treated women or, vice versa, equating woman and nature. In 1972, in the written report 'World Conversation Strategy' prepared by Conservation of Nature and Natural Resources (IUCN) which is an international organization working in the field of nature conservation and sustainable use of natural resources, the concept of sustainable development was evaluated in terms of conservation of nature. In 1974, 'eco-feminism' was first used as a term by Francoise d'Eaubonne in her work Feminism or Death. D'Eaubonne was a former member of the French Communist Party and took part in the founding of FHAR, which was a homosexual revolutionary movement. The same year, Shelia Colins in her work 'Another Paradise and World', evaluating gender discrimination and ecological destruction in the same context, said 'Racism, sexism, class exploitation, and ecological destruction are structures which shoulder patriarchal construction and they are firmly clasped together'.[3]

The second impact of the eco-feminism wave was seen in the 1990s. Plumwood has captured the precedence of nature through her considerations on the relations between gender and capitalism, racialism and colonialism in the framework of feminism in her books *Feminism and the Mastery of Nature* (1993)[4] and *Environmental Culture: The Ecological Crisis of Reason* (2002). The reasons for the dilemma between humans and nature are expressed by an anthropocentric approach. Plumwood accepted that all these dilemmas are contrary to the approaches of environmental ethics. In order to overcome these dilemmas coming from the power-dependent polarizations, people should build up empathy with all others.[5] Another eco-feminist researcher, Shiva Vandana, pointed out that the Western kind of development aims only to increase capital without considering the competence of nature for restructuring itself. Vandana has evaluated the exploitation of women in the framework of the destruction of produc-tive lands (Mies and Vandana, 1993: 113).

Women in development approach (WID)

In the framework of the women in development approach, women are considered as a distinct and vulnerable group in projects and programmes, where women's knowledge has been utilized in areas related to family or community health (ensuring medical plans and food security) and environmental conservation (the protection of forest products). This approach also ignores the required strategies needed to pursue the various objectives involved in the use and management of environmental resources that will require the contributions of women and men alike. This approach first came to prominence in the early 1970s. Research and information collected throughout the UN Decade for Women (1975–85) highlighted the existing poverty and disadvantages of women and their invisibility in the development process. Different policy responses and interventions focused on women as a separate group resulting in women's con-cerns being 'added on' and peripheral to mainstream development efforts. WID poli-cies have proposed actions targeted only to women rather than integrating them fully into the project activities. WID policies and interventions have concentrated on wom-en's productive work. Failure to make an explicit link to women's reproductive work has often added to women's workload. Gradually, it was recognized that an approach that focused on women in isolation was inadequate and not sustainable, because it did not take into account the overall project objectives or integrate women fully into their implementation. Moreover, it did not address or change unequal gender relations in various social and economic settings. However, there are shortcomings to this approach because by WID women are not available in the use and management of environmen-tal resources. Many policy-makers tend to follow the WID approach to development discourses and programmes (Moser, 1993: 3–4). Although the WID approach may be successful when implementing projects on a small scale, to ensure long-term and sus-tainable results, it is better to utilize the gender and development approach.

Gender and development approach (GAD)

The gender and development (GAD) perspective emerged in the late 1980s as a response to the failure of WID projects. The aims of GAD are to provide qualitative and long-lasting changes in women's social status. GAD focuses on social, economic, political and cultural forces that determine how men and women participate in, ben-efit from and control project resources and activities differently (*Cornell Journal of Law and Public Policy*, 22: 672). This approach shifts the focus from women as a group to the socially determined relations between women and men. GAD uses the term 'gender' instead of 'women'. It also takes into account participation of men as well as women (Buvinic, Gwin and Bates, 1996). However, several key analytical principles, relating to gender roles and practical and strategic gender needs, as well as control over resources and decision making in the household, civil society and the state, were determined and translated into tools and techniques for a gender-planning process at the policy, programme and project levels (Moser, 1993). Table 14.3 indicates the major differences between the WID and GAD approaches.

Table 14.3 WID or GAD?

Description	Women in Development	Gender and Development
Approach	An approach that views women as the problem.	An approach to development.
Focus	Women.	Relations between men and women.
problem	The exclusion of women (half of the productive resources) from the development process.	Unequal relations of power (rich and poor, women and men) that prevent equitable development and participation.
Goal	More efficient, effective development.	Equitable, sustainable development with both women and men as decision makers.
Solution	Integrate women into the development process.	Empower the disadvantaged and women; transform unequal relations.
Strategies	Women's projects. Women's components. Integrated projects. Increase women's productivity. Increase women's income. Increase women's ability to look after the household.	Identify/address practical needs determined by women and men to improve their condition. At the same time, address women's strategic interests. Address strategic interests of the poor through people-centred development.

Source: Dayal, Parker and Svendsen, 1993.

Towards Gender Mainstreaming in Environmental Policies

With 2015 as the target date for achieving the MDGs, it will not be possible to end gender-based injustices that create barriers to women's and girls' opportunities. Some practical approaches should be used to put women's rights at the heart of the MDGs such as increasing the rate of access to services for women (including reproductive health, using stipends and cash transfers), encouraging girls to go to school, delaying marriage, amplifying women's voices in decision making, enhancing women's ability to accumulate assets including through laws and affirmative action, ensuring policies which reflect the realities of women's lives.

Women in Ecosystem Management

Although women have played a leadership role to minimize and reuse environmental wastes, consumption of natural resources and to develop environmental ethics in their daily life, the number of women is very low in professional areas such as city planners, environmentalists, agriculturalists and oceanographers. If women are educated as professionals for the management of natural resources, equal participation has not been provided at decision-making levels in local, national, regional or international organizations, or public institutions and parliaments. On the other hand, there is a traditional weakness in the means of cooperation among non-governmental organizations and public bodies. Furthermore, the participation of women in local governments is extremely low although women have incredibly high experience in environmental protection, ecosystem management and ecological interaction at local levels.

Gender Mainstreaming in Environmental Policy

One implies that gender mediates human/environment interactions and use, knowledge and assessment of environmental issues. According to the second precept, gender roles, responsibilities, expectations and norms predict the human–environment relationship. A gender-sustainable development perspective should be infused with a commitment to change cultural values. United Nations Environmental Program (UNEP) feels that the issue of concern should be 'gender and environment' rather than 'women and environment'. The two broad principles noted above manifest themselves in a variety of environmental relations and interactions.

An analysis conducted by Castaneda and Martin[6] in the Country Analysis Report for CEDAW (Convention on the Elimination of all forms of Discrimination Against Women) points out that the inclusion of sustainable development and the environment in the gender agenda is still weak in many countries. While some reports presented sex-disaggregated data to contextualize gender gaps in rural and urban contexts, most of the reports did not. The situation is not better at international level. When we revised global indices that measure progress in gender equality in different policy areas, the number of indices that show the advancement of women in relation to environmental and development concerns (see Table 14.4 for global indices) is very limited.

Table 14.4 Global indices

Title	Type	Dimension	Observations
Global Gender Gap Report (WEF)	Index Annual 135 Countries	Economic Participation, Educational Attainment, Health and Survival, Political Empowerment	2011 and previous: Does not include or measure any environmental dimension such as use of and access to natural resources, climate change, water and sanitation.
Human Development Report (UNDP)	Index Annual 187 Countries	Human Development Index, Gender Inequality Index (Before 2010 known as Gender Development Index), Multidimensional Poverty Index)	2006: Focused on water scarcity, emphasising gender inequalities and time-use. 2007/2008: Focused on climate change and recognized that climate changed will aggravate existing inequalities (including gender inequality). 2011: Focused on sustainability and equity. Great attention to women's productivity health.
Humanitarian Response Index (HRI)	Index Annual Donor Countries	Responding to Humanitarian Needs, Integrating Relief and Development, Working with Humanitarian Partners, Implementing International Guiding Principles, Promoting Learning and Accountability	2008: Focused on donor accountability in humanitarian action. Women and gender mentioned in relation to violence and development. 2009: Focused on clarifying donor's priorities. 2010: Focused on the problems of politicization. 2011: Focused on addressing the gender challenge. Heavy focus on women and gender issues in relation to humanitarian responses.

Source: *Cornell Journal of Law and Public Policy*, 22: 677.

Conclusion

Gender is a key organizing principle in the distribution of all kinds of resources. When we focus on the definition of 'environmental justice' as 'the fair treatment and meaningful involvement of all people regardless of race, colour, sex, national origin, or income with respect to the development, implementation and enforcement of environmental laws, regulations, and policies',[7] we easily understand that it couldn't be possible to provide environmental justice without using gender mainstreaming strategy. On the other hand, socio-economic classifications are made according to access to global resources. Poverty is generally thought of in terms of deprivation, either in relation to some basic minimum needs or in relation to the resources necessary. However, gender-based data show that 1.3 billion people in developing countries living on less than one dollar a day are women. This is because energy poverty has a disproportionate effect on women. In many countries, women have the responsibility to provide basic family needs through close contact with natural resources such as crops, water, trees and animals.

The UN 2012 Report in Human Development in Africa (UN, 2012) observes that food security and human development reinforce each other. The report notes that, 'To accelerate food security, countries in sub-Saharan Africa must boost agricultural productivity and enhance nutrition to improve availability, access and use of food . . . and empowering women and the rural poor are critical enablers of food security'. Another dramatic example is about the relation between women and access to water. According to the Organization of Few Resources, in just one day, 200 million work hours are consumed by women collecting water for their families. This lost productivity is greater than the combined number of hours worked in a week by employees at Walmart, United Parcel Service, McDonald's, IBM, Target and Kroger.

Findings

In 1995, governments across the world signed the Beijing Platform for Action to achieve gender equality, and gender mainstreaming was defined as the most important strategy to reach the goal. Twenty one years later, it is impossible to say that gender mainstreaming strategy is widely used in different agendas of sustainable development. When we focus on gender mainstreaming in environmental politics, it is becoming more complicated. Although the history of the feminist movement is very old, the conceptual evolution regarding gender equality was realized in recent times. However, it is possible to say that gender equality is also the third-generation human right like the rights for a healthy environment, natural resources, intergeneration, equity, sustainability, cultural heritage, collective movements, self-determination, economic and social development, communication. Certainly, overlapping these two new concepts is taking up time because it requires systemic change in the stated and unstated rules of the game. These rules can be formal, such as constitutions, laws, policies and school curricula, or informal such as cultural arrangements, religious practices and norms (Goetz, 1998; North, 1990; Rao and Kelleher, 2002). Figure 14.1 indicates what we are trying to change.

Discussion

Many researchers have pointed out the importance of effective implementation of gender mainstreaming strategies (Hannan, 2003; Subrahmanian, 2004). The

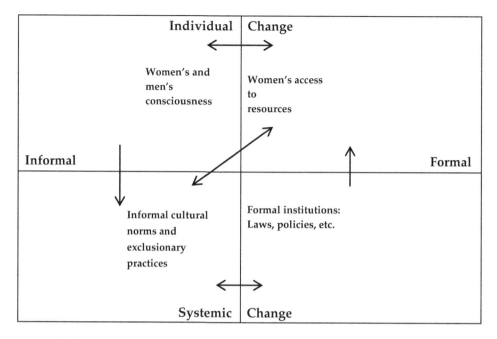

Figure 14.1 What are we trying to change?

Source: *Mainstreaming Gender in Development: A Critical Review.*

fundamental mistake comes by accepting that gender mainstreaming is completely different from work on women's empowerment. However, they are very close to each other as a means of providing gender equality. It is because women have time constraints and burdens due to their traditional roles. Moreover, they have limited access to land and other natural resources.

Another challenge for effective implementation of gender mainstreaming strategies is related to obtaining sex-disaggregated data. The data are needed to examine the access to resources and the impacts of environmental factors on both women and men. On the other hand, gender mainstreaming and organizational culture are intrinsically linked. An organizational culture which is male biased, in terms of attitudes, recruitment, working conditions, structures and procedures, discriminates against female staff and clients (Minh-Chau-Nguyen, 2004).

Gender training programmes always recommended increasing awareness about gender equality at all levels. Gender training needs to be not a one-off event but ongoing and consistently refreshed. It needs to be more tailored to operational activities and culturally sensitive (Wallace, 1998). As both DAC (1998) and UNIFEM (1997) stated, gender mainstreaming should not be considered without women's participation at all levels. Cornwall (2003) argues that to provide development without participatory mechanisms can exacerbate existing exclusion and unequal gender roles. Although women's representation at all levels is necessary, it is not sufficient. The following questions should be answered on the process of gender mainstreaming: Are women's voices actually heard? What is the participation and representation of women in general? Does their presence simply legitimize decisions made by men? What of the differences among women? How are gender issues raised in participatory processes? Who shapes the processes of policy-making?

Recommendations

The World Bank's approach for mainstreaming gender and development is an applicable tool to apply gender mainstreaming in environmental policies. Five recommendations of the World Bank to achieve gender mainstreaming in environmental policies are summarized below:

Recommendation 1. Define a rationale framework for gender and environment

Men and women have different positions, different social roles and different needs within the household. They have differences regarding access to and control over resources as well. Because of the differences, solutions should be developed for different needs through varying participatory planning, processes and procedures. On the other hand, gender planning should be accepted as an operational procedure at the policy, programme and project levels. Gender planning is mainstreamed into existing institutions rather than establishing separate gender-specific organizational structures.

Recommendation 2. Gender-based data collection

Gender analysis looks at quantitative and qualitative data on different roles, activities, needs and opportunities of men and women. Gender-based data collection is a vital part in determining how they differ and how they affect and, in turn, are affected by interventions and policies. The starting point is to examine the access to and control over resources for men and women besides the effects of environmental factors that influence both women and men.

Recommendation 3. A world of women's activism

Around the world, the women's movement and many non-governmental organizations have mobilized around gender and livelihood issues. Many groups have identified environmental issues and gender equality as a priority and placed them on top of their political agenda. In the process, women have acquired a wide range of expertise, including their experiences on the ground. However, the importance of women's participation in policy-making and relevant implementations should be accepted.

At the international level, the Women's Environment and Development Organization (WEDO) continues to be a strong advocate for women in sustainable development; the United Nations Commission on Sustainable Development facilitates women as a major group. The Gender and Water Alliance looks specifically at water-related subjects; the International Network on Gender and Sustainable Energy (ENERGIA) advocates around energy; and Diverse Women for Diversity specialize in agro-biodiversity. GROOTS organizes grassroots women's organizations from around the world on livelihood issues, while the International Network of Indigenous Women is a strong voice on biodiversity and environment-related issues. In 2002, the international network Women Leaders for the Environment was launched, bringing together women ministers of environment and other leaders. Regionally, prominent groups include Women in Europe for a Common Future (WECF), the Platform on Land and Water Rights in Southern Africa and the Gender and Environment Network in Latin America and the Caribbean. Innumerable national and local organizations have flourished as well. Involvement of these civil society organizations is needed at all levels and in all phases of development. (UNEP, 1996)

Recommendation 4. Gender budgeting for infrastructure investments

Gender budgeting does not aim to produce a separate budget for women. Instead it aims to produce a budget in which gender has been mainstreamed. It means that the formulation of the budget incorporates an analysis of public expenditure and methods of raising public revenue from a gender perspective, identifying the implications and impacts for women and girls as compared to men and boys. The key question is: what impact does this fiscal measure have on gender equality? Does it reduce gender inequality, increase it or leave it unchanged?

There are two principles[8] which are mostly used in doing gender budget analysis. The first principle is to assess the budget from the point of view of poor households as compared to rich households. But it is also important to assess the budget for each person in a family, although households do share some resources. According to the second principle, social and economic objectives of a country depend not only on the amount of paid work its people do, but also on the amount of unpaid work its people do caring for their family members and neighbours, and upon the amount of free time people have for leisure and for civic activities. Unpaid care work is still unequally shared between women and men in most countries and this is one of the major obstacles to equality in paid work and to the full development of the talents of both women and men. A key dimension of a budget's impact on gender equality is the impact on the amount of unpaid care work that has to be done.

Recommendation 5. Define the components of gender analysis

The main components of gender analysis which are critical regarding to gender mainstreaming in environmental policies are summarized in Table 14.5.

Table 14.5 Potential components of gender analysis in environmental policy

Component	Description
Need assessment	What are the priority needs of men and women? What are the underlying causes of the problem? How can these problems be addressed? Which problems can be solved at the local level? Which need external intervention?

Component	Description
Activities profile	Who does what?
	What do women, men and children do?
	When do they do it? Daily? Seasonally?
	Where is the activity performed?
	How flexible or rigid is the division of labour?
Resources, access and control	What resources are available to men and women to conduct their activities?
	What resources (land, knowledge, cash and institutions) do women and men have access to (use)?
	Which resources do they control, who has power to decide whether a resource is used, how it is used, and how it is allocated?
Benefits and incentives	Benefit resources refers to resources; access and control and goes further to analyse who controls outputs or benefits.
	Incentive analysis taps into user preferences, values placed on output, and the risks involved, which affect motivation.
	Incentives include: taste, risk, convenience, time savings, reduced conflict, marketability, prestige and by-products.
Institutional analysis	The household is a system of resource allocation.
	All members of a household have different roles, skills, interests, needs, priorities, access to and control over resources.
	Policies, laws, regulations and procedures.
	Planning and evaluation procedures.
	Participatory mechanisms.

Sources: Derbyshire (1996), Kabeer (1999), Moser (1993), Overholt (1985).[9]

Notes

1 http://www.un.org/womenwatch/daw/cedaw/
2 http://www.iucn.org/content/environment-and-gender-equality-keys-achieving-millennium-development-goals
3 https://systemicalternatives.org/2016/01/19/ecofeminism/
4 https://books.google.com.tr/books?id=hU8JAVq0ip4C&printsec=frontcover#v=onepage&q&f=false
5 https://books.google.com.tr/books?id=3V4SCHer39MC&pg=PA275&dq=Environmental+Culture:+The+Ecological+Crisis+of+Reason+(2002).&hl=en&sa=X&ved=0ahUKEwi63vW4g6XNAhWCbhQKHYi9BWIQ6AEIJTAA#v=onepage&q=Environmental%20Culture%3A%20The%20Ecological%20Crisis%20of%20Reason%20(2002).&f=false
6 http://www.lawschool.cornell.edu/research/JLPP/upload/Castaneda-et-al-final.pdf
7 The definition of environmental Justice by the United States Environmental Protection Agency.
8 http://ec.europa.eu/education/programmes/llp/jm/more/confgender03/elson.pdf/.
9 http://www.kitpublishers.nl/net/KIT_Publicaties_output/ShowFile2.aspx?e=1456/.

References

Aguilar, S. (2002), Environmental Non-Government Organisations in Argentina. *Review of European, Comparative and International Environmental Law (RECIEL)* 22(3): 281–90.

Buvinic, M., Gwin, C. and Bates, L. (1996), *Investing in Women: Progress and Prospects for the World Bank.* ICRW Policy Essay 19. Washington, DC: International Center for Research on Women.

Cornwall, A. (2003), Whose Voices? Whose Choices: Reflections on Gender and Participatory Development. *World Development* 31(8): 1325–42.

DAC. (1998), *DAC Source Book on Concepts and Approaches Linked to Gender Equality*. Paris: OECD.

Dayal, R., Parker, R. and Svendsen, D.S. (1993), *Gender Analysis and Planning in the Bank Project Cycle*. Washington, DC: World Bank, Asia Technical and Human Resources Division.

Derbyshire, H. (1996), *Summary Sheets: Gender Training Frameworks and Methods*. London: ODA.

Goetz, A.M. (1998), *Getting Institutions Right for Women in Development*. London: Zed Publication.

Hannan, C. (2003), *Gender Mainstreaming: Some Experience from the United Nations*. Paper presented at the conference Gender Mainstreaming: A Way towards Equality, Bern, 20 June.

Kabeer, N. (1999), Resources, Agency Achievement: Reflections on the Measurement of Women's Empowerment. *Development and Change* 30: 435–64.

———. (2003), *Gender Mainstreaming in Poverty Eradication and the Millennium Development Goals: A Handbook for Policy-Makers and Other Stakeholders*. Ottawa, ON: International Development and Research Centre.

Mies, M. and Vandana, S. (1993), *Ecofeminism*. Halifax, NS: Fernwood Publications.

Minh-Chau-Nguyen. (2004), *Gender Analysis in the CAS Process*. Washington, DC: The World Bank Research Center.

Moser, C. (1993), *Gender Planning and Development: Theory, Practice and Training*. London: Routledge.

North, D. (1990), *Institutions, Institutional Change and Economic Performance*. Cambridge: Cambridge University Press.

Overholt, C., Anderson, M., Cloud, K. and Austin, J. (1985), *Gender Roles in Development Projects*. West Hartford, Conn.: Kumarian Press.

Rao, A. and Kelleher, D. (2002), *Unravelling Institutionalized Gender Inequality*. AWID Occasional Paper, No. 8. Toronto, ON: AWID.

Subrahmanian, R. (2004), Making Sense of Gender in Shifting Institutional Contexts: Some Reflections on Gender Mainstreaming. *IDS Bulletin* 35(4): 89–94.

Wallace, T. (1998), Institutionalising Gender in UK NGOs. *Development in Practice* 8(2): 159–72.

Internet Sources

United Nations. (1997), Mandates For Gender Focal Points in the United Nations. Available at: http://www.un.org/womenwatch/osagi/gmrolesmadtgenfp.htm/ (Retrieved 4 April 2014).

———. (2007), Gender Mainstreaming: Strategy for Promoting Gender Equality. Available at: http://www.un.org/womenwatch/osagi/pdf/factsheet1.pdf/ (Retrieved 2 May 2013).

———. (2012), Africa Human Development Report 2012 Towards a Food Secure Future. Available at: http://www.un.org/womenwatch/directory/north_africa_and_the_middle_east_10476.htm/ (Retrieved 5 January 2014).

———. (2013), Put Nature at the Heart of Sustainable Development Goals. Available at: http://www.iucn.nl/en/?13750/Put-nature-at-the-heart-of-sustainable-development-goals/ (Retrieved 27 September 2013).

United National Environmental Programme. (1996), Towards Gender Mainstreaming in Environmental Policies. Available at: www.unep.org/PDF/Women/ChapterSix.pdf (Retrieved 17 July 2014).

Chapter 15

The Influence of Boards of Directors, Ownership Structures and Women on Boards on the Extent of Corporate Social Responsibility Reporting in Malaysian Public Listed Companies

Roshima Said, Syahiza Arsada and Rahayati Ahmad

Introduction

Corporate social reporting in Malaysia is lagging far behind compared to other Asian countries such as Singapore, Thailand and South Korea. Chambers, Moon and Sullivan (2003) investigated Corporate Social Responsibility (CSR) reporting in seven countries through website analysis of the top 50 companies in Asia through the penetration of CSR reporting within countries, the extent of CSR reporting within companies and the waves of CSR engaged in. The findings showed that there were fewer CSR companies in the seven selected Asian countries compared to the UK and Japan. The mean for the seven countries studied gives a score of 41 per cent, which is below half the score for the UK (98 per cent) and Japan (96 per cent). From the study, Malaysia showed fewer CSR companies compared to Singapore, Thailand and South Korea.

CSR covers three key areas: environmental, economic and social performance. Environmental reporting is part of CSR reporting, where Global Reporting Initiatives (GRI) guidelines vision is that companies should report on economic, environmental and social performance as routine and comparable as financial reporting. Tilt (2004) showed that there was a link between environmental activities undertaken by organizations and their subsequent reporting. The statement showed that the link always provides the motivation for firms to report. As affirmed by Tilt (2004), as managers become more aware of the environmental challenges and activities, they are likely to disclose more. Companies should rethink and recognize their way of doing business to benefit shareholders and specifically, other stakeholders.

Environmental pollution problems in Malaysia have a long history. River pollution by mine wastewater and sludge began with the rapid development of tin mining, a traditional industry that started at the beginning of the twentieth century. In later years, other traditional industries such as natural rubber and palm oil production began in earnest, and wastewater from the factories caused further pollution of rivers and seas. Malaysia also pursued rapid industrialization supported by foreign investment, but the result of industrialization was a raft of pollution problems, caused by industrial wastewater and other wastes, which is still apparent today. Environmental reporting in Malaysia is generally low. Nik Ahmad and Sulaiman (2004) examined the extent and type of voluntary environmental disclosures in the annual reports of Malaysian companies in selected industries. They found that only 27.54 per cent of the annual reports examined contained some environmental disclosures while 72.46 per cent had none. Their study concluded that the level of current environmental reporting and disclosures in Malaysia appears to be low and restricted to very general environmental issues.

The government's incentive to further promote CSR among public listed companies (plcs) in Malaysia is very encouraging. This can be seen in the introduction of Bursa Malaysia's CSR framework for public listed companies in 2006. Past studies had shown that there are various factors that act as the drivers for both CSR and environmental reporting. The Association of Chartered Certified Accountants (ACCA, 2002) emphasized that among the driving forces for environmental reporting in Malaysia are the introduction of the Malaysia Code on Corporate Governance listing requirements, the National Annual Corporate Award (NACRA) and the ACCA Award called the Malaysian Environmental Reporting Award (MERA), changed in 2004 to the Malaysian Environmental and Social Reporting Award (MESRA).

A board of directors is one of the elements of corporate governance. Hermalin and Weisbach (2003: 7) define boards of directors as 'an economic institution that, in theory, helps to solve the agency problems inherent in managing an organization'. The agency theory framework foresees boards of directors as the ultimate mechanism of corporate control. Boards monitor and review the agents who may have acting on behalf of the principal (owner). Without a board's monitoring, agents might pursue their own interests at the expense of the principal (Jensen, 1986; Jensen and Meckling, 1976).

The number of female directors on boards is increasing. In 1995, there were only 9.6 per cent female directors on board in Fortune 500 companies and the number increased to 13.6 per cent in 2004 (Speedy, 2004). Furthermore, Anonymous (2000) found that 73 per cent of corporate boards had at least one female member in year 2000, that 25 per cent of corporate boards had more than one woman, and that in 2004, 87 per cent of companies had at least one female director on a board. In 2008, 90 per cent of Fortune 500 companies had at least one woman on corporate boards and below 20 per cent had three or more women on the board. Clearly there has been a constant increase in the number of female directors on corporate boards. A study on the effect of female boards in CSR reporting by Feijoo, Romero and Ruiz (2012) supports the finding that boards have at least three women and that these are determinant to the quality of CSR reporting. Different genders may have different thinking, sensitivities and ethical values. Studies by O'Fallon and Butterfield (2005) and Becker and Ulstad (2007) found that women tend to be more ethical than men. Thus boards with a higher proportion of women directors tend to have more board meetings and had better attendance records at board meetings (Adams and Ferreira, 2004). Adams and Ferreira (2004) also concluded that companies with gender diversity on boards will be more profitable than companies with homogeneous boards and can also enhance their business reputations (Bernadi, Bosco and Vassill, 2006; Brammer, Millington and Pavelin, 2009). This is due to the unique character of women, who are more sensitive and more inclined to share and discuss with others or network before making decisions (Hersby, Ryan and Jetten, 2009).

Furthermore, women's thought and sensitivity towards CSR is different compared to that of male boards of directors due to feminist characteristics. Ewert and Baker (2001) examined whether there are links between environmental concerns and gender, and their results indicated a positive correlation with the female gender. This finding contradicts Bernadi and Threadgill (2010) because their analyses indicate that the presence of female directors was not significant on the environmental variable of CSR. Williams's (2003) result is consistent with a charitable contribution variable and he found that the higher the number of female directors on boards, the larger the amount given to charity.

Women's sensitivity towards social signals will increase the level of CSR rating. Bear, Rahman and Post (2010) examine the effect of board diversity and gender composition on firms' reputations of 689 selected companies from Fortune 2009 through improved CSR. In their study, a dependent variable is a firm's reputation; CSR is a moderating variable and the number of women on the board is an independent variable. Their study indicates that the number of female board members was positive and statistically significant with CSR strength rating. Their study showed that female board contribution to the firm's CSR can enhance corporate reputation. In other words, we can summarize that the existence of CSR as a moderating variable gives high impact to the firm's reputation when the number of female directors is higher on corporate boards.

Barako, Hancock and Izan (2006), Haniffa and Cooke (2005) and Huafang and Jianguo (2007) found a significant relationship between disclosure and foreign ownership. Thus the involvement of foreign shareholders is one way in which Malaysian companies can use Corporate Social Disclosure (CSD) as a legitimate strategy to obtain continued inflows of capital and to please ethical investors in the markets. Government interventions may generate pressure for companies to disclose additional information because the government is a body that is trusted by the public. Amran and Devi (2008) and Eng and Mak (2003) found that government ownership was associated with increased voluntary disclosure. Thus the objectives of the study are to investigate the relationship between the board of directors, ownership structure (government and foreign ownership) and women on boards on the extent of CSR reporting in Malaysian publicly listed companies.

Literature Review

Haniffa and Cooke (2005) also added that the way to reduce legitimacy gaps between organizations and stakeholders was through additional disclosure. Haron et al. (2006) found that although the board of directors considered that they had embarked on a lot of CSR activities pertaining to an environmental theme, it was not supported by evidence of the disclosure level in the annual report which ranked environmental themes fourth.

Beekes and Brown (2006) argued that governance quality is related to how informative financial disclosure is. In their study, they examined whether a listed company's corporate governance 'quality' is related to information reports of the share market and how its agents respond to it. They studied six variables that influence the informativeness of financial disclosure: the frequency with which the firm makes price-sensitive announcements to the share market, the extent of its security analyst following, the accuracy, bias, and disagreement in the analysts' earnings forecasts for that firm, and the speed with which its share price reflects value-relevant information.

Corporate Governance Quality (CGQ) is sourced from the Horwath University of Newcastle Corporate Governance Report. Their study demonstrated that five out of six predictions were supported: the frequency with which the firm makes price-sensitive announcements to the share market, the extent of its security analyst following, the accuracy, bias, and the speed. The results of their study demonstrated that better-governed firms in Australia make more informative disclosures.

Krüger (2009) examined the cross-sectional relationship between positive and negative CSR events with a US firm's board of directors (BOD) for the years 1998 to 2007. Three independent variables of BOD were studied: inside directors, female directors and director tenure. While CSR is a dependent variable and seven areas (corporate governance, community, diversity, employee relations, environment, human rights and product) were tested in this study. The results indicated that the higher the number of female directors on the board, the higher the positive CSR events that were found. This demonstrates that female directors are more concerned about stakeholders' welfare with higher altruism.

In Nigeria, Fodio and Oba (2012) conducted a study to investigate whether the presence and proportion of female directors on a board had an impact on environmental responsibility information disclosure. To examine this, multiple regression analysis has been employed and a content analysis method has been used to explore environmental information. The result demonstrated that 50 per cent (48) of the sample firms for the period 2005–7 had a female director and the proportion of female directors to board size was 7 per cent. Furthermore, the result revealed that presence of female directors and the proportion of female directors had a positive association with the extent of environmental responsibility of information disclosure. This implies that women are more concerned and inclined to be socially and environmentally oriented than men (Ibrahim and Angelidis, 1994).

The issue of women as directors on boards was documented as early as 1977 by Burson-Marsteller and continues to be a salient issue to the researcher because the numbers of female directors appointed on boards is increasing year by year. Although it is apparent that men dominated on boards, the presence of few women on boards might have some impact on the companies. The majority of the studies also showed a positive effect of gender diversity on corporate boards to the companies. According to Harrigan (1981), female directors are more sensitive to CSR and the welfare of various stakeholders: he found that women and minority directors are non-profit oriented. Wang and Coffey (1992) also found the proportion of women and minority directors is positively correlated to corporate giving, and they suggest that women and minority directors are more sensitive to CSR issues but less business-oriented. Although nowadays women are more highly educated than men and increasingly enter the workforce, according to Scholz (2012) women do not reach corresponding leadership positions. Furthermore, males are profit-driven and business-oriented. These findings agree with those of Van Der Laan Smith, Adhikari and Tondkar (2005); they found a negative relationship between masculinity levels and CSR quality because men are more concerned with material achievement and less with community solidarity.

Female directors on boards are highly recommended in order to ensure that companies are economically and socially responsible because both activities can lead to financial success and a good business reputation. Additionally, when there is a higher number of a female directors in a company it gives a positive signal to investors.

Hypotheses Development

Board Size

A board of directors is one important characteristic of corporate governance mechanisms in managing the conduct of the company's business, to ensure the company is being properly directed by their agents. Past studies have found that board size increases communication and coordination problems, decreases the ability of the board to control management and spreads the cost of poor decision-making among a larger group (Eisenberg, Sundgren and Wells, 1998; Lipton and Lorsch, 1992; Raheja, 2003; Yermack, 1996). Raheja (2005) revealed that the optimal board structure and effectiveness of the board in monitoring depend on the characteristics of the firm and its directors.

Xie, Davidson and Dadalt (2003) found that a larger board size may bring a greater number of experienced directors to the board and would cover various services and interests for their shareholders. In contrast, Chaganti, Mahajan and Sharma (1985) claimed that smaller boards are more manageable and more often play a role as a controlling function whereas larger boards may not be able to function effectively because the board leaves the management relatively free of control. Thus, it is proposed that:

H1: There is a significant positive relationship between the size of a board of directors and the extent of CSR disclosure in annual reports of Malaysian companies.

Board Independence

The Malaysian Code of Corporate Governance suggests the board of directors be made up of one-third of independent members (MCCG, 2001). The board of directors has a direct responsibility to prepare and execute corporate strategy (Weir and Laing, 2001). Roshima, Yuserrie and Hasnah (2009) found that independent directors play an important role in enhancing corporate image and have a monitoring role in ensuring that the company is properly managed. Leung and Horwitz (2004) found that board independence is significantly positive related to voluntary disclosure. On the other hand Barako, Hancock and Izan (2006) and Haniffa and Cooke (2005) found a negative correlation. As environmental reporting is one of the voluntary segments of disclosure, it is hypothesized that:

H2: There is a positive significant relationship between board independence and the extent of CSR disclosure in annual reports of Malaysian companies.

Proportion of Female Directors

The studies conducted by Ewert and Baker (2001) and Kollmuss and Agymen (2002) found that there are links between environmental concerns and human capital characteristics such as age and gender. Ewert and Baker (2001) suggested that environmental concerns have positively correlated with a younger age and being female. A number of studies by O'Fallon and Butterfield (2005) and Becker and Ulstad (2007) found that women tend to be more ethical than men. Thus a higher proportion of women directors on boards leads to more board meetings and a better attendance record at board meetings (Adams and Ferreira, 2004). Addams and Ferreira also concluded that gender-diverse boards will be more profitable than companies with homogeneous boards and can also enhance business reputations (Bernadi, Bosco and Vassill, 2006; Brammer, Millington and Pavelin, 2009). This was due to characteristics common among women, including being sensitive and more inclined to share and discuss with other members or engage in networking before making decisions (Hersby, Ryan and Jetten, 2009). We propose hypothesis H3:

> H3: There is a significant positive relationship between the proportion of female directors and the extent of CSR disclosure in annual reports of Malaysian companies.

Foreign Ownership

Barako, Hancock and Izan (2006), Haniffa and Cooke (2005) and Huafang and Jianguo (2007) found a significant relationship between disclosure and foreign ownership. Involving foreign shareholders is one way Malaysian companies can use CSD as a legitimate strategy to obtain continued inflows of capital and to please ethical investors in the markets. It is hypothesized that:

> H4: There is a significant positive relationship between foreign ownership and the extent of CSR disclosure in annual reports of Malaysian companies.

Government Ownership

Mohd Ghazali and Wheetman (2006) state that government ownership of shares is a particular feature of Malaysian companies, where the government retains shares in privatized companies. In December 2000, government ownership in privatized entities was 49.5 per cent. In their study, they examined the relationship between government ownership with voluntary disclosure in Malaysia and found that government ownership was not significant in explaining the extent of voluntary disclosure.

Government interventions may generate pressures for companies to disclose additional information because the government is a body that is trusted by the public. Amran and Devi (2008) and Eng and Mak (2003) found that government ownership was associated with increased voluntary disclosure. It is hypothesized that:

> H5: There is a significant positive relationship between government ownership and the extent of CSR disclosure in annual reports of Malaysian companies.

Methodology

Unit of Analysis and Population

The unit of analysis is the annual report of public listed companies in the main market of Bursa Malaysia Berhad. The population of this study consists of the total available 2006 annual reports of main market companies published in Bursa Malaysia Berhad. The annual report for the year 2006 was selected because it is the year of the implementation of Bursa Malaysia CSR Framework. This study includes all industries in the main market except for financial companies due to their different regulatory framework and governance environment. The industries in the main market include construction, consumer products, industrial products, plantation, technology and trading/services industries.

Sample Size

A proportionate stratified random sampling of 150 Malaysian companies has been taken. Based on Roscoe's rule of thumb (Sekaran, 2003) for determining sample size, our sample size should be not less than 60 companies. However, we selected 150 companies: thus the sample represents 25 per cent of the target population with a representation of above 20 per cent in every sector.

The study is based on secondary data collected from the annual reports of companies in the main market of Bursa Malaysia Berhad. The sample data selected is from non-financial companies listed on the main market of Bursa Malaysia in 2006.

The Process of Constructing a CSR Index

A preliminary checklist with 100 items was constructed based on items selected by Ernst and Ernst (1978); Hackston and Milne (1996); Haniffa and Cooke (2005); Manasseh (2004); and Shaw Warn (2004). The list was then screened to eliminate the mandatory items required by the approved Accounting Standards, Companies Act, 1965, Bursa Malaysia Listing Requirement. The CSR checklist was sent to experts (auditors and academics) to verify all the selected items. The final checklist with 86 items was used in this study to construct the CSR disclosure index after taking into consideration the experts' opinion and to eliminate the mandatory items required by the approved Accounting Standards in Malaysia. According to Hooks, Coy and Davey (2002), an expert is someone who has special knowledge about a specific subject. A chosen panellist in the process of constructing the CSR index is one who knows more about the topic than most people would.

In order to construct a disclosure index, the researchers used the Corporate Social Responsibility Disclosure Checklist that covered the five themes: environment, community, human resources, energy and product. Sources of data in constructing the CSR disclosure index were collected from annual reports. A corporate annual report can be viewed as a formal public document produced by public companies largely as a response to the mandatory corporate reporting requirements. In order to ensure consistency and stability throughout the process of constructing disclosure index, the selected annual reports were read twice. The second examination on the selected annual report was done after the first round had taken place. Where differences appeared, a third investigation was done in order to check the stability and consistency of the process.

Measurement of Variables

The independent variables of board characteristics are board size, board independence and the chairman's independence. The measurement of each variable is described in Table 15.1.

Table 15.1 Measurement of variables

No.	Independent variables	Measurement
1.	Board size	Number of board members.
2.	Board independence	Number of independent non-executive directors divided by total number of directors on the board (%).
3.	Proportion of female directors	Number of female directors divided by total number of directors on the board.
4.	Foreign ownership	Percentage of shares owned by foreign shareholders to total number of shares issued.
5.	Government ownership	The proportion of ordinary shares owned by the government.
6.	Firm's size	Total assets.
7.	CSR index	The CSR disclosure index was developed by adding all the items covering the five themes: environment, community, human resources, energy and product. The process will add all the scores and they will be equally weighted.

Findings of the Study

Table 15.2 Descriptive analysis

	No.	Minimum	Maximum	Mean	Standard deviation
CSR index	150	0.00	61.63	8.35	13.03
Board size	150	4.00	15.00	7.81	2.06
Board independence	150	0.25	1.00	0.63	0.18
Proportion of female directors	150	0.00	0.40	0.12	0.10
Foreign ownership	150	0.00	45.99	6.31	8.66
Government ownership	150	0.00	70.60	8.45	11.60
Total assets	150	46,678,000	29,745,724,000	1,681,489,997	3,730,644,654

Table 15.3 Correlation between variables

	CSR index	Board size	Board independence	Proportion of female directors	Foreign ownership	Government ownership
CSR Index	1	0.294*	−0.111	0.150†	0.271*	0.268*
Board size	0.294*	1.00	−0.165†	−0.217†	0.130	0.190†
Board independence	0.092	−0.165†	1.00	0.05	−0.110	−0.175†
Proportion of female directors	0.150†	−0.217†	0.050	1.00	−0.120	−0.204†
Foreign ownership	0.271*	0.130	−0.110	−0.120	1.00	0.060
Government ownership	0.268*	0.190†	−0.175†	−0.204†	0.060	1.00

*Correlation is significant at the 0.01 level (2-tailed).
†Correlation is significant at the 0.05 level (2-tailed).

Table 15.4 Regression model

Variables	Standard beta Model 1	Standard beta Model 2
Control variables		
Total assets (LnTA)	0.327[*]	
Model variables		
Total assets (LnTA)		0.192[†]
Board size		0.228[*]
Board independence		0.004
Proportion of female directors		0.155[‡]
Government ownership		0.192[†]
Foreign ownership		0.195[†]
R square	0.107	0.254
Adjusted R square	0.100	0.212
R square change	0.107	0.148
F value	15.535[*]	6.041[*]
F change	15.535	4.089
Sig. F change	0.000	0.001
Durbin Watson		2.013

[*]$p<0.01$, [†]$p<0.05$, [‡]$p<0.10$.

Table 15.4 shows the descriptive statistics for the dependent variables of Corporate Social Responsibility index, control variable (total asset) and independent variables (board size, board independence, proportion of female directors, foreign ownership and government ownership) from the source of data – the annual report. The descriptive statistics includes statistics such as minimum, maximum, mean and standard deviation. The mean for the disclosure level of CSR Index is 8.35 per cent.

From the sample of 150 Malaysian listed companies, the descriptive statistics of board size varies from 4 to 15 with a mean of 8. The proportion of non-executive directors varies from 25 per cent to 100 per cent with a mean of 63 per cent. The proportion of female directors varies from 0 per cent to 40 per cent with a mean of 12 per cent. The mean value for foreign ownership is 6.31 per cent and government ownership is 8.45 per cent.

Correlation Analysis

In this study, the Pearson Product-Moment correlation coefficient (r) was used to measure the extent of the relationship between variables. Correlation value is expected to be between +1 to –1. Pallant (2005: 123) states that: 'correlation analysis is used to describe the strength and direction of the linear relationship between two variables. A correlation of 0.0 indicates no relationship, a correlation of 1.0 indicates a perfect positive correlation, and a value of –1.0 indicates a perfect negative correlation'.

The Pearson correlation coefficient reported in Table 15.3 suggests that the multi-colinearity is not serious for the independent variables. As suggested by Gujarati (1988), simple correlations between independent variables are considered harmful when they exceed 0.80 or 0.90. The Pearson correlation (r value) between independent variables in this study ranged between 0.05 to 0.294, which does not exceed 0.80 or 0.90.

The correlation coefficients between CSR reporting index and board size, foreign ownership and government ownership are positively and significantly related or correlated at p<0.01 significance levels. The positive sign between CSR reporting index and board size, foreign ownership and government ownership are in line with what had been hypothesized. The correlation coefficient between CSR reporting index and board size is r = 0.294, for foreign ownership r = 0.271 and for government ownership r = 0.268.

The correlation coefficients between the CSR reporting index and proportion of female directors are positively and significantly related or correlated at p<0.05 significance levels. The positive sign between CSR reporting index and the proportion of female directors is in line with what has been hypothesized. The correlation coefficient between CSR reporting index and proportion of female directors is r = 0.150. The correlation coefficient between CSR reporting index and board independence is r = 0.092 and it is not significant.

Hypotheses Testing

The regression model in Table 15.4 shows regression analysis with one control variable, namely Total Assets (Natural log Total Assets). The model is significant with R square = 0.107, adjusted R square = 0.100, R square change = 0.107 and F value = 15.535.The result shows that the control variable namely Total Assets (Natural log Total Assets) is significant (β = +0.327, p<0.01).

In model 2, the independent variables are included in the model together with the control variable. The model shows the evidence of direct relationship between independent variables and dependent variables after statistically controlling the control variable, namely Total Assets (Natural log Total Assets). In Table 15.4, the model improved significantly with R square = 0.254, adjusted R square = 0.212, R square change = 0.148, F value = 6.041. As mentioned earlier, the control variable was found to be significant. In this model, the most significant independent variable that influenced the CSR disclosure is board size, which is positively correlated with β = +0.228, p<0.01,while government ownership is positively and significantly correlated with β = +0.195, p<0.05. The result also indicates that the higher the percentage of government ownership, the higher the CSR disclosure. Foreign ownership is positively and significantly correlated, with β = +0.192, p<0.05. In addition, the proportion of female directors is positively correlated with β = +0.155, p<0.10; whereas board independence is positively correlated with β = +0.004, p>0.05 and it is not significant.

In model 2, by adding the model variables together with the control variable, the R square has increased to 25.4 per cent and the R square change is 14.8 per cent and is significant. This implies that the additional 14.8 per cent of the variation in environmental disclosure is explained by model variables. In addition, the R square change of 14.8 per cent means that the model variables explain an additional 14.8 per cent of the variance in CSR disclosure even when the effect of the firm's size is statistically controlled for.

Discussion

Table 15.5 summarizes the findings of hypotheses testing on the relationship between model variables and dependent variable. The results of this study shows that board size, the proportion of female directors on boards, foreign ownership and government ownership have significant relationships in the extent of CSR disclosure.

While, board independence is not significant. The objective of this study was to examine the relationship between board size, board independence and the proportion of female directors to total directors, foreign ownership, government ownership and CSR disclosure in Malaysian public listed companies. The significant result of the influence of board size towards CSR disclosure shows that the board of directors is one of the most important elements of the corporate governance mechanism in overseeing the conduct of the company's business, i.e. that it is being properly managed by their agents. Past studies proposed that board size will increase communication and coordination problems, decrease the ability of the board to control management and spread among a larger group the cost of poor decision-making (Eisenberg, Sundgren and Wells, 1998; Lipton and Lorsch, 1992; Raheja, 2003; Yermack, 1996).

As for the relationship between women on boards and CSR disclosure, the results of the study showed that there is a significant relationship between the proportion of female directors on a board and the extent of CSR disclosure. Different genders might have different thinking, sensitivity and ethical values. Studies by O'Fallon and Butterfield (2005) and Becker and Ulstad (2007) found that women tend to be more ethical than men, thus a higher proportion of women directors on boards leads to more board meetings and a better attendance record at board meetings (Adams and Ferreira, 2004). They also concluded that gender-diverse boards will be more profitable than companies with homogeneous boards and can also enhance their business reputations (Bernadi, Bosco and Vassill, 2006; Brammer, Millington and Pavelin, 2009). This was due to women's unique character, which is more sensitive and more inclined to share and discuss issues with other members or networking contacts

Table 15.5 Summary of hypotheses: the relationship between model variables and dependent variables

H	Hypotheses	Result
H1	There is a significant positive relationship between board size and the extent of CSR disclosure in annual reports of Malaysian companies.	Significant
H2	There is a significant positive relationship between board independence and the extent of CSR disclosure in annual reports of Malaysian companies.	Not significant
H3	There is a significant positive relationship between proportion of female directors to total directors and the extent of CSR disclosure in annual reports of Malaysian companies.	Significant
H4	There is a significant positive relationship between foreign ownership and the extent of CSR disclosure in annual reports of Malaysian companies.	Significant
H5	There is a significant positive relationship between government ownership and the extent of CSR disclosure in annual reports of Malaysian companies.	Significant

before making any decisions (Hersby, 2009). On the other hand, women's thought and sensitivity towards CSR are also different. The result of the study is consistent with Ewert and Baker (2001), who found that there is a link between environmental concern and gender; the result indicates a positive correlation with the female gender.

As for the relationship between government ownership and the extent of CSR disclosure, the results of the study showed that there is a significant relationship between the two. Government ownership is the most significant variable that influences the level of CSR disclosure: the higher the government shareholding in a company, the higher the level of CSR disclosure will be. The result of the study is consistent with Eng and Mak (2003) and Amran and Devi (2008), who found a positive relationship between government ownership and CSR disclosure. Government interventions may generate pressures for companies to disclose additional information because the government is a body that is trusted by the public, and the government acts as a control system that determines the regulatory philosophy of the country. Pressure from government can boost transparency and disclosures among public listed companies. The mean for government ownership, and foreign ownership in this study is 8.45 per cent and 6.31 per cent respectively, which is generally low, but the impact of government and foreign stakes significantly influence the level of CSR disclosure in Malaysian publicly listed companies for the year ended 2006. Barako, Hancock and Izan (2006), Haniffa and Cooke (2005) and Huafang and Jianguo (2007) found a significant relationship between disclosure and foreign ownership. Thus, involving foreign shareholders is one way Malaysian companies can use CSD as a legitimating strategy to obtain continued inflows of capital and to please ethical investors in the markets.

The study also shows an insignificant relationship between board independence and CSR reporting. The findings perceived it as a requirement for Malaysian companies to follow the Malaysian Code of Corporate Governance to have a board composition of non-executive directors of 1:3. In addition, the majority of the listed companies selected in this study are complying with the Bursa Malaysia and Malaysian Code of Corporate Governance for a balanced board structure with the mean of 63 per cent of board independence. Thus the term *independence* should be redefined back by the listed companies in order to maintain the quality of independence among non-executive directors in Malaysia. The revised Code of Corporate Governance 2007 provides greater clarity on those aspects a nominating committee should consider when recommending candidates for directorship, including the core competencies which non-executives directors should bring to the board. In addition, the revised code has advised that the nominating committee should annually assess the effectiveness of the board as a whole, the committees of the board and the contribution of each individual director, including independent non-executive directors and the CEO.

Conclusion

This study examines the specific characteristics of the corporate governors of the company in relation to the disclosure of activities pertaining to CSR that the company has undertaken. As for the relationship between corporate governance characteristics and CSR disclosure, foreign ownership, government ownership, and the proportion of female directors to total directors and board size significantly influence the level of CSR disclosure of public listed companies in Malaysia. The most significant variable that influences the level of CSR disclosure is foreign ownership. It implies that the higher the foreign shareholding in a company, the higher the level of CSR disclosure will be.

This study has demonstrated that in order to mitigate the agency problems between firms and shareholders, society and stakeholders, pressure from government and foreign shareholders can help to reduce the expected costs and the negative impact on firm value and indicate to society and stakeholders that individual firms are doing their part to help in solving society's social problems through additional disclosures. Additionally, the women directors' roles are an important factor in CSR disclosure level in Malaysian public listed companies. Proportions of female directors on boards are highly recommended in order to ensure that companies are economically and socially responsible: both activities can lead to financial success and a good business reputation. A higher number of a female directors in the company will give a positive signal to investors.

Finally, this study has brought up a number of implications which may be applied in many countries irrespective of whether they are developing or developed. First, it provides strong evidence to show that board size, the proportion of female directors on boards and government and foreign ownership are significant variables in the extent of CSR disclosure. Second, it is useful to managers, especially to the board of directors in Malaysia, in identifying those governance characteristics that could improve the company's CSR activities and thus disclose them to stakeholders and the public. Third, this study can also be used as an initial step for the companies in Malaysia to get involved in CSR activities which have been proven by prior studies to enhance the company's image and reputation. Furthermore, a new guideline should be issued by regulatory bodies in relation to the involvement of foreign and government ownership and women on boards in order to mitigate agency problems between companies, environment and society.

References

ACCA. (2002), *The State of Corporate Reporting in Malaysia*. Kuala Lumpur: ACCA Malaysia.

Adams, R.B. and Ferreira, D. (2004), Gender Diversity in the Boardroom. *European Corporate Governance Institute, Finance Working Paper* 57: 30.

Amran, A. and Devi, S. (2008), The Impact of Government and Foreign Affiliate Influence on Corporate Social Reporting: The Case of Malaysia. *Managerial Auditing Journal* 23(4): 386–404.

Anonymous. (2000), Board Diversity Increases. *Association Management* 52(1): 25.

Barako, D.G., Hancock, P. and Izan, H.Y. (2006), Relationship Between Corporate Governance Attributes and Voluntary Disclosures in Annual Reports: The Kenyan Experience. *Financial Reporting, Regulation and Governance* 5(1): 1–25.

Bear, S., Rahman, N. and Post, C. (2010), The Impact of Board Diversity and Gender Composition on Corporate Social Responsibility and Firm Reputation. *Journal of Business Ethics* 97(2): 207–31.

Becker, D.A. and Ulstad, I. (2007), Gender Differences in Student Ethics: Are Females Really More Ethical? Plagiary. *Cross-Disciplinary Studies in Plagiarism, Fabrication, and Falsification* 2: 77–91.

Beekes, W. and Brown, P. (2006), Do Better-Governed Australian Firms Make More Informative Disclosures? *Journal of Business Finance & Accounting* 33(3&4): 422–50.

Bernadi, R.A. and Threadgill, V.H. (2010), Women Directors and Corporate Social Responsibility. *Electronic Journal of Business Ethics and Organisation Studies* 15(2): 15–21.

Bernadi, R., Bosco, S. and Vassill, K. (2006), Does Female Representation on the Board of Directors Associate with Fortune's 100 Best Companies List? *Business and Society* 45(2): 235–48.

Brammer, S., Millington, A. and Pavelin, S. (2009), Corporate Reputation and Women on the Board. *British Journal of Management* 20(1): 17–29.

Chaganti, R.S., Mahajan, V. and Sharma, S. (1985), Corporate Board Size, Composition and Corporate Failures in Retailing Industry. *Journal of Management Studies* 22(4): 400–17.

Chambers, E., Moon, W.C.J. and Sullivan, M. (2003), *CSR in Asia: A Seven Country Study of CSR Website Reporting*. Research Paper Series conducted at the International Centre for Corporate Social Responsibility. Available at: http://www.nottingham.ac.uk/business/ICCSR/pdf/ResearchPdfs/092003.PDF/ (Retrieved 18 July 2006).

Eisenberg, T., Sundgren, S. and Wells, M. (1998), Larger Board Size and Decreasing Firm Value in Small Firms. *Journal of Financial Economics* 48(1): 35–54.

Eng, L.L. and Mak, Y.T. (2003), Corporate Governance and Voluntary Disclosure. *Journal of Accounting and Public Policy* 22(4):325–45.

Ernst and Ernst. (1978), Social Responsibility Disclosure surveys, Ernst and Ernst, Cleveland, OH.

Ewert, A. and Baker, D. (2001), Standing for Where You Sit: An Exploratory Analysis of the Relationship between Academic Major and Environment Beliefs. *Environment and Behavior* 33(5): 687–707.

Feijoo, B.F., Romero, S. and Ruiz, S. (2012), Does Board Gender Composition Affect Corporate Social Responsibility Reporting? *International Journal of Business and Social Science* 3(1): 31–8.

Fodio, M.I. and Oba, V.C. (2012), Board's Gender Mix and Extent of Environmental Responsibility Information Disclosure in Nigeria: An Empirical Study. *European Journal of Business and Management* 4(14): 163–9.

Gujarati, D.N. (1988), *Basic Econometrics*, International edn. Singapore: McGraw-Hill.

Hackston, D. and Milne, M. (1996), Some Determinants of Social and Environmental Disclosures in New Zealand Companies. *Accounting, Auditing and Accountability Journal* 9(1): 77–108.

Haniffa, R.M. and Cooke, T.E. (2005), The Impact of Culture and Corporate Governance on Corporate Social Reporting. *Journal of Accounting and Public Policy* 24(5): 391–430.

Haron, H., Ibrahim, D.A., Ismail, I., Quah, C.H., Kader Ali, N.N., Zainuddin, Y. and Nasruddin, E. (2006), Governance, Ethics and Corporate Social Responsibility of Listed Companies in Malaysia. Unpublished Research, Universiti Sains Malaysia.

Harrigan, K.R. (1981), Numbers and Positions of Women Elected to Corporate Board. *Academy of Management Journal* 24(3): 619–25.

Hermalin, B.E. and Weisbach, M.S. (2003), Boards of Directors as an Endogenously Determined Institution: A Survey of Economic Literature. *Economic Policy Review: Federal Reserve Bank of New York* 9(1): 7–26.

Hersby, M.D., Ryan, M.K. and Jetten, J. (2009), Getting Together to Get Ahead: The Impact of Social Structure on Women's Networking. *British Journal of Management* 20(4): 415–30.

Hooks, J., Coy, D. and Davey, H. (2002), The Information Gap in Annual Reports. *Accounting, Auditing & Accountability* 15(4): 501–22.

Huafang, X. and Jianguo, Y. (2007), Ownership Structure, Board Composition and Corporation and Corporate Voluntary Disclosure: Evidence from Listed Companies in China. *Managerial Auditing Journal* 22(6): 604–19.

Ibrahim, N.A. and Angelidis, J.P. (1994), Effect of Board Members' Gender on Corporate Social Responsiveness Orientation. *Journal of Applied Business Research* 10(1): 35–40.

Jensen, M. (1986), Agency Costs of Free Cash Flow, Corporate Finance, and Takeovers. *American Economic Review* 76, 323–9.

Jensen, M. C. and Meckling, W.H. (1976), Theory of the Firm: Managerial Behavior, Agency Costs and Ownership Structure. *Journal of Financial Economics* 3(4): 305–60.

Krüger, P. (2009), *Corporate Social Responsibility and the Board of Directors.* Job Market Paper. Toulouse, France: Toulouse School of Economics.

Kollmuss, A. and Agymen, J. (2002), Mind the Gap: Why do People Act Environmentally and What are the Barriers to Pro-environmental Behavior? *Environmental Education Research* 8(3): 239–60.

Lipton, M. and Lorsch, J. (1992), A Modest Proposal for Improved Corporate Governance. *The Business Lawyer* 48(1): 59–77.

Leung, S. and Horwitz, B. (2004), Director Ownership and Voluntary Segment Disclosure: Hong Kong Experience. *Journal of International Financial Management and Accounting* 15(3): 235–60.

Malaysian Institute of Corporate Governance. (2001), Malaysian Code on Corporate Governance (MCCG). *Malayan Law Journal Sdn. Bhd.,* Kuala Lumpur.

Manasseh, S. (2004), Study on the Level of Corporate Social Disclosure Practices in Malaysia. Unpublished Master's thesis in Accounting, Universiti Sains Malaysia.

Mohd Ghazali, N.A. and Wheetman, P. (2006), Perpetuating Traditional Influences: Voluntary Disclosure in Malaysia Following the Economic Crisis. *Journal of International Accounting, Auditing and Taxation* 15(2): 226–48.

Nik Ahmad, N.N. and Sulaiman, M. (2004), Environmental Disclosures in Malaysian Annual Reports: A Legitimacy Perspective. *International Journal of Commerce & Management* 14(1): 44–58.

O'Fallon, M. and Butterfield, K. (2005), A Review of the Ethical Decision-making Literature 1996–2003. *Journal of Business Ethics* 59(4): 375–413.

Pallant, J. (2005), *SPSS Survival Manual: A Step by Step Guide to Data Analysis Using SPSS for Windows Version 12.* Crows Nest, NSW: Allen & Unwin.

Raheja, C. (2003), *The Interaction of Insiders and Outsiders in Monitoring: A Theory of Corporate Boards.* Working Paper, Vanderbilt University, Available at: http://tkyd.org/ . . . /board_structure_and_agency_costs_ameziane_lesfer_2002.pdf/ (Retrieved May 2005).

Raheja, C.G. (2005), Determinants of Board Size and Composition: A Theory of Corporate Boards. *Journal of Financial and Quantitative Analysis* 40(02): 283–306.

Roshima, S., Yuserrie, Z. and Hasnah, H. (2009), The Relationship Between Corporate Social Responsibility Disclosure and Corporate Governance Characteristics in Malaysian Public Listed Companies. *Social Responsibility Journal* 5(2): 212–26.

Scholz, K.M. (2012), The Importance of Gender Equality in Corporate Social Responsibility Reporting. *Sustainability. Thomson Reuters.* Available at: www.sustainability.thomsonreuters.com.

Sekaran, U. (2003), *Research Methods for Business: A Skill Building Approach.* New York: John Wiley & Sons.

Shaw Warn, T. (2004), *Determinants of Corporate Social Reporting in Malaysia.* Unpublished M.Sc. thesis, Universiti Putra Malaysia.

Speedy, B. (2004), Diverse View: Women Directors are Good for the Bottom Line. *The Australian*, 5 October, p. 24.

Tilt, C.A. (2004), A Note on Linking Environmental Activity and Environmental Disclosure. Paper presented at the Fourth Asia Pacific Interdisciplinary Research in Accounting Conference, Singapore, 4–6 July, 2004.

Van Der Laan Smith, J., Adhikari, A. and Tondkar, R.H. (2005), Exploring Differences in Social Disclosures Internally: A Stakeholder Perspective. *Journal of Accounting and Public Policy* 24(2): 123–51.

Wang, J. and Coffey, B.S. (1992), Board Composition and Corporate Philanthropy. *Journal of Business Ethics* 11(10): 771–8.

Weir, C.M and Laing, D. (2001), Governance Structures, Director Independence and Corporate Performance in the UK. *European Business Review* 13(2): 86–94.

Williams, R. (2003), Women on Corporate Boards of Directors and their Influence on Corporate Philanthropy. *Journal of Business Ethics* 42(1): 1–10.

Xie, B., Davidson III, W.N. and Dadalt, P.J. (2003), Earnings Management and Corporate Governance: The Role of the Board and the Audit Committee. *Journal of Corporate Finance* 9(3): 295–316.

Yermack, D. (1996), Higher Market Valuation of Companies with a Small Board of Directors. *Journal of Financial Economics* 40(2): 185–211.

Chapter 16

Women Start-up Businesses Utilizing Web 2.0, MOOC, ePortfolio and Ice House Entrepreneurship Mindset

Milena Krumova

Introduction

Women's entrepreneurship has garnered recognition in many parts of the world, calling attention to the value women entrepreneurs offer society. According to European Training Foundation research, to strengthen the entrepreneurial competences and business potential of women it is necessary to broaden business advisory structures for women engaged in various stages of entrepreneurial activity (ETF, 2013). According to the US Chamber of Commerce Foundation (2014) there are six best practices for creating female entrepreneurship programmes: advocacy on women's business issues; networking; business management assistance and support; access to contracts; leadership development and mentoring; access to capital. According to the Global Entrepreneurship Monitor 2012 Women's Report, the most comprehensive research about the entrepreneurial activity of women across the globe, more than 126 million women entrepreneurs were starting or running new businesses in 67 economies in 2012 (Kelley et al., 2012; Watson, 2013). Research shows that on the next step after start-up business – growth factors influencing the growth of women-owned businesses – are motivation for entrepreneurship, motivation for wealth, work–life balance and outside advisers (NWBS, 2013).

For example in Europe, women constitute 52 per cent of the total European population but only one-third of the self-employed or of all business starters in the EU (Eurostat, 2007). Women thus represent a large pool of entrepreneurial potential in Europe. The study shows that when establishing and running a business, women face more difficulties than men, mainly in access to finance, training, networking, and in reconciling business and family (EU Commission, 2013). The EU Entrepreneurship 2020 action plan's accent on the better use of information and communication technology (ICT) can be a significant help for new businesses to thrive, including female entrepreneurship. ICT is the key source of growth for national economies, and European small- and medium-sized enterprises (SMEs) grow two to three times faster when they embrace ICT. As indicated in the Commission's industrial policy communication, 'entrepreneurs need to exploit the full potential of the digital single market in the EU that is expected to grow by 10% a year up to 2016' (EU Commission, 2013). Because the ICT sector is fast-paced and dynamic, the skills of the ICT workforce also need to keep up with the pace of change. This suggests that ICT qualifications need to be extended to include a much broader spectrum, which in turn suggests that there may potentially be more employment openings that might attract the attention and interest of girls and women. Along with better use of ICT, a source of business potential for women entrepreneurs is access to the Internet and networks. This is important for formal, non-formal and informal learning, for exchange of good practices, for sharing knowledge and building confidence and for resolving real-life business problems.

The research question of this study is to identify how women can utilize ICT, Web-based technologies and Massive Open Online Courses (MOOCs) successfully for start-up businesses. The methodology undertaken in this study is a literature review and desk analysis, and connecting concepts in a conceptual model.

Women's Entrepreneurship and ICT

The information technology revolution and networks make communication systems of special importance to indigenous peoples – for sharing, informing and educating, for generating income and reinforcing self-reliance. Indeed, new ICTs, with their potential to break through social and geographic obstacles, have considerably increased communities' capacity to access information and to share experience and practices in almost any part of the world. The ICT sector opens a broad spectrum of creativity, innovation and entirely new ways of working, interacting and learning that should appeal to women and men alike. The Institute for the Future identifies six drivers most likely to shape the future workforce, including women entrepreneurs (Tandon et al., 2012):

- longer life spans;
- a rise in smart devices and systems;
- advances in computational systems such as sensors and processing power;
- new multimedia technology;
- the continuing evolution of social media;
- a globally connected world.

Female entrepreneurship can enforce gender-specific awareness, e.g. in technology incubators, in public and private financing institutions and significantly increasing the number of girls and women in science, innovation and technology. According to the ITU 2013 report, over 2.7 billion people are using the Internet, which corresponds to 39 per cent of the world's population. More men than women use the Internet: globally, 37 per cent of all women are online, compared with 41 per cent of all men. This corresponds to 1.3 billion women and 1.5 billion men (ITU, 2013a). The report shows that the gender gap is more pronounced in the developing world, where 16 per cent fewer women than men use the Internet, compared with only 2 per cent fewer women than men in the developed world. However, despite the disparities, the gender gap continues to close, with access to mobile technology increasingly within reach of women worldwide (ITU, 2013b). For example, an initiative about women Web entrepreneurs aims to empower women around the globe to start and grow their businesses using technology through organizing global series of meet-ups, events, speakers and training. These community-led initiatives are part of a network of Google Business Groups, groups of entrepreneurs who come together to share business and technical knowledge.

Goldman Sachs also has a best practice women's initiative which operates through a network of more than 80 academic and non-profit institutions. Research conducted by Goldman Sachs has shown that investing in education for women has a significant multiplier effect, leading to more productive workers, healthier and better-educated families, and ultimately to more prosperous communities. The same results are explained in the Global Perspective on Entrepreneurship Education and Training study (Martinez et al., 2010), which shows that people who have taken up entrepreneurship training are three times more confident about having the skills to run a business.

Women entrepreneurs are becoming more and more aware of the power of ICT, the Internet and social networking potential for discovering and sharing knowledge, participating in open online courses, developing new skills, networking and being successful. Along with technologies innovation, a key concept which broadens women entrepreneurs' opportunities is that of openness, where the Web-based applications are taking a leading role. Those are open data, open knowledge (open knowledge reality brings many more advantages vs traditional practices of knowledge sharing), open science and open courses – MOOCs – which are aimed at unlimited participation and open access via the Web.

Web-based Applications

Appearance and dissemination of Web 2.0 technologies shifted the role of a user from consuming content and information to creating content and knowledge and being social around information (McKinsey Global Institute, 2011). Web 2.0 is a set of Internet services and practices that give a voice to individual users. Such services encourage Internet users to participate in various communities of knowledge-building and knowledge-sharing. This has been made possible by the ever-extending reach of the (worldwide) 'Web'. Meanwhile, navigating and exploring this web of knowledge has been greatly facilitated by the increased functionality of the Web browser. Browsers have become the network reading/display tool that offers a universal point of engagement with the Web.

The core principles around the Web 2.0 concept are of the Web as a platform; harnessing collective intelligence; data as the next 'Intel inside', the end of software release cycles; lightweight programming models; software above the level of a single device; and rich user experiences (O'Reilly, 2005). However, Anderson laid down the modified Web 2.0 ideas basing some of these principles in a more social rather than technological perspective and a global information space perspective (Anderson, 2007): individual production and user-generated content; harnessing the power of the crowd; data on an epic scale; an architecture of participation; network effects and openness. Participation controls every aspect of Web 2.0. The transition to Web 2.0 was due to the emergence of platforms such as blogging, social networks, and free image and video uploading that collectively allowed easy content creation and sharing by everyone (Future Exploration Network, 2008).

Currently there is a broad diversity of social tools for learning – software, platforms or services that enable women at different locations to communicate and work with each other in a secure, self-contained environment, using them to build online communities of people who share interests and activities; services are primarily Web-based and provide multiple ways for users to interact, such as chat, messaging, email, video, file sharing, blogging, discussion groups and so forth (Table 16.1).

Table 16.1 Web 2.0 tools and functions

Type	Function	Tools	Web applications
Communicative	To share ideas, information and creations	Social networking, blogs, audio blogs, video blogs, IM tools, podcasts and Web-conferencing	Facebook, Blogger, YouTube, MySpace, Twitter, Bumping, Tumblr, Vidipedia, etc.
Collaborative publishing	To work with others for a specific purpose in a shared work area	Authoring, editing tools, virtual communities of practice (VCOPs), Wikis	Wikipedia, Vidipedia, Netcipia, Wordpress, PBworks, Edmodo,
Documentative (content management)	To collect and/or present evidence of experiences, thinking over time, etc.	Blogs, video blogs, ePortfolios, open journalism	SeeNReport, Calameo, Drupal, Joomla
Generative	To create something new that can be seen and/ or used by others	Mashups, VCOPs, virtual learning worlds (VLWs)	Amazon (customer comments), Second Life, Flickr, YouTube, Voci, Animoto, Flipsnak
Interactive	To exchange information, ideas, resources, materials	Social bookmarking, Really Simple Syndication (RSS), VCOPs, VLWs	StumbleUpon, Delicious, Facebook, MySpace, Tiki-toki

A core function of Web 2.0 services is to support communication between users. These tools allow individuals on the shared infrastructure of the Internet to coordinate their activities in various degrees of depth. This can range from the relatively trivial level of participating in anonymous recommender systems to the more intense level of interpersonal, verbal debate. At one end of this continuum, some of the exchange is better termed 'coordination', rather than 'collaboration'.

However, Web 2.0 offers women entrepreneurs a set of tools to support forms of sharing knowledge and learning that can be more strongly collaborative and more oriented to the building of communities. There is a growing argument that decisions emerging from the human 'crowds' of Web 2.0 coordination are the key to innovative thinking and problem-solving (Crook et al., 2008; Surowiecki, 2004). The most familiar and widely recognized types of Web 2.0 activity include:

- Blogging – an Internet-based journal or diary in which a user can post text and digital material while others can comment, e.g. Blogger, Technorati, Twitter.
- Conversing – one-to-one or one-to-many between Internet users, e.g. MSN.
- Media sharing – uploading or downloading media files for purposes of audience or exchange, e.g. Flikr, YouTube.
- Online gaming and virtual worlds – rule-governed games or themed environments that invite live interaction with other Internet users, e.g. Second Life, World of Warcraft.
- Social bookmarking – users submit their bookmarked Web pages to a central site where they can be found and tagged by other users, e.g. del.icio.us.

- Social networking – websites that structure social interaction between members who may form subgroups of 'friends', e.g. MySpace, Bebo, Facebook.
- Syndication – users can subscribe to RSS (Really Simple Syndication) feed-enabled websites so that they are automatically notified of any changes or updates in content via an aggregator, e.g. bloglines, podcast.
- Trading – buying, selling or exchanging through user transactions mediated by Internet communications, e.g. Craigslist, eBay.
- Wikis – a Web-based service allowing users unrestricted access to create, edit and link pages, e.g. Wikipedia.

As a set of technologies, delivery, models, and philosophies that use the Web as a platform to deliver information products and services, Web 2.0 emphasizes user participation. It signifies a drastic shift from a closed, data-hoarding, product-based online society where the Web was a restricted medium for conducting limited business (Stone, 2010). Web 2.0 continues to evolve into an open, trusting, service-based society which provides a unique platform for developing new ways of working.

Besides different social roles or levels of participation, Web 2.0 users can also utilize them according to their purposes – networking, learning, sharing knowledge, and many more, e.g. participating in open online courses.

Massive Open Online Courses

Massive Open Online Courses offer free online college-level classes, open to anyone and everyone that wants to take them. MOOCs have captured the imagination and attention of entrepreneurial newcomers and traditional incumbents alike. In addition to traditional course materials such as videos, readings and problem sets, MOOCs provide interactive user fora that help build a community.

The use of teaching materials like MOOCs that feature women entrepreneurs in a greater variety of industries and with high growth aspirations can expand the horizons and stimulate aspirations of women students while broadening the perspectives of their male colleagues who are likely to be their future spouses, bankers, investors and employees. Multiple ways to expand business experiences can also be considered, including programmes of personal coaching and mentoring. Training programmes to address specific tasks and skills can not only address increased expertise but also enhance levels of self-confidence. A broader education can also help young women understand their unique situation regarding historical, economic, ethnic, legal and religious contexts (Oppedisano, 2003).

MOOCs represent the latest stage in the evolution of open educational resources. First was open access to course content, and then access to free online courses. Many accredited institutions are now accepting MOOCs as well as free courses and experiential learning as partial credit toward a degree (Harden, 2013). Start-ups such as Coursera, edX and Udacity have led the charge, expanding course offerings and rapidly signing up partners, from individual faculty members to prestigious institutional partners (Jarrett, 2012).

MOOCs can be seen as an extension of existing online learning approaches in terms of open access to courses and scalability, and they also offer an opportunity to think afresh about new business models that include elements of open education.

This includes the ability to disaggregate teaching from assessment and accreditation for differential pricing and pursuit of marketing activities (Educause, 2012). Some of the most popular MOOCs are:

- Founded by Harvard University and MIT in 2012, edX is an online learning destination and MOOC provider, offering high-quality courses from the world's best universities and institutions to learners everywhere. With Open edX, educators and technologists can build learning tools and contribute new features to the platform, creating innovative solutions to benefit students everywhere.
- **Coursera** is a for-profit company. It has 197 courses in 18 subjects, including computer science, mathematics, business, humanities, social science, medicine, engineering and education. Some partner universities offer credit for their Coursera classes to those who want to pay a fee to have some extra assignments, work with an instructor and be assessed.
- **Udacity** is for-profit start-up, which offers 18 online courses in computer science, mathematics, general sciences, programming and entrepreneurship. When students complete a course, they receive a certificate of completion indicating their level of achievement, signed by the instructors, at no cost. Some universities have begun to offer transfer credit for Udacity students who then take the final examination at a Pearson centre.
- **Udemy** offers over 5,000 courses, 1,500 of which require payment.
- **P2Pu** offers some of the features of MOOCs, but is focused on a community-centred approach to provide opportunities for anyone who is willing to teach and learn online. There are over 50 courses available, and the process of improving the quality of the courses relies on community review, feedback and revision. There are no fees or credits, but P2PU's school of Webcraft adopted a badge reward system to integrate elements of gamification into the learning process.
- **Khan Academy**, another well-known free online learning platform, is a not-for-profit educational organization with significant backing from the Bill and Melinda Gates Foundation and Google. The Khan Academy, started by Salman Khan in 2008, offers over 3,600 video lectures in academic subjects with automated exercises and continuous assessment.

Although MOOCs share many of the same benefits as conventional online learning, such as the ability to overcome barriers of time and place, they also promote, model and scaffold digital literacy skills (Glance, Forsey and Riley, 2013). Some of the major benefits of MOOCs are that they:

- expand the pool of applicants prepared to undertake education;
- promote the participating universities;
- improve the professional standing and reputations of the faculty and departments involved;
- attract donors and collaborators;
- encourage user contributions in the form of source code and supplementary software;
- may lead to more multi- and interdisciplinary undergraduate education as students are provided with access to courses that they might not otherwise have; and

- may enhance on-campus education by reducing the time required to lecture and assess, providing faculty with more time for student interaction (Hardesty, 2012).

Before starting up entrepreneurship initiatives, women can enrol in an entrepreneurship MOOC course to be aware of the approaches, principles and best practices. Women entrepreneurs can also enrol in a MOOC course within their field of business interest.

MOOCs influence the curriculum, platform and assessment "opens" within:

- Open curriculum: learners mix educational resources, activities, and/or packages for different disciplines to meet their needs. This places learners in charge of their own learning and ensures that they will learn what they need to meet their personal desires and requirements.
- Open learning: instructors, experts and/or peers will, through various activities, generate and share new ideas and new understanding during the learning process. This provides learners with opportunities for self-determined, independent and interest-guided learning.
- Open assessment: instead of the 'monopoly' on formal evaluation of learning results, previously led by accredited education providers, assessment of what learners have learned is carried out by their instructors, others and peers during the learning process via peer-to-peer or crowd-sourced assessment with 'on-demand accreditation' for learners.
- Open platform: supports a dynamic and interactive open education community by creating and maintaining an engaging, intuitive and stable user interface for educators and learners. Cloud-based provision and the use of open standards make it easier for different platforms and services to exchange information and data (Yuan and Powell, 2013).

MOOCs support self-organization, critical thinking and collaboration, connect people and knowledge across disciplines, value interest and willingness to learn over academic credentials, and reduce financial and cultural barriers to participation. They build personal learning networks and improve lifelong learning skills. MOOCs not only bring value via their access to open knowledge, but also provide an environment for networking, and bring together people who share the same fields of interest. An excellent example for reflection about courses enrolled, new ideas, networking and professional development of women entrepreneurs is ePortfolio, where artefacts about what they have achieved can be saved, analysed, reflected, changed and/or shared among the entrepreneur communities.

ePortfolio

ePortfolio is a collection of authentic and diverse evidence, drawn from a larger archive representing what a person or organization has learned over time on which the person or organization has reflected, and designed for presentation to one or more audiences for a particular purpose. There are a variety of purposes for developing ePortfolios – as an assessment tool, for marketing or employment, and to document the learning process and growth for learners of all ages, from preschool through graduate school and into the professions. The purposes and goals for the portfolio determine the content (Barrett, 2005). ePortfolios emphasize the importance of the evidence they contain for the development of the individual (Burek et al., 2009). In its core, ePortfolio-based learning finds increasing implementation in a variety of educational and professional learning contexts (van Wesel and Prop, 2008). It is used to stimulate and monitor professional learner's development and to stimulate their ability to become lifelong learners. The ePortfolio process consists of four stages.

There are six major types of ePortfolios (Information Management System): assessment; presentation; learning; personal development; multiple owner; working. Costa and Laranjeiro (2008) describe possible stages as follows:

- Stage 1. Collection of evidence, which will be decided by the objectives and abilities expressed in the portfolio: (a) information with different types of content (conceptual, procedural and attitudinal or normative); (b) tasks undertaken inside or outside the classroom (mind maps, press cuttings, exams, reports, interviews, etc.); (c) documents on different physical media (digital, paper, audio, etc.).
- Stage 2. Selection of evidence, where the users choose the best works or those questions which best represent them and which demonstrate the positive developments and learning that is to be presented to the learning community.
- Stage 3. Reflection on the evidence. Where both the weak and the strong points of the process are highlighted and proposals drawn up for improvement.
- Stage 4. Publication of the portfolio based on a design and an orderly, clear and well-arranged structure that assists understanding and innovative thinking.

ePortfolio can be utilized as a tool for women entrepreneurs to organize knowledge resources when participating in MOOCs, evidence of research projects, attendance at learning events and activities, learning plans, acquisition and understanding of essential skills as observed by a senior expert, discussions of varied case management and reflection on key activities and experiences of specific importance to the individual. One of the best options for women entrepreneurship start-ups, along with MOOCs and ePortfolio, is the utilization of the Ice House entrepreneurship mindset.

Ice House Entrepreneurship Mindset and Start-up 2.0 Model

Entrepreneurship is all about the opportunity discovery process. The decision to become an entrepreneur is often viewed as a process largely motivated by profit: an individual has an idea for a business and, before founding a firm and investing in the creation of an innovative product, service or process, does research to evaluate the size of the market opportunity, the competition and the feasibility of developing a cost-effective solution. However, the entrepreneurial process is widely varied: individuals traverse a wide variety of paths on the road to entrepreneurship and are motivated by a variety of factors. Distinguishing amongst these paths – and the differential effects of these paths on economically and societally relevant outcomes – remains a relatively unexplored area of inquiry (Shah, Smith and Reedy, 2012).

The Ice House entrepreneurship mindset focuses on cultivating and growing the ability of an individual to think entrepreneurially, which is something that isn't really taught conventionally. An Ice House entrepreneurship mindset is based on nine building block elements. The mindset starts with thinking about describing a problem being solved or needing to be solved and ends with a test of the assumption in practice.

Before starting a business, it is necessary to create a personal vision statement:

- Dare to dream: creating a vision statement is a powerful tool, one that separates entrepreneurs from the crowd. A personal vision statement guides life. It provides a source of inspiration that will energize the entrepreneur. It will help guide the decisions an entrepreneur makes and help determine how to invest time and energy in ways that will bring them closer to their goals.

  ○ Without a personal vision, one is much more likely to follow the crowd rather than steer towards a destination of one's own choosing. Without a clear vision of where the entrepreneur wants to go, she is more likely to squander time and effort on things; those who write down their goals are much more likely to accomplish their goals than those who do not.

- Create vision: find a time and place where one can focus attention on developing an effective personal vision statement. Write the statements as if the entrepreneurship is already making them happen in your life. Try to limit your statement to a single page. And remember, there are no wrong answers.
- Commit to vision: once the entrepreneur has created a vision statement, it is important to commit to the vision and stay focused on goals. Share the vision with a trusted friend. Print a statement and post it where you can see it often. Include inspiring pictures.

When women entrepreneurs define a clear vision for the business, they can apply the proposed four steps start-up 2.0 model. It starts with *T*argeting MOCC, *I*nitiating e-Portfolio, *M*anaging Web 2.0 applications and *E*xploring the Ice House entrepreneurship mindset (TIME).

As a dynamic process, entrepreneurship creates incremental wealth. The wealth is created by individuals who assume the major risks in terms of equity, time and/or career commitment to provide value for some product or service. The implementation of the women start-up 2.0 model can be followed by the entrepreneurial process, which involves finding, evaluating and developing opportunities for creating a new venture (Table 16.2).

Each step is essential to the eventual success of the new venture. Once the opportunity is identified, the evaluation process begins. Basic to the screening process is the understanding of factors that create the opportunity: technology, market changes, competition or changes in government regulations.

Table 16.2 Entrepreneurship project

Identify and evaluate the opportunity	Develop a business plan	Resources required	Manage the enterprise
Opportunity assessment Creation and length of opportunity Real and perceived value of opportunity Risk and returns of opportunity Opportunity versus personal skills and goals Competitive environment	Title page Table of Contents Executive Summary Major Section 1. Description of Business 2. Description of Industry 3. Technology Plan 4. Marketing Plan 5. Financial Plan 6. Production Plan 7. Organization Plan 8. Operational Plan 9. Summary Appendixes (Exhibits)	Determine resources needed Determine existing resources Identify resource gaps and available suppliers Develop access to needed resources	Develop management style Understand key variables for success Identify problems and potential problems Implement control systems Develop growth strategy

Conclusion

The current advancement in the technologies and web 2.0 allow women to start-up business and to become a successful entrepreneur. On the one hand, the diversity of Web 2.0 offers many ways for sharing, archiving, retrieving, combining and generating new knowledge; on the other hand, the MOOC offers not only open access to knowledge, but much more – it is a new way of working together, networking and using technology that is effective and accessible and may contribute to balancing work, family and social life. ePortfolio is a useful tool which can cover a comprehensive range of material, demonstrating women's progress in terms of development, critical thinking, professional identity and acquisition of skills and competencies. By utilizing Web-based technologies and recording achievements in ePortfolio, women can develop their knowledge, skills and competencies effectively. The implementation of the proposed conceptual start-up 2.0 model can help women develop their own business. The first step is to identify the MOOC and start learning, then to create an ePortfolio and manage Web 2.0 tools, and to implement the Ice House mindset. The Ice House mindset is a useful tool for generating ideas as a first step in the identification and evaluation of business opportunities in the market. Further research should examine the implementation of the model in practice and determine how social media can be utilized to enhance the model's values.

References

Anderson, P. (2007), *What is Web 2.0? Ideas, Technologies and Implications for Education.* JISC Technology and Standards Watch, 2–64, Joint Information Systems Committee, UK. Available at: http://www.jisc.ac.uk/media/documents/techwatch/tsw0701b.pdf (Retrieved 8 November 2014).

Barrett, H. (2005), *Researching Electronic Portfolios and Learner Engagement, The Reflect Initiative*. Available at: http://www.taskstream.com/reflect/whitepaper.pdf (Retrieved 8 November 2014).

Burek, G., Berlanga, A., Kalz, M., Braidman, I., Smithies, A., Wild, A., Osenova, P., Simov, K., Hoisl, B., Lemnitzer, L., Stoyanov, S., van Rosmalen, P., Hensgens, J., Regan, M., Van Bruggen, J. and Armitt, G. (2009), D4. 1 Positioning Design. LTfLL-project. Available at: http://dspace.ou.nl/bitstream/1820/1761/1/D4.1%20final%20EC.pdf (Retrieved 26 July 2014).

Costa, F. and Laranjeiro, M. (2008), ePortfolio in Education Practices and Reflections, Associação de Professores de Sintra. Imprensa de Coimbra, Lda, Oslo. Available at: http://digifolioseminar.org/pt/?download=ePortfolio_in_Education.pdf (Retrieved 8 November 2014).

Crook, C., Cummings, J., Fisher, T., Graber, R., Harrison, C., Lewin, C., Logan, K., Luckin, R., Oliver, M. and Sharples, M. (2008), *Web 2.0 Technologies for Learning: The Current Landscape – Opportunities, Challenges and Tensions*. Becta Research Reports. Available at: http://dera.ioe.ac.uk/1474/1/becta_2008_web2_currentlandscape_litrev.pdf (Retrieved 8 November 2014).

Educause. (2012), *What Campus Leaders Need to Know About MOOCs*. Available at: http://tinyurl.com/c7gqj65 (Retrieved 26 July 2014).

ETF (European Training Foundation). (2013), *Training for Women Entrepreneurs: An Imperative for Growth and Jobs*, INFORM. Available at: http://www.etf.europa.eu/webatt.nsf/0/541576CCB06E2F1EC1257B28004846C2/$file/INFORM_14_Women%20entrepreneurs.pdf (Retrieved 26 July 2014).

EU Commission. (2013), *Communication from the Commission to the European Parliament, the Council, the European Economic and Social Committee and the Committee of the Regions, Entrepreneurship 2020 Action Plan*. Brussels: European Commission. Available at: http://www.unescochair.uns.ac.rs/sr/docs/enterpreneurship2020ActionPlan.pdf (Retrieved 26 July 2014).

Eurostat. (2007), *European Communities Statistics in Focus: The Entrepreneurial Gap Between Men and Women*. Available at: http://epp.eurostat.ec.europa.eu/cache/ITY_OFFPUB/KS-SF-07–030/EN/KS-SF-07–030-EN.PDF (Retrieved 8 November 2014).

Future Exploration Network. (2008), *WEB 2.0 Framework*. Future Exploration Network, Sydney, Australia. Available at: http://www.futureexploration.net/images/Web2_Framework_E2EF.pdf (Retrieved 26 July 2014).

Glance, D., Forsey, M. and Riley, M. (2013), *The Pedagogical Foundations of Massive Open Online Courses*. Available at: http://firstmonday.org/ojs/index.php/fm/article/view/4350/3673 (Retrieved 26 July 2014).

Harden, N. (2013), The End of the University as We Know It. *The American Interest LLC Magazine* 8(3). Available at: http://www.the-american-interest.com/articles/2012/12/11/the-end-of-the-university-as-we-know-it/ (Retrieved 8 November 2014).

Hardesty, L. (2012), Is MIT Giving Away the Farm? *MIT Technology Review*. Available at: http://www.technologyreview.com/article/428698/is-mit-giving-away-the-farm/ (Retrieved 26 July 2014).

ITU. (2013a), *ICT Facts and Figures, The World in 2013*. Available at: http://www.itu.int/en/ITU-D/Statistics/Documents/facts/ICTFactsFigures2013-e.pdf (Retrieved 26 July 2014).

———. (2013b), *ITU Releases Latest Global Technology Development Figures*. Available at: http://www.itu.int/net/pressoffice/press_releases/2013/05.aspx#.Ux7XqPmSx1Z (Retrieved 26 July 2014).

Jarrett, J. (2012), *What Are MOOC's and Why Are Education Leaders Interested in Them?* Available at: http://www.huffingtonpost.com/impatient-optimists/what-are-moocs-and-why-ar_b_2123399.html (Retrieved 26 July 2014).

Kelley, J., Brush, C., Greene, P., Litovsky, Y. and Global Entrepreneurship Research Association. (2012), *Global Entrepreneurship Monitor: 2012 Women's Report*. Available at: http://gemconsortium.org/docs/download/2825 (Retrieved 26 July 2014).

Martínez, A. Levie, J., Kelly D., Samundsson, R., Schott T. and Global Entrepreneurship Monitor Special Report A Global Perspective on Entrepreneurship Education and Training (2010), *Global Entrepreneurship Monitor Special Report: A Global Perspective on Entrepreneurship Education and Training*. Available at: http://www.babson.edu/Academics/centers/blank-center/globalresearch/gem/Documents/gem-2010-special-report-education-training.pdf (Retrieved 8 November 2014).

McKinsey Global Institute. (2011), *Big Data: The Next Frontier for Innovation, Competition, and Productivity*. Washington, DC: McKinsey Global Institute. Available at: http://www.mckinsey.com/mgi/publications/big_data/pdfs/MGI_big_data_full_report.pdf (Retrieved 26 July 2014).

NWBS (National Women's Business Council). (2013), *2013 Annual Report (NWBS)*. Available at: http://nwbc.gov/sites/default/files/NWBC_2013AnnualReport-spreads_FINAL.pdf (Retrieved 26 July 2014).

Oppedisano, J. (2003), *The Invisible Wall: Implications for Researching, Teaching, & Understanding Women's Multidisciplinary Entrepreneurship*. Paper presented at US Association of Entrepreneurship and Small Business. Hilton Head, South Carolina.

O'Reilly, T. (2005), *What Is Web 2.0 Design Patterns and Business Models for the Next Generation of Software*. Available at: http://www.elisanet.fi/aariset/Multimedia/Web2.0/What%20Is%20Web%202.doc (Retrieved 8 November 2014).

Shah, S., Smith, S. and Reedy, E.J. (2012), *Who Are User Entrepreneurs? Findings on Innovation, Founder Characteristics, and Firm Characteristics*. The Kauffman Firm Survey. Available at: http://faculty.washington.edu/skshah/Shah,%20Winston%20Smith,%20Reedy%20-%20Who%20are%20User%20Entrepreneurs.pdf2 (Retrieved 26 July 2014).

Stone, T. (2010), *100+ Tips on the Use of Blogs, Wikis, and, Forums in Organizations, Web 2.0 and Social Learning Best Practices*. Available at: http://www.training-partners.com/downloads/elearning/Web2_bestpractices_0910v1.pdf (Retrieved July 26, 2014).

Surowiecki, J. (2004), *The Wisdom of Crowds: Why the Many are Smarter than the Few*. London: Abacus.

Tandon, N., Pritchard S., Savelieva V., Smith R. and Vogt Ei. (2012), *A Bright Future in ICTs Opportunities for a New Generation of Women*. ITU, Telecommunication Development Sector Report. Available at: http://girlsinict.org/sites/default/files/pages/itu_bright_future_for_women_in_ict-english.pdf (Retrieved 8 November 2014).

US Chamber of Commerce Foundation. (2014), *Women-owned Businesses – Carving a New American Business Landscape*, p. 23. Available at: http://www.uschamberfoundation.org/sites/default/files/legacy/cwb/ccfwib.pdf (Retrieved 26 July 2014).

van Wesel, M. and Prop, A. (2008), *The Influence of Portfolio Media on Student Perceptions and Learning Outcomes*. Paper presented at Student Mobility and ICT: Can E-LEARNING overcome barriers of Life-Long learning? Maastricht, The Netherlands. Available at: http://www.personeel.unimaas.nl/maarten.wesel/documenten/the%20influence%20of%20portfolio%20media%20on%20student%20perceptions%20and%20learning%20outcomes.pdf (Retrieved 26 July 2014).

Watson, E. (2013), *126 Million Women Entrepreneurs Active Worldwide*. Available at: http://www.prowess.org.uk/gem-2012 (Retrieved 26 July 2014).

Yuan, L. and Powell, S. (2013), *MOOCs and Open Education: Implications for Higher Education*. Available at: http://publications.cetis.ac.uk/wp-content/uploads/2013/03/MOOCs-and-Open-Education.pdf (Retrieved 26 July 2014).

Chapter 17

Women-run Companies' Growth and Finance

Milen Baltov

Introduction

Considering the nature of family businesses with varying types and degrees of family involvement, one might expect research on management practices of owners to include not only business management but also family/business interface management. However, that has not been the case (Bird et al., 2001). Additionally, not much is known about the interaction of gender and management practices and the effect of that interaction on family business performance.

Chell and Baines (1998) indicate that the gender and performance interaction is not clear because previous studies focus exclusively on women or use simple male/female comparisons with a gender dummy or parallel female/male analyses. These authors also indicate that studies need to incorporate owner demands at the family/business interface and ways owners meet those demands, because those patterns, and not gender, may be what affect family business performance.

Chell and Baines (1998) further question whether the concept of 'performance' is itself gendered. Their challenge arose because most research on gender and performance assumes financial performance as the standard and therefore fails to consider the complexities of the socialized perspective of gender (Bird and Brush, 2002). For example, women may not measure success according to traditional financial indicators; they may prioritize family business decisions based on balancing work and family because of their primary responsibility for children. One result has been that females gravitate to smaller and more manageable firms.

With financial performance as the standard for family business success, a 'female underperformance' theme has surfaced in the literature. Although findings are mixed, female owners are often found to underperform their male counterparts using a financial performance standard. Olson et al. (2003) utilize a national, representative household sample of family businesses to investigate both business and owning family success for family businesses. The most important result of that study is that business success depends, in part, on family processes – such as how the family responds to disruptions – rather than simply how owners manage the family business. This study extends Olson et al. (2003) by (a) adding business innovations, a critical entrepreneurial behaviour in family business performance, (b) utilizing the National Family Business Survey (NFBS) panel data to facilitate the use of a dependent business performance variable three years after the explanatory variables, and (c) incorporating both main and moderating effects of gender. Thus, the current study investigates whether the gender of the family business owner moderates the relationship between business and family/business interface management practices and gross revenue.

Understanding differences in how the genders operate their family businesses and utilize family/business interface resources, and incorporating those nuances into family business education programmes and consultations should increase the probability for successful outcomes for both female- and male-owned family businesses.

Theoretical Foundation: The Sustainable Family Business Theory

The sustainable family business theory (SFB; see Figure 17.1) draws from general systems theory, giving equal recognition to family and business and to their interplay in achieving mutual sustainability (see Stafford et al., 1999 for in-depth explanation).

The theory is considered an 'innovative approach to the study of family business' (Trent and Astrachan, 1999: v). In the theory, both family and business are purposive, rational social systems. The systems transform available resources and constraints via interpersonal and resource transactions into achievements (Olson et al., 2003). The theory assumes that business sustainability is a function of both business success and family functionality; individuals in either system may affect both systems (Stafford et al., 1999). Family/business overlap varies, as does the divergence of goals and achievements.

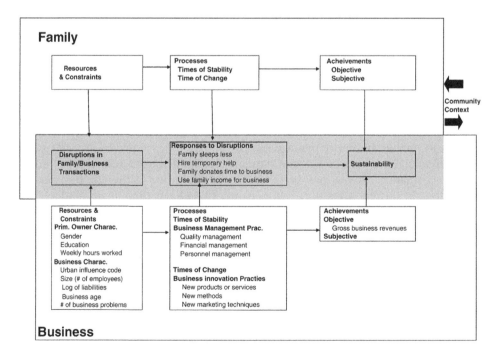

Figure 17.1 Family business

Family and business systems are affected by environmental and structural change. During stable periods, systems are managed within their boundaries, but during periods of disruption, the other system's resources are used. In general systems theory, when encountering disruptions, resources are exchanged at system boundaries (Stafford et al., 1999).

Therefore, responses to disruptions are placed at the interface in the SFB theory. Olson et al. (2003) found disruption responses explain 20 per cent of the variance in family business revenues. One of the most important implications of this result is that aspects of family outside the firm impacted revenue. Resilience capacity against disruptions, a type of human capital, can be built in both the family and business. When needed, resilience capacity can be transmitted across boundaries to the family business. Resilience is the owning family's use of an ability to adjust resource and interpersonal processes to disruptions (Danes, 2006). If families have built a stored capacity for resilience, when a disruption is encountered, the store of trust and creativity in problem-solving can be more easily and quickly tapped and adapted to new situations (Danes et al., 2002).

Business and/or family managers must perceive, process and respond to a changing environment and reconstruct processes to ensure sustainability over time (Danes et al., 2005). Concrete resources and interpersonal transactions from either the business or family may facilitate or inhibit family business sustainability. Gender is an inescapable element of the owner's management context because gender carries the socialized perspectives that are a basis for disruption responses.

In recent years, the resource-based view has been applied to family firms. These studies hold that family resources in firms constitute unique resources and capabilities for competitive advantage. This resource-based view focuses on family resources within the firm only. The systems nature of the SFB theory focuses on how family members exchange resources across systems (Stafford et al., 1999). The SFB theory is compatible with the resource-based view but is broader. Unlike the resource-based view of the firm and firm management, the SFB theory provides a mechanism to examine aspects of the owning family and business owner that are not within the firm but affect firm achievement and long-term sustainability.

Female-owned businesses generally underperform those headed by males using financial performance measures such as earnings, survival or growth (Bird et al., 2001; Brush and Hisrich, 1991; Olson et al., 2003). When other explanatory variables are controlled, differences in financial measures of business success often disappear. These variables include industry, firm size, business experience, innovation activity, managerial attributes risk aversion, assets and equity.

Many of these studies have methodological shortcomings such as small or non-random samples from industries where either males or females are underrepresented. Using a large Swedish sample, female underperformance is much weaker in larger firms and non-existent in firms with only one employee. For many female owners, maintaining a 'small and stable' business is not a transitory phase but rather a consciously chosen business state. Doing so represents an adaptation to their professional, social, family and personal demands.

On the whole, however, these performance studies do not investigate the varied ways in which females might manage their family business differently from males. Bird and Brush (2002) describe masculine management as strategic and competitive with centralized decision-making, low people commitment with clear boundaries between owners and employees, and growth leading to hierarchy. On the other hand, feminine management is personal and influenced by familial history, has participative decision-making and high commitment to people, and resists growth. Bird and Brush (2002) further indicate that resources are managed differently by gender; the masculine approach to resources is to find ways to obtain and use them by leveraging rather than sacrificing the owner's resources. The feminine approach is more personal; the individual is fully at risk and makes a deeper personal commitment to both the opportunity and the resources, including employees.

In addition to gender, education, managerial skills and experience contribute to firm income, profitability and growth. Owner's training and hours worked in the firm contribute to sales, and men work significantly more hours than women (Bird and Brush, 2002). Olson et al. (2003) found that new, small and home-based firms have less gross revenue than firms that are older, larger and are located outside of the home. A business' geographic location has a significant effect on economic opportunities by virtue of differential access to larger economies and centres of information, communication, trade and finance.

Research on gender differences and business practices focuses on strategic management, values held by entrepreneurs, managerial styles, and firm bureaucracy and employment relationships; of four planning measures – market, financial, personnel and inventory – only market and inventory planning reveal significant gender differences. Innovation practices adopted in businesses have been classified into three categories: administrative and technical; product and process; and radical and incremental. In this chapter more the product and process category is regarded, with focus on the introduction of new products or services and the introduction of new elements into a firm's operations, process innovations.

This study includes a third type of innovation, introduction of improved business and marketing practices. The family business literature implies that management decisions about resource exchanges are made within the boundaries of either the family or business. Recent research, however, finds support for the premises that resources are shared between business and family systems, and that family businesses are, indeed, cross-system organizations. Olson et al. (2003) find that family business success depends on family processes and the family's responses to disruptions rather than simply how the owner manages the business. In fact, responses to disruptions have a greater effect on family business revenues (20 per cent of variance) than the family's resources (2 per cent). Nearly half of home-based businesses that use or trade family resources to spend more time on business the female business owners are more likely to reallocate family resources to the business than male business owners, and the use of family financial resources in the business occurs more when the business owes money to financial institutions or when the owner is older, more experienced and without children.

Based on the discussion of SFB theory and literature on gender, management, innovation, responses to disruptions and family business performance, several hypotheses are tested. Business and owner characteristics and business management and innovation practices are the control variables. Independent variables of interest are primary owner gender and responses to disruptions at the family/business interface. Figure 17.1 places the study variables within the sustainable family business theory.

Gender of the primary owner explains variance of gross revenues, ceteris paribus. Responses to disruptions explain variance of gross revenues. Its gender moderates the relationship between business innovation practices and gross revenue. It moderates the relationship between business management practices and gross revenue, ceteris paribus, and it moderates the relationship between responses to disruptions and gross revenue.

After verifying family business ownership in the household, business and household manager interviews occurred. Gender of the primary business owner was established through a series of questions and probes in the screening interview. If the interviewer encountered a spouse who insisted that they owned the business equally, the person was probed as to who was most involved in the day-to-day business management. If the respondent indicated they were equally involved in management, the interviewer recorded the household manager's name.

This chapter also applied at least one of these criteria: owner perceived their business to be a family business, at least one other family member was a major business decisionmaker, at least one other family member was an owner, at least one other family member worked in the business and future family ownership was considered likely. The measure of family business performance used in this study was family business gross revenue, a measure of financial performance. This simple measure was chosen, in part, because most of the family businesses in this sample were small. Revenue is the simplest of the ratio measures of financial performance, and financial performance is the narrowest conception of business performance.

Quality management might be regarded as analysing customer satisfaction on a continual basis and evaluating product and service quality. Financial management is to be composed of: planning advertising and promotion budgets or strategies; estimating cost and expense figures; preparing financial records such as cash flow statements, balance sheets, or inventory control methods; determining numerical objectives such as sales or earnings; and developing or updating a written strategic plan, including a mission statement. Personnel management is composed of estimating or setting personnel needs, labour costs, or performance standards; evaluating employee performance; and motivating workers to become better employees.

"Family sleeps less was a transfer of time" from a family system activity to make time for business activities. Family members, other relatives and friends were a source of free labour when the business was busy (family donates time to business). Less frequently, the family business owners reported that they hired temporary help for either business or home. "Use family income for business" indicated transfer of family financial resources to meet business needs; "cash flow problems" were assumed to be non-routine.

Discussion and Implications

The chapter focuses on the moderating effect of gender on the management processes of business planning, innovations and responses to disruptions in family businesses. It provides evidence for a gender difference in gross revenue of female- and male-owned family firms after controlling for family business management and innovation practices. Inclusion of responses to disruptions significantly increases the explanation of variance in gross revenue, and a significant gender difference in gross revenue still remains. Thus, in this study, the effect of gender does not disappear when other explanatory variables are controlled, as described by Chell and Baines (1998).

However, only 'hire temporary help' is significant. The direction of causality in this study is clearer than in the Olson et al. (2003) study, but the results indicate that some ways of managing disruptions may not have long-lasting effects on gross revenues. The only business innovation practice with a significant effect on gross revenue is new methods of production; however, the effect is large and positive. Gender does not have a significant moderating effect on innovation practices. Introducing new methods of production has a large positive effect for females as well as males.

Gender has a significant moderating effect on business management practices. Gender has a significant moderating effect on only personnel management, and that effect is large and very significant. Personnel management has a much larger effect on gross revenue for females than for males. The positive effect of personnel management on gross revenue for female owners is over nine times greater than for males. Further, the significant main effects for business management practices in prior models became statistically insignificant; the main effects for financial management and personnel management retain their previous signs, however.

Gender has moderating effects on responses to disruptions, explaining more variance than any other except controls. Furthermore, when including the moderating effects of gender in the model, the previously insignificant main effects for two of the responses become significant. The moderating effects of gender on responses to disruptions are large and have signs that are opposite the signs of the main effects. The moderating effects of gender on responses to disruptions are so large that the effects of responses to disruptions on gross revenue are opposite for females and males. Sleeping less negatively effects gross revenue for males, but has an even larger positive effect on gross revenue for females.

For male owners, hiring temporary help has the largest effect on gross revenue of all responses to disruptions, yet that practice has little or no effect on gross revenue for female owners. Perhaps male owners hire temporary help for the business and female owners hire temporary help for the family. Or, perhaps males are more likely to own seasonal businesses. Gender has a moderating effect on family members donating their time to the business during disruptions. Donating time is associated with less gross revenue for male owners and more gross revenue for female owners. Perhaps male owners accept the unpaid labour of family members when they believe they have little choice, whereas female owners view unpaid labour of family members as a gesture of affection and respect, a way to bond and be with family even though busy, which exemplifies the feminine perspective outlined by Bird and Brush (2002).

Gender has a significant moderating effect on using family income to meet business cash flow needs, but the main effect is not significant. Using family income for the business has little or no association with gross revenue for males, but has a very large negative association with gross revenue for females. Perhaps females use family income only when necessary; whereas, males view family income as relatively cheap capital to be used when advantageous.

Working harder, putting in more weekly hours, is related to higher gross revenues for females, but previous research indicates many of them started businesses to have more time for their families. This study's results indicate that females have better alternatives than simply putting in more time. 'Smarter' alternatives are feasible for most female owners. Increasing that score slightly might not be as easy as increasing the personnel management score and would not result in as much extra revenue, but doing so would be more productive than working an extra hour or two. However, low average scores and high variability on these practices may help explain the large effects for females. To expect this effect to remain constant as females increase the prevalence of practices would be unrealistic.

The implications of the gender moderating effect for using family income are not as straightforward. Other research has found that female owners take more money for the family out of the business than male owners do. Such a practice is more likely to result in cash flow problems, and retaining earnings is a cheap source of capital. Female owners may focus too much on family support and not enough on building a sound set of financial practices for the business. Their perspective might be more personal. This finding might be interpreted to imply that female business owners are less likely to practice personnel management than males. However, the typical industries of female-owned firms may provide a better explanation. According to US statistics, more than half (55 per cent) of female-owned businesses are in the service sector (U.S. Department of Labor, 2002). These family business types naturally benefit from personnel management since their sales are more dependent on the direct delivery of services from human resources.

The findings reinforce those of Olson et al. (2003); during periods of disruption, family resources outside the firm impact firm revenues. The sustainable family business theory provides additional support for causal inferences. Nevertheless, the discussion in this chapter avoids making firm causal linkages between the explanatory variables and gross revenue. Future research that uses growth in gross revenue as the dependent variable would strengthen the foundation for causal inferences.

Furthermore, the results indicate that the socialized gender perspective of the business owner is a key contextual construct when analysing family businesses. More specifically, the chapter provides evidence to support two central tenets of the sustainable family business theory: that family and business systems exchange resources during times of disruption and that owning families manage family and business resources together to meet the demands of both systems. However, results indicate that effective resource exchange processes to sustain the family business are not necessarily homogeneous. Chell and Baines (1998) question whether family demands on the owner and the family's involvement in the business are responsible for what have previously been called gender effects.

The gender effect, in addition to an effect from the family's resource exchanges with the business, leads to the conclusion that both the gender of the owner and family resource exchanges with the business affect family firm performance. Family business managers must perceive, process and respond to changing environments and reconstruct processes to ensure sustainability over time (Danes et al., 2005). Further research is needed on how family resources and actions outside the firm impact family business performance and how resilience capacity against disruptions is built and maintained in both the owning family and the business. That research should examine the relationship between the amount and types of all management practices and the moderating effect of gender, not simply traditional business management. However, the conceptual difference between the stock of resilience capacity and taking actions that draw on that capacity needs to be considered in pursuing that line of research. Much family business research incorporating constructs authors described as family management (Gimeno, 2005) use indicators of structures such as presence of a family council rather than the flow measures of family management practices that are used in this study. The moderating effects of gender on structures may be different.

Future research needs to study the management structure and practice relationship. Structures and management practices that impact family business performance may differ by family values, role expectations of owners, level and type of family involvement in the business, business size, business goals and motivations as well as the socialized gender perspective of the owner. This chapter does not control for these constructs. Neither does this study control for resource exchanges between the family and business without a disruption. Future research would benefit from inclusion of these constructs and gender moderating effects on them.

Conclusions

The complexities of the socialized perspective of gender within family businesses can no longer be ignored in family business research. To investigate gender differences in management practices with solely a gender dummy is no longer sufficient. With varying types and degrees of family involvement in family businesses, investigating management practices at the family/business interface is imperative, especially with female-owned businesses. Also, research needs to ascertain whether gender affects other outcomes and measures of performance. Multiple, simultaneous measures of family business success need to be considered such as congruity within the owning family about desired attributes and actions of the family business. Such research might discover management practices that contribute simultaneously to the sustainability of both the family and business systems. If certain management practices are found to contribute to business success but hinder family success, strategic family business decisions could be made that mitigate the effects on the family system.

References

Bird, Barbara and Brush, Candida. (2002), A Gendered Perspective on Organizational Creation. *Entrepreneurship Theory and Practice* 26(3): 41–65.
Bird, Sharon R., Sapp, Stephen G. and Lee, Motoko Y. (2001), Small Business Success in Rural Communities: Explaining the Sex Gap. *Rural Sociology* 66(4): 507–31.
Brush, Candida and Hisrich, Robert. (1991), Antecedent Influences on Women-Owned Businesses. *Journal of Managerial Psychology* 6(2): 9–16.
Chell, Elizabeth and Baines, Susan. (1998), Does Gender Affect Business 'Performance'? A Study of Microbusinesses in Business Services in the UK. *Entrepreneurship & Regional Development* 10(2): 117–35.
Danes, Sharon M. (2006), Tensions within Family Business-owning Couples Over Time. *Stress Trauma and Crisis* 9(3–4): 227–46.

Danes, Sharon M., Haberman, Heather R. and McTavish, Donald. (2005), Gendered Discourse About Family Business. *Family Relations* 54(1): 116–30.

Danes, Sharon M., Reuter, Martha A., Kwon, H.K. and Doherty, William. (2002), Family FIRO Model: An Application to Family Business. *Family Business Review* 15(1): 31–43.

Gimeno, Alberto (2005), Performance in the Family Business: A Causal Study of Internal Factors and Variables. Unpublished doctoral thesis, ESADE Universitat Ramon Llull, Spain.

Olson, Patricia D, Zuiker, Virginia S., Danes, Sharon M., Stafford, Kathryn, Heck, Ramona, K.Z. and Duncan, Karen A. (2003), The Impact of Family and Business on Family Business Sustainability. *Journal of Business Venturing* 18(5): 639–66.

Stafford, Kathryn, Duncan, Karen A., Danes, Sharon M. and Winter, Mary. (1999), A Research Model of Sustainable Family Businesses. *Family Business Review* 12(3): 197–208.

Trent, Elizabeth and Astrachan, Joseph. (1999), Family Businesses from the Household Perspective. *Family Business Review* 12(3): v–vi.

U.S. Department of Labor. (2002), *Facts on Working Women*. Available at: http://www.dol.gov/wb/factsheets/wbo02.htm/ (Retrieved 31 October 2013).

Index

Note: Italicized page numbers indicate a figure on the corresponding page. Page numbers in bold indicate a table on the corresponding page.

For Product Safety Concerns and Information please contact our EU
representative GPSR@taylorandfrancis.com Taylor & Francis Verlag GmbH,
Kaufingerstraße 24, 80331 München, Germany

Printed and bound by CPI Group (UK) Ltd, Croydon, CR0 4YY
01/05/2025
01858385-0004